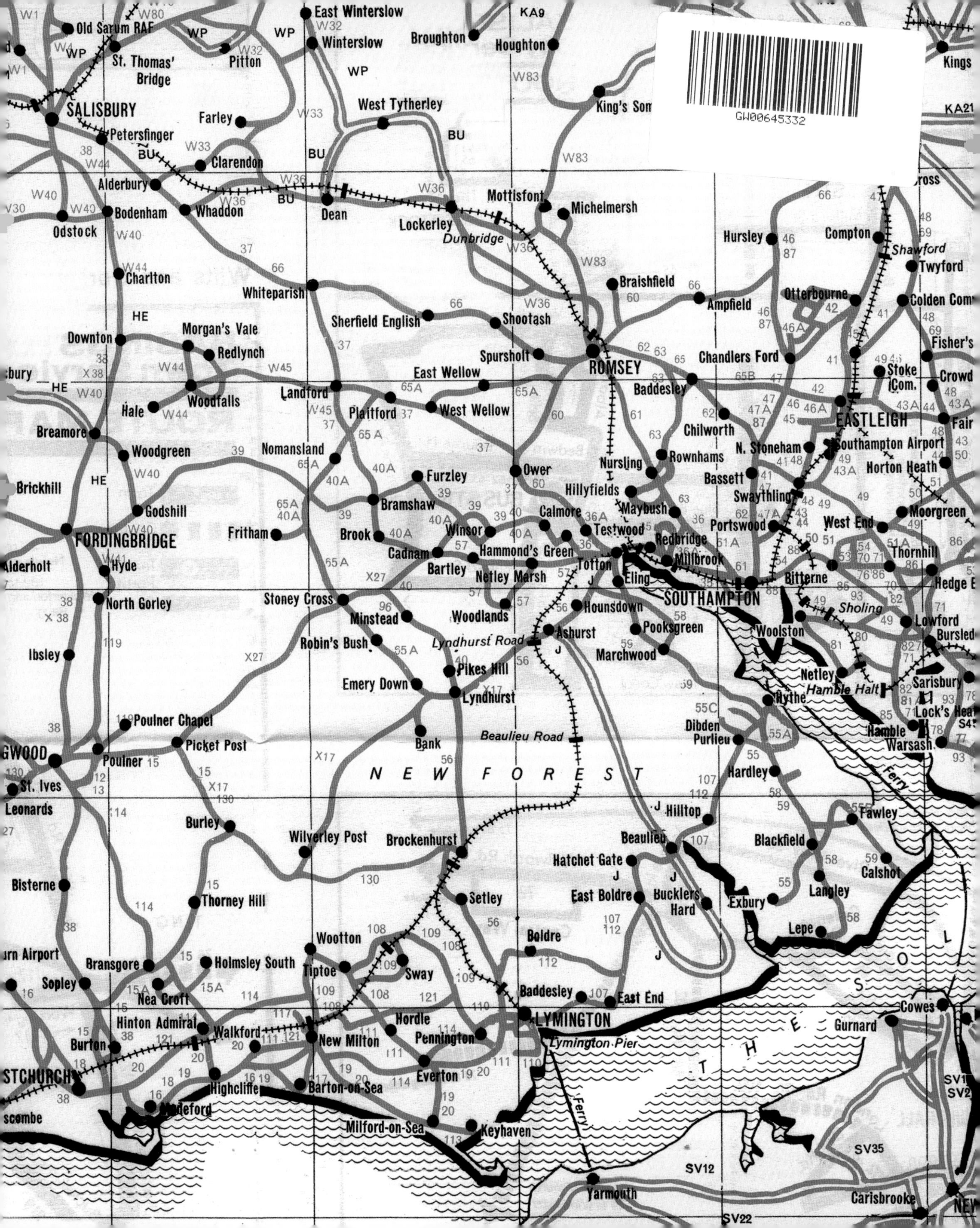

East Winterslow
Old Sarum RAF
Winterslow
Broughton
Houghton
Kings
St. Thomas' Bridge
Pitton
SALISBURY
Farley
West Tytherley
King's Som
Petersfinger
Clarendon
Alderbury
Bodenham
Whaddon
Dean
Lockerley
Mottisfont
Michelmersh
Dunbridge
Odstock
Hursley
Compton
Shawford
Twyford
Charlton
Whiteparish
Braishfield
Ampfield
Otterbourne
Colden Com
Sherfield English
Shootash
Chandlers Ford
Downton
Morgan's Vale
Redlynch
Spursholt
ROMSEY
Fisher's
East Wellow
Baddesley
Stoke Com.
Crowd
Hale
Woodfalls
Landford
Plaitford
West Wellow
Chilworth
EASTLEIGH
Fair
Breamore
Woodgreen
Nomansland
N. Stoneham
Southampton Airport
Horton Heath
Brickhill
Godshill
Furzley
Ower
Nursling
Rownhams
Bassett
Hillyfields
Swaythling
Bramshaw
Maybush
Moorgreen
Fritham
Brook
Winsor
Calmore
Testwood
Portswood
West End
FORDINGBRIDGE
Cadnam
Hammond's Green
Redbridge
Thornhill
Alderholt
Hyde
Bartley
Netley Marsh
Totton
Millbrook
Bitterne
Hedge E
Eling
SOUTHAMPTON
North Gorley
Stoney Cross
Minstead
Woodlands
Hounsdown
Sholing
Lowford
Ashurst
Pooksgreen
Woolston
Bursled
Robin's Bush
Lyndhurst Road
Ibsley
Marchwood
Pikes Hill
Netley
Sarisbury
Hamble Halt
Emery Down
Lyndhurst
Hythe
Lock's Hea
Poulner Chapel
Dibden Purlieu
Bank
Hamble
Warsash
Picket Post
Beaulieu Road
GWOOD
Poulner
NEW FOREST
St. Ives
Hardley
Ferry
Leonards
Hilltop
Fawley
Burley
Wilverley Post
Brockenhurst
Beaulieu
Blackfield
Hatchet Gate
Calshot
Bisterne
Setley
East Boldre
Bucklers Hard
Exbury
Langley
Thorney Hill
Wootton
Boldre
Lepe
rn Airport
Bransgore
Holmsley South
Tiptoe
Sway
Sopley
Nea Croft
Baddesley
East End
Cowes
LYMINGTON
Hinton Admiral
Walkford
Hordle
Gurnard
Burton
New Milton
Pennington
Lymington Pier
STCHURCH
Highcliffe
Barton-on-Sea
Everton
Mudeford
scombe
Milford-on-Sea
Keyhaven
THE SOL
Yarmouth
Carisbrooke
NE

Sir,

When operating the 5.44pm Canal-Bemerton Heath relief (51) on Tuesday Nov. 25th I accidently tore a gentleman's mackintosh.

The passenger was sitting at the end of the second row from the back, on the upper deck, which was also occupied by three other passengers. There was very little room for me to squeeze past him and in doing so the handle of my machine caught in the pocket of his mackintosh. I did not realize what had happened until I heard a tearing sound, when I looked I found I had torn his mac. about four inches near the pocket.

J. Bailey

26.11.58

A CENTURY OF SERVICE

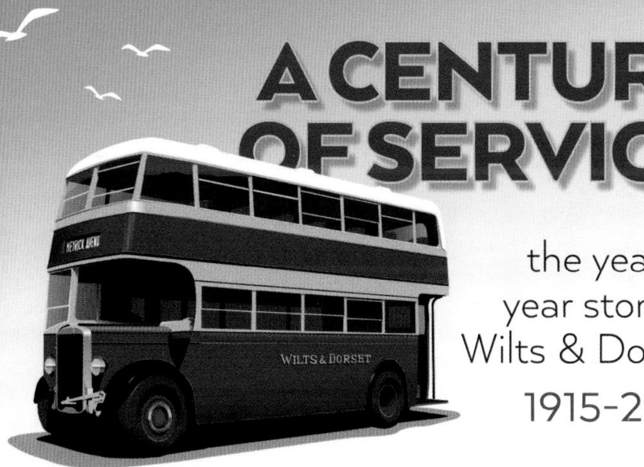

the year by year story of Wilts & Dorset

1915-2015

written by
Chris Harris

edited & designed by
Ray Stenning

commissioned by
Go South Coast

printed by
Lavenham Press

published by
Best Impressions
15 Starfield Road London W12 9SN

ISBN 978 0 9565740 3 9

Fare collection on the top deck of a lowbridge bus with a sunken side gangway and bench seats each seating four passengers could be difficult when the bus was crowded.

Conductress Joan Bailey, who worked for Wilts & Dorset from 1947 until 1979, had to submit a report about a rather unfortunate incident that took place in November 1958. Her report is shown on the opposite page.

It's a pleasure for me to write the foreword to this excellent book, which records so well our journey from 1915 to today. Although our company now looks very different to those early days, our core purpose is still very much the same - to provide safe, reliable and economical transport for customers throughout our area.

Over the last hundred years we have very much become part of the social and economic fabric of Wiltshire, Dorset and Hampshire. We've made a difference to people's lives: taking them to school, to first dates, to work, on holiday and shopping.

This book superbly illustrates the huge variety of buses and coaches we have operated over the years, which are of great interest to many readers. However our biggest asset is of course our people, who have done, and still do, a fantastic job whatever the weather and despite the pressures and difficulties of shift work.

The contribution of our staff was highlighted in the Second World War, when many left their secure and safe career on the buses to go abroad and fight for their country. Tragically some made the ultimate sacrifice and never returned. We still remember these colleagues with memorial plaques in Salisbury Travel Shop and in Poole.

We continue to innovate and develop our business. It was a pleasure to launch brand new buses for Salisbury recently, with more due later this year. Our predecessors would not recognise the advanced technology we now employ for ticketing, maintenance and information, but of course we do all this to give the best possible service for our customers, so as to sustain and develop our business.

It's been a great hundred years. We are all now looking forward to the next hundred.

Andrew Wickham
Managing Director
Go South Coast
Poole, Dorset

March 2015

a word from the Managing Director & the author

One hundred years ago, on 4 January 1915, Wilts & Dorset Motor Services Limited was registered at Companies House as company number 133876. This centenary is being proudly celebrated by Go South Coast in 2015 by the publication of this book and other special events.

A purist may assert that although serving some of the same area, Salisbury Reds and More are not, and indeed the 1983 formed Wilts & Dorset Bus Company Limited (company number 01671355) was not, the same organisation as the original Wilts & Dorset Motor Services. It is possible to dispute that assertion. When the company's title or branding has been changed, the same friendly staff have continued to provide the services, giving a continuity that has been much valued by many local people. There are loyal, long-serving staff who have worked for Wilts & Dorset Motor Services, Hants & Dorset (National Bus Company), Wilts & Dorset Bus Company and Salisbury Reds without changing their workplace. Taking the view that for most people the company is the people and the services provided, rather than a registration number, we can properly celebrate the centenary in 2015.

In this book I have traced the history of the company for the hundred years from 1915 to 2014 inclusive. Each of the 100 years has its own section, complete with contemporary photographs, while items from the news and the popular music scene for each year help to put the story into perspective.

My research has been based on original documents, including minute books and other material held in the National Archive at Kew and by the Kithead Trust at Hampton Lovett, near Droitwich. My warm thanks go to the very kind people at both locations who have been so helpful to this project, and also to the staff at Swindon Library and the Wiltshire History Centre in Chippenham. There is a list of other people without whom I could not have completed this task at the back of the book.

Throughout my own lifetime's career in the bus industry, from starting as a conductor with Hants & Dorset at Poole through to retirement a few years ago as Public Relations Manager for Go South Coast, and in my continuing role of producing the staff magazine, I've always valued the privilege of being part of an excellent company and working with some great colleagues. I hope you will enjoy reading this book as much as I have enjoyed writing it.

Chris Harris, Poole, Dorset
March 2015

The brass plate of the former Wilts & Dorset Bank was still in place on the Blue Boar Row, Salisbury, branch of Lloyds bank in 2014.

in 1915

Photographs became a requirement in British passports.

A railway accident at Quintinshill resulted in 226 deaths, mostly of troops – the highest death toll from a rail crash in the UK.

In the circumstances of war, Liberal Prime Minister Herbert Asquith formed an all party coalition government.

The Women's Institute was founded.

Popular music included It's a Long Way to Tipperary by John McCormack and Listen to the Mocking Bird by Alma Gluck.

in 1916

The Military Service Act introduced conscription.

The Easter Rising took place in Dublin.

The Battle of the Somme resulted in thousands of casualties.

Prime Minister Herbert Asquith resigned; his place was taken by David Lloyd George.

Popular music included Good Bye, Good Luck, God Bless You by Henry Burr and Somewhere A Voice Is Calling by John McCormack.

1915

In August 1914 a man called Edwin Coombes started a bus service between Amesbury and Salisbury under the name of Wilts & Dorset, using a bus built locally by a company called Scout. However, earlier the same year the Salisbury-based Wilts & Dorset Bank had been absorbed into Lloyds Bank, and the story runs that Coombes did not want to see the old name disappear completely, so named his operation Wilts & Dorset Motor Services. During the autumn of 1914 Alfred Cannon and Douglas Mackenzie, directors of Worthing Motor Services, got into discussions with Edwin Coombes, and these culminated in Cannon and Mackenzie buying Coombes' Wilts & Dorset undertaking.

Thus it was that Wilts & Dorset Motor Services Limited was registered at Companies House on 4 January 1915. The registered office was in Amesbury; Percy Lepherd was Company Chairman, Douglas Mackenzie became Company Secretary and Alfred Cannon a director, while Edwin Coombes was retained as Manager. During 1915 Mackenzie and Cannon were also involved in the formation of Southdown Motor Services, but there was no financial connection between the two companies.

The original route between Salisbury and Amesbury had been extended to serve Bulford and Larkhill too, and in March 1915 the operations of A A Brewer of Ringwood were taken over. By December 1915 an additional four locally-built Scout buses had been bought by the company.

1916

A historic precedent was made in August 1916 when Wilts & Dorset acquired a 40hp McCurd bus, registration number IB 806; this was the first Wilts & Dorset bus to be painted red, the earlier Scout vehicles bought new by the Company having carried a yellow livery. The McCurd, which carried a secondhand body, was collected from the Thomas Tilling premises in London and proved to be an excellent investment,for it lasted ten years in the Company's service before being sold to another operator.

Salisbury Market Square is the location of the picture at the top of the opposite page. The bus, registered IB 802, is a 37hp Scout chassis with a charabanc body by Marks of Wilton. It was bought new by Wilts & Dorset in March 1915 but only stayed in the fleet until 1917.

In the lower picture in Guildhall Square in Salisbury, which in 1915 was the terminus of the Wilts & Dorset route from Amesbury via Woodford, was IB 804. This was also a 37hp Scout, but carried a body of unknown origin, the design of which resulted in this vehicle being nicknamed '*the greenhouse*'. This bus was also was withdrawn in 1917.

Received by Wilts & Dorset in August 1916, IB 806 was a 40hp McCurd that carried a rear-entrance bus body that provided perimeter seating for 26 passengers; this body had originally been carried by a Southend-on-Sea Corporation Tilling-Stevens. Seen with its crew in Salisbury's Guildhall Square above, IB 806 was the first Wilts & Dorset vehicle to be painted red. It was in the fleet for ten years, being withdrawn in 1926. It saw further service with Jeanes in Weymouth and eventually ended its days as a garden summer house in Chickerell.

DAVID PENNELS COLLECTION

This is the Certificate of Incorporation for Wilts & Dorset Motor Services Limited, dated 4 January 1915.

courtesy of IAN GRAY

No. 138876.

Certificate of Incorporation

I HEREBY CERTIFY that Wilts and Dorset Motor Services, Limited, is this day Incorporated under The Companies Acts, 1908 and 1913, and that the Company is Limited.

Given under my hand at London this Fourth day of January, One Thousand Nine Hundred and Fifteen.

GEO. J. SARGENT,
Assistant Registrar of Joint Stock Companies.

Fees and Deed Stamps .. £6 : 10 : 0.
Stamp Duty on Capital .. £12 : 10 : 0.

in 1917

An Imperial War Cabinet was set up by Prime Minister David Lloyd George to co-ordinate military policy in the British Empire during the First World War.

The Women's Army Auxiliary Corps was formed and the Women's Royal Naval Service established.

The People's Dispensary for Sick Animals was founded by Marie Dickin; the first free dispensary was at Whitechapel in the East End of London.

Popular music included Pack Up Your Troubles in Your Old Kit Bag by Reinald Werrenrath and Keep the Home Fires Burning by John McCormack.

in 1918

The Representation of the People Act gave women over 30 the right to vote.

The school leaving age was raised to 14.

An epidemic of influenza caused many deaths.

The First World War ended at 11am on 11 November.

Popular music included Over There by Enrico Caruso and Smiles by Joseph C Smith's Orchestra.

in 1919

The Treaty of Versailles was signed.

The Cenotaph in London, designed by Edwin Lutyens, was unveiled as a memorial to those who had lost their lives in the First World War. In November the first Remembrance Day was observed, with two minutes silence at 11am.

Popular music included A Pretty Girl is like a Melody by John Steel and I'm Forever Blowing Bubbles by Henry Burr.

1917

Manager Edwin Coombes had been called up for military service during the First World War; his role at Wilts & Dorset was taken by George Wallis who transferred from Worthing. On 5 February 1917 the registered office of Wilts & Dorset was changed from 46 High Street, Amesbury to 2 St Thomas's Square, Salisbury, the latter also being the office of Mr George Davis, who was now Company Secretary.

Mainly because of a shortage of drivers because of the war, Wilts & Dorset had to suspend all services with the exception of the Amesbury route. This was worked by the McCurd bus that had been bought the previous year, and the Scout buses were disposed of.

Thus Wilts & Dorset remained afloat with just one bus running on the one route, a very narrow escape from becoming a casualty of the First World War and disappearing altogether.

Six out of the first seven vehicles bought by Wilts & Dorset featured locally built Scout chassis. The origins of Scout Motors went back to 1902, when a company called Dean & Burden Brothers was formed to manufacture motorboat and motorcycle engines. The company name became Scout Motors in 1904, and production switched from marine engines to commercial vehicles in 1909.

It could be said that Scout Motors was a casualty of the First World War, the company's machinery being requisitioned and removed by the government during the course of the conflict. Production could not restart until 18 months after the Armistice, and Scout Motors was soon swamped by competitors who had taken advantage of modern mass production methods. Scout Motors was wound up in June 1921.

In happier days for Scout Motors, this advertisement was produced, showing what it described as '*the old order versus the new*' at Salisbury Market. And although all of the company's Scout buses were taken out of service by the end of 1917, it can be truthfully said that it was Scout Motors vehicles that first put Wilts & Dorset on the road.

DAVID PENNELS COLLECTION

1918

By 1918 the total Wilts & Dorset fleet amounted to just two vehicles, one of which was hired from Southdown. Following the Armistice in November the Company placed orders for new buses to re-establish the fleet, but as production at that time was still geared to military vehicles, it was to be well into the following year before it got any.

1919

The first new post-war vehicle for Wilts & Dorset arrived in June 1919, a 3-ton AEC Y with a 31-seat charabanc body by Harrington. The following month saw the delivery of the first double- deck bus, another 3 ton AEC Y but with a Brush body. A further double deck followed in September, this time a Leyland S5 carrying a Dodson body. Both double-deck buses were, of course, open top with an outside staircases rising from the rear platform.

The double deck buses were put to work on a new route between St Mark's Church, Salisbury and Wilton, which started in September 1919, while the charabanc was used for local excursions, including to Stonehenge.

At the end of the First World War only one bus of the original six bought by the company remained in service, a McCurd. The original six - five Scouts and the McCurd - had been (as was often the practice of Worthing - later Southdown - Motor Services) registered with Armagh County Council in Northern Ireland by Wilts & Dorset's Amesbury office. Armagh County Council records show IB 805 to have been registered by Wilts & Dorset on 29 May 1915 and to have subsequently been transferred to Southdown at 23 Marine Parade, Worthing from 12 March 1916. This is where this vehicle was later photographed in Southdown livery, shown on the left.

DAVID PENNELS COLLECTION

Wilts & Dorset's first double deck bus was built by AEC with a 45-seat body by Brush. In the picture at the top the driver, leaning on the nearside mudguard, is Bert Cooper, who brought this vehicle from Worthing to Salisbury in July 1919 - and never went back! CD 2555 was in service with Wilts & Dorset until December 1929.

DAVID PENNELS COLLECTION

Becoming part of the Wilts & Dorset fleet in June 1919, CD 3330 was a 3 ton AEC YC that initially carried a 31-seat charabanc body by Harrington. It is seen above during its early days with the company, well loaded for a private hire outing.

PHIL DAVIES COLLECTION

When delivered to Wilts & Dorset in May 1920, AEC YC CD 5249 carried the 45-seat Tilling open-top double-deck body seen in the picture on the right. In late 1923 this chassis was rebodied as a single-deck bus, and rebodied again as a charabanc in 1928. It was withdrawn from service the next year.

DAVID PENNELS COLLECTION

in 1920

The first Hornby model trains were produced - clockwork at O gauge.

The children's cartoon character Rupert Bear appeared for the first time.

Conscription was ended.

For the first time, women were admitted to study for full degrees at Oxford University.

Popular music included Whispering by Paul Whiteman and his Orchestra and Swanee by Al Jolson.
The light orchestral piece In a Persian Market written by Albert Ketelbey was also enjoying great popularity.

1920

When Edwin Coombes returned from war service he had expected to resume his previous job as Manager at Wilts & Dorset, but the company - who had brought in George Wallis from Worthing to fill the position - denied him this. So, on 10 March 1920 Coombes launched Salisbury & District Motor Services Limited, trading as The Yellow Victory, and was soon competing with Wilts & Dorset in Salisbury.

It was in June 1920 that the signature of Mr Raymond Longman first appeared on a Wilts & Dorset document; at that time an assistant to George Davis, Mr Longman was to be deeply involved in the company for more than 40 years.

Five new buses entered the fleet in 1920; a Leyland and three AECs were received during April and May, while in December a Maxwell with a 16 seat charabanc body by Salisbury Carriage Works arrived. November saw the acquisition of a garage in Castle Street, Salisbury. It was also in 1920 that Wilts & Dorset became a public limited company.

New in April 1920, CD 3177 had a Dodson 35-seat bus body on its AEC YC 3-ton chassis. It was photographed on the right operating from Salisbury to Ringwood and Bournemouth, a route that was started in 1920.

DAVID PENNELS COLLECTION

Route developments during the year included a service between Wilton and Harnham Bridge and one from Salisbury to Bournemouth via Fordingbridge, Ringwood and Christchurch.

This happy group above are certainly enjoying their day out by Wilts & Dorset charabanc. The front vehicle is CD 5247, a Leyland S5 with a 33-seat Harrington body. This vehicle entered service with Wilts & Dorset in May 1920 and was seen here when new.

Salisbury
Fordingbridge
Ringwood
Christchurch
Bournemouth

An unusual vehicle purchase in December 1920 was HR 3186, shown on the left. It was a Canadian built Maxwell chassis with 16-seat charabanc body by Salisbury Carriage Works. It seems this vehicle was displayed in the showroom of S & E Collett of Catherine Street, Salisbury, in a very similar red livery to that used by Wilts & Dorset.

Realising the danger of this red liveried vehicle getting into the hands of a competitor, Wilts & Dorset decided to buy it. Sadly, HR 3186 proved unreliable; it was withdrawn in 1923 and sold to W F Hancock of Corsham in Wiltshire.

DAVID PENNELS COLLECTION

During 1920-21 Wilts & Dorset faced competition from Salisbury & District Motor Services, operated by Edwin Coombes, who had first used the name Wilts & Dorset on the sides of buses. Coombes is seen standing in the centre of this group (in front of the word DISTRICT) beside Salisbury & District's HR 1952, a Thornycroft double decker that came into the Wilts & Dorset fleet when the Company bought Salisbury & District in August 1921.

DAVID PENNELS COLLECTION

1921

Two new Leyland buses – a double deck and a single deck – joined the Wilts & Dorset fleet in May. But more importantly, on 2 August 1921 Wilts & Dorset bought the Salisbury & District (Yellow Victory) operation from Edwin Coombes and his fellow directors. The deal included seven Thornycroft and two Crossley buses. This eliminated the serious competition that Wilts & Dorset had been facing on the Salisbury to Wilton, Salisbury to Amesbury and Salisbury to Fordingbridge roads.

The cost to Wilts & Dorset, almost £10,000, was a very substantial sum at that time, but very satisfying to Coombes and the Yellow Victory directors & staff, all of whom were shareholders in the enterprise.

Territorial development in 1921 included the establishment of routes from Salisbury to Southampton, Salisbury to Warminster and Salisbury to Dorchester.

in 1921

Car tax discs were introduced.

The British Legion was founded

Cambridge University admitted women to study for full degrees.

Registration of dentists became compulsory, making dentistry a fully regulated profession.

Popular music included Margie by Eddie Cantor and Song of India by Paul Whiteman and his Orchestra.

Salisbury & District's HR 2275 had an interesting history; the Crossley chassis had been built for the War Department in 1918, and the original WD tender body was adapted by Salisbury Carriage Works in 1920 to carry 14 passengers on perimeter seating; this can be seen in this photograph showing the bus while it was in service with Salisbury & District. In August 1921 HR 2275 passed to Wilts & Dorset when the company bought Salisbury & District.

DAVID PENNELS COLLECTION

This outing by a party of young ladies on the left was transported by Wilts & Dorset's CD 2556 on a sunny day in 1921. This vehicle had entered the fleet in 1919 with a double-deck body, but early in 1921 had been rebodied as a 33- seat charabanc by Harrington. Wonder how many hats were blown off along the way.

On the other hand, CD 3330 in the picture below it, which had been new as a 31-seat charabanc in 1919, was rebodied as a double-deck bus in 1921; it carried that body (as seen here) until 1925 when it was again rebodied as a single-deck bus.

Entering service in May 1921, Leyland G7 HR 4483 seated 45 passengers; the double deck body was also built by Leyland. It is seen when new at the bottom left, marked up for route 2A from Harnham Bridge to Wilton via Salisbury. Note the reference to 'Stations'; at that time Salisbury still had separate London & South Western Railway and Great Western Railway stations.

Also acquired with the Salisbury & District fleet was HR 5605; this had a Crossley chassis built for the War Department in 1915, but in this case fitted with a new Salisbury Carriage Works charabanc body in 1921. Wilts & Dorset clearly thought it ideal transport for this gentlemen's outing below.

DAVID PENNELS COLLECTION

Another vehicle acquired with the Salisbury & District fleet in August 1921 was HR 3037, a Thornycroft with an Acton 42-seat double-deck body. Here in Wilts & Dorset livery, HR 3037 carries an advertisement for Salisbury's Style & Gerrish, the department store beside the bus stops in Blue Boar Row. It's now part of the Debenhams organisation.

DAVID PENNELS COLLECTION

1922

Just one new vehicle - a Leyland G7 with a Harrington charabanc body - joined the fleet in 1922. By the autumn, as well as the routes from St Mark's Church and Harnham Bridge to Wilton, Wilts & Dorset were running bus services from Salisbury to:

Amesbury, Durrington and Larkhill
Fordingbridge, Ringwood and Bournemouth
Whiteparish and Southampton
Codford and Warminster
Blandford and Dorchester
Porton
Fovant

1923

For the second year in succession just one new vehicle joined the Wilts & Dorset fleet, but this time it was a double deck for the Salisbury city routes. HR 9541 had a 51-seat body by Harrington, and at the time of purchase was the Company's highest capacity vehicle to date.

Like a number of bus operators at the time, Wilts & Dorset often swapped bodies around between chassis, or rebodied vehicles, simply to suit operating needs; in the case of HR 9541 the chassis received a Harrington charabanc body in 1929, the removed double deck body passing to a scrap merchant near Andover in February of that year.

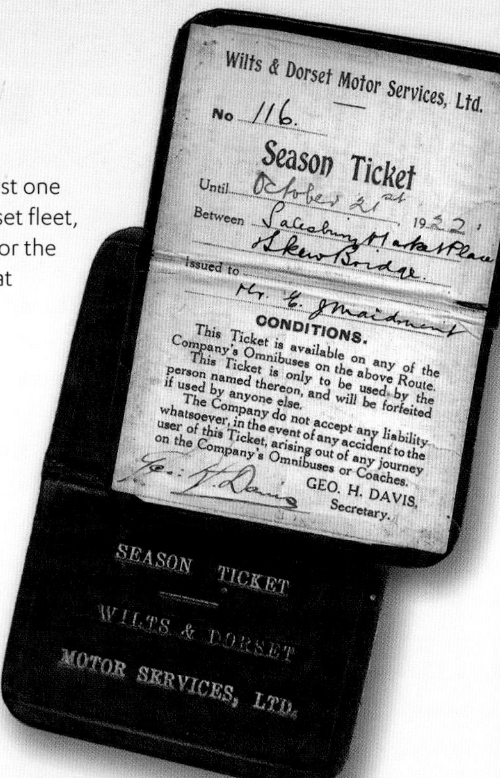
Wilts & Dorset Motor Services, Ltd.

No 116.

Season Ticket

Until October 21st 1922.

Between Salisbury Market Place Skew Bridge.

Issued to Mr. E. J Maidment

CONDITIONS.

This Ticket is available on any of the Company's Omnibuses on the above Route.

This Ticket is only to be used by the person named thereon, and will be forfeited if used by anyone else.

The Company do not accept any liability whatsoever, in the event of any accident to the user of this Ticket, arising out of any journey on the Company's Omnibuses or Coaches.

Geo. H. Davis
GEO. H. DAVIS, Secretary.

SEASON TICKET
WILTS & DORSET
MOTOR SERVICES, LTD.

This season ticket, with an expiry date of 21 October 1922, was issued to a Mr E J Maidment for travel between Salisbury Market Place and Skew Bridge. Note that it's signed in ink by the Company Secretary George H Davis. This ticket was pasted into a leather season ticket wallet embossed with Wilts & Dorset Motor Services Ltd in gold.

IVOR WEST

in 1922

The British Broadcasting Company (BBC) was formed, and began radio broadcasts.

Production of Branston Pickle began.

The Transport & General Workers Union (TGWU) was formed, Ernest Bevin being the first general secretary.

The Irish Free State came into being.

Popular music included April Showers by Al Jolson and Sheik of Araby by Ray Miller and his Orchestra.

in 1923

Britain's railways was grouped into four large companies: the Great Western Railway, the Southern Railway, the London, Midland & Scottish Railway and the London & North Eastern Railway.

Prime Minister Andrew Bonar Law resigned owing to ill health; his place was taken by Stanley Baldwin.

Radio Times published for the first time.

A general election resulted in a hung parliament and Stanley Baldwin remained Prime Minister.

Popular music included Yes! We have no Bananas by Ben Selvin and Barney Google by Billy Jones and Ernest Hare.

1922-1923

By the time the photograph on the left was taken in 1922, CD 2556 had this Harrington 33-seat charabanc body, fitted to it the previous year. In this guise it was to remain in service with the company until 1930.

Bought new by Wilts & Dorset early in 1922 was Leyland G7 HR 6404 with 26-seat Harrington charabanc bodywork, shown in the lower picture on the left.. This was no doubt a jolly outing; notice that one of the gentlemen has brought along a banjo to enliven the journey.

Among the vehicles taken over with Salisbury & District in August 1921 had been Thornycroft J HR 4559. This vehicle had originated as a War Department lorry in 1917; after overhaul by Thornycroft in 1920, it had a Strachan & Brown charabanc body mounted on to it the following year.

After acquisition by Wilts & Dorset, a Harrington single- deck bus body was put on it instead in 1923, and then two years later replaced by a Dodson double-deck body! HR 4559 remained in the Wilts & Dorset fleet until 1929.

Below are driver and conductor in the time-honoured pose, leaning against the radiator between trips.

DAVID PENNELS COLLECTION

in 1924

The shipping forecast was broadcast on radio for the first time.

The Government lost a vote of confidence; James Ramsay MacDonald became Prime Minister, leading a minority Labour Government.

The Greenwich Time Signal ('pips') was first heard on the radio.

A general election was won by the Conservative Party, Stanley Baldwin becoming Prime Minister.

Popular music included It Had to be You by Isham Jones and his Orchestra and Somebody Stole My Gal by Ted Weems & his Orchestra. Also selling many records was Rhapsody in Blue, written in 1924 by American composer George Gershwin.

in 1925

John Logie Baird transmitted the first television images in greyscale.

The first double deck buses with covered tops ran in London.

Benito Mussolini took dictatorial powers in Italy.

Popular music included If You Knew Susie by Eddie Cantor and Tea for Two by Marion Harris.

in 1926

John Logie Baird gave the first public demonstration of a television.

Countrywide general strike during May.

First British Grand Prix held at Brooklands Circuit, near Weybridge, Surrey.

Council for the Preservation of Rural England formed.

Popular music included Bye Bye Blackbird by Gene Austin, I'm Sitting on Top of the World by Al Jolson and Valencia by Paul Whiteman & his Orchestra.

1924

In September 1924 joint Managing Director and Secretary George Davis died. The position of Secretary was then taken by Raymond Longman, who went on to play a key role in conduct of the Company for the following 38 years. A new Managing Director was not appointed then.

Two vehicles joined the fleet that year; a Leyland G7 with charabanc body that entered service in March and a 2-ton AEC single-deck chara/saloon that came in June. The latter was the first vehicle bought new by the company to have pneumatic (as opposed to solid) tyres.

1925

Two AEC single decks received in March were of interest in that their 24-seat bodies were built by United Automobile Services at Lowestoft. This coachbuilding department of the United Automobile company was later transferred to the Eastern Counties Omnibus Company in 1931, then in 1936 formed the basis of Eastern Coach Works, which provided the bodywork for the majority of new Wilts & Dorset buses bought between 1940 and 1980.

In September a Leyland single deck - MR 4867 - was Wilts & Dorset's first forward-control vehicle; because of its design it soon gained the nickname *'the tram'*. It was used mainly on the Salisbury to Bournemouth route, but was withdrawn in 1930 and sold to a garage in London where it was converted to a lorry which survived until after the Second World War.

Traffic on the routes north of Salisbury was light, partly owing to the fact that fewer troops were now training on Salisbury Plain. To match the service to the level of demand some curtailment of routes and journeys became inevitable.

1926

Wilts & Dorset employees did not take part in the general strike which afflicted the country during May 1926. The company's directors were pleased by this display of staff loyalty and later recorded, *"During the national crisis in May no man left his work, and every scheduled journey was run."* The board extended a hearty vote of thanks, which was conveyed to employees by suitable notices at the garage and in offices.

McCurd bus registration number IB 806, which had been new in 1916 and which had been the first Wilts & Dorset bus to be painted red, was withdrawn in 1926 and sold to a Mr P Jeanes of Weymouth for £85.

It was decided to position a couple of buses at Larkhill to act as chasers, so that when a rival operator's bus departed for Salisbury, a Wilts & Dorset bus also ran direct to the city, with a particular aim of getting the military traffic. It was also agreed to establish a garage in Fordingbridge; this was built by Sidney Horsey of that town to Wilts & Dorset's requirements. The company then rented the garage from him for £33 per year.

New vehicles received during 1926 included two Leyland charabancs and a 54-seat Leyland double-deck bus. Advertising rights on the Company's vehicles were let to Salisbury Billposting Company with effect from December 1926.

In view of the condition of the company's finances, it was stated that it would be impossible to pay a staff bonus for the year.

Under the provisions of the Military Lands Act of 1892, large areas of Salisbury Plain were acquired by the military authorities for training purposes. From time to time in past years open days and demonstrations have been held for the information and entertainment of the public.

Thee two Wilts & Dorset charabancs in the picture at the top of the opposite page were among the vehicles providing transport - and spectator seating - for this display at Larkhill. MR 994 on the right is a Harrington bodied Leyland G7 new in March 1924; the other vehicle, CD 5247, is also a Leyland/Harrington charabanc but this vehicle had joined the Wilts & Dorset fleet in May 1920.

In 1924 Wilts & Dorset's first bus with pneumatic, rather than solid, tyres was delivered. Retro-fitting to older vehicles in the fleet soon followed, including CD 2555. This AEC had started life as a double-deck bus in 1919, but in 1923 was given the Dodson single deck body seen in the picture at the bottom of the opposite page. The crew on this journey from Salisbury to Larkhill and Shrewton were no doubt pleased by the more comfortable ride provided by their newly re-shod bus.

Some of the vehicles operated by the company during the early years had an interesting history, exemplified by HR 4559. This Thornycroft J had started life as a War Department lorry in 1917, overhauled by Thornycroft in 1920 and fitted with a Strachan & Brown charabanc body in 1921, passing to Wilts & Dorset in August of that year.

The charabanc body was replaced by a Harrington single-deck bus body in late 1923. In this guise it had been a regular performer on the Salisbury to Bournemouth route. But in 1925 this was replaced by a 45-seat Dodson double-deck body. It was photographed the following year on a Salisbury city route with driver and conductor posing rather seriously for the camera, seen here on the left. This bus was in service with Wilts & Dorset until the spring of 1929.

DAVID PENNELS COLLECTION

During 1927 Wilts & Dorset took delivery of eight 30cwt Dennis buses with 19-seat bodies by Short. Capable of being one-man-operated when necessary, and particularly suited to either lightly trafficked or highly competitive routes, these small buses soon became known as 'chasers'. The first three were delivered in February 1927; an example is seen here when new.

DAVID PENNELS COLLECTION

1927

The directors met with Mr W W Graham of Hants & Dorset to agree to an even frequency for the Salisbury to Bournemouth route, over which both companies ran.

In February some small capacity Dennis buses were delivered; these soon became known as 'chasers', and later in the year came the first of the company's Leyland Lion PLSC buses. Then in April Wilts & Dorset bought the goodwill, two single-deck buses and the garage of B&C Motor Services of Bulford. The proprietor, Mr A J Corp, was taken on by Wilts & Dorset as Traffic Superintendent for a wage of £4 per week plus a commission of 2.5% on private hire work gained.

Company Secretary Raymond Longman was made a director of Wilts & Dorset after Douglas Mackenzie resigned his directorship, and that summer, competitor Sparrow & Vincent, trading as Victory, started competition on the Salisbury to Wilton route just after Wilts & Dorset had increased the frequency to six buses an hour.

Wilts & Dorset agreed to rent a portion of Mr B Haskell's shop at 31 Market Square, Salisbury, for use as a booking and parcel office at a rent of £60 per year. Agreement was also reached with HM Postmaster General for the carriage of mail on certain of the company's routes.

A route from Salisbury to Marlborough began on 1 November, and one between Salisbury and Romsey on 5 December.

1928

The year opened well, with a new route from Salisbury to Shaftesbury via the Chalke Valley beginning on 2 January. The Secretary of the British Legion Salisbury Branch sent a letter on 8 February expressing appreciation of the manner in which Wilts & Dorset staff had turned out on parade for the memorial service of the late Sir Douglas Haig; copies were posted in the garage and offices for staff to read.

Competition with Victory intensified in the Salisbury area, with timetables changing frequently as each operator vied for the maximum business, and buses sometimes ran off schedule to be just in front of their competitor. This was confusing for the public and led to strained relationships between the bus companies and the local authorities.

in 1927

The first transatlantic telephone call was made between New York and London.

Christopher Stone became the first radio disc jockey, with a record programme on what was then universally called the wireless.

The first experiment was made, in Wolverhampton, with automatic traffic lights.

Popular music included Me and My Shadow by Whispering Jack Smith and My Blue Heaven by Gene Austin.

in 1928

Parts of London were badly flooded when the River Thames overflowed in January; 14 people drowned and many were left homeless.

The voting age for women was reduced from 30 to 21, giving them equal suffrage rights with men.

British Home Stores opened its first department store, in London.

Alexander Fleming, by accident, discovered penicillin.

Popular music included Sonny Boy by Al Jolson and Among My Souvenirs by Paul Whiteman and his Orchestra

During the year Wilts & Dorset bought an area of land in Castle Street, Salisbury, for the construction of a new garage; also agreement was made with the WD Land Agent to rent a bus parking site at Porton for £13 per year.

New in October 1928, MW 3052, shown above, was a Leyland Lion PLSC3 with a body also built by Leyland .

BRIAN JACKSON COLLECTION

Three more 30cwt Dennis 'chasers' entered service early in 1928, MW 957 being received in January of that year. The crew on the left look proud of their new steed, and are ready to go into action against the competition between Salisbury and Wilton.

DAVID PENNELS COLLECTION

From the summer of 1927 Wilts & Dorset faced competition from Victory, initially on the Salisbury to Wilton route. One of Victory's vehicles was MR 9964, an Albion single decker new in July 1927, and shown on the left.

DAVID PENNELS COLLECTION

Victory also competed on coach and charabanc hire. In the picture on the left the driver holds a baby towards the camera as this party stop for a posed photograph by the Pheasant Inn on the corner of Salt Lane and Rollestone Street in Salisbury.

The Daimler charabanc, HR 6408, eventually passed to Wilts & Dorset in December 1933, but was withdrawn six months later.

DAVID PENNELS COLLECTION

The weather was not kind when these Wilts & Dorset vehicles working a private hire job were lined up for a photo-shoot on the North Walk of Salisbury Cathedral Close late in 1929.

At the front is MW 4594, a Leyland Tiger TS1 with a 32-seat Harrington coach body that incorporated a canvas roof. It was subsequently rebodied by Harrington in 1936, and stayed in service with Wilts & Dorset until November 1952.

DAVID PENNELS COLLECTION

1929

Wilts & Dorset bought 6 Endless Street, Salisbury for £1,700, with the intention of using the premises for offices. Under the provisions of the Railway (Road Transport) Acts passed the previous year, discussions began in May with the Southern Railway Company; in due course the latter was to hold 50% of Wilts & Dorset's share capital.

Mr E J Gulliver of Bowerchalke agreed to relinquish his bus service to Salisbury at the end of March on condition that he was employed by the Company at 50/- (£2.50) per week for a period of at least two months. In April The Tidworth Motor Service was acquired from H R Bartley.

Towards the end of the year, Wilts & Dorset's Charabanc Superintendent wrote to the board requesting an increase in salary together with recognition of his past season's work by way of a bonus. His request for a salary increase was refused, but it was agreed that he would be paid a bonus of £15.

At the end of the year, staff gratuities were paid: £5 each to the Garage Manager and Traffic Manager; £1 each to Inspectors and 10/- (50p) each to all other employees ; apprentices and those with less than 12 months service received 5/- (25p).

1930

Wilts & Dorset's first double deck buses to feature enclosed top decks entered service in January 1930. MW 6050 and MW 6051 were Leyland Titan TD1s fitted with lowbridge bodywork which reduced the height of the vehicle by having a sunken side gangway along the offside of the upper deck, with passengers sitting in rows of four. Lowbridge bodywork became standard for the Company's new double deck buses for the next 24 years.

The new offices, passenger waiting hall and buffet at 6 Endless Street, Salisbury, were formally opened by Cllr Harry Medway, Mayor of Salisbury, on 21 February 1930. The buffet was let to Mr W Shipsey at a rental of £50 for the first year and £100 per year thereafter.

Three buses and the goodwill of his Romsey – Andover route were bought from Mr H Wolstenholme for £1,650.

in 1929

The general election resulted in a hung parliament; J Ramsay MacDonald formed a Labour government (below).

The first Tesco shop opened at Burnt Oak, Middlesex.

The Wall Street crash during late October in the USA also led to a sharp fall on the London Stock Exchange.

Popular music included Tiptoe Through the Tulips by Nick Lucas and Honey by Rudy Valee.

in 1930

Yorkshire born Amy Johnson became the first woman to fly solo from England to Australia.

Unemployment rose to over two million.

On its maiden overseas voyage from Cardington, Bedfordshire, to India, the British airship R101 crashed in France, with the loss of 48 lives.

The first YHA hostel opened – at Llanwrst, North Wales.

Popular music included Ten Cents A Dance by Ruth Etting and On the Sunny Side of the Street by Ted Lewis & his Orchestra.

The 1930 Road Traffic Act (see page 22) was a very significant piece of legislation for the bus industry. The country was segmented into Traffic Areas, each presided over by a Traffic Commissioner. Bus routes required Road Service Licences issued by the Traffic Commissioner, whose authorisation was now needed to start or alter a service.

Objections to the issue of a licence could be made on the grounds of competition or for other reasons. In such instances it was the Traffic Commissioner who decided whether or not to grant the Road Service Licence. The procedures for regulating local bus services laid down in this legislation remained in force until October 1986.

Wilts & Dorset's first fully enclosed double deck buses entered service in January 1930 on Salisbury city routes. They were Leyland TD1s with Leyland lowbridge bodywork seating 48 passengers. One of these impressive vehicles is seen in a photograph taken for Leyland before delivery to Wilts & Dorset.

DAVID PENNELS COLLECTION

Deliveries of new Leyland double deck buses continued, four more being received during the summer of 1930. The photograph on the left was taken with the crew of an Andover local service.

ARTHUR BLAKE
DAVID PENNELS COLLECTION

During the 1920s and early 1930s Wilts & Dorset used the Bell Punch ticket system. When issuing a ticket the conductor punched a hole in the stage number indicating the start of the passenger's journey. Conductors carried the tickets in wooden racks, with stocks of each value of ticket being held in place by a metal spring clip.

WILTS & DORSET.

Competition with Sparrow & Vincent continued; Wilts & Dorset driver Oliver Blake (who was later to preside over Blandford and subsequently Amesbury depots) and his conductor will soon depart for Meyrick Avenue with their new Leyland LT1 saloon; a competing Sparrow & Vincent bus can just be seen in the background.

DAVID PENNELS COLLECTION

The poster advertising the Tidworth Tattoo that was taking place in August 1930 - it's in the middle of the righthand window - enables us to accurately date this photograph of Wilts & Dorset's waiting room and enquiry office in Andover High Street.

The large display timetable to the right of the door that lists buses to a number of destinations is excellent, and you can see that information was available about the services of other operators, including Hants & Dorset and Venture. There was also catering, run by Salisbury based Shipsey's catering.

EDITH S HOWARD
DAVID PENNELS COLLECTION

EGULAR DAILY BUS SERVICES IN THIS DISTRICT
HANTS & DORSET MOTOR SERVICES LTD
BUSES START FROM HERE FOR WINCHESTER WITH DIRECT CONNECTIONS FOR GOSPORT. PORTSMOUTH. AND OTHER POINTS ON THE COMPANY'S SYSTEM.
PARTICULARS WITHIN.
BOOK HERE FOR ROYAL BLUE
AUTOMOBILE SERVICES.
COVERING:
THE SOUTH OF ENGLAND
THE MIDLANDS
THE SOUTH EAST
THE NORTH AND SOUTH DEVON COASTS.

VENTURE LIMITED
BUSES START FROM HERE FOR
LONGPARISH.
WHITCHURCH.
OVERTON.
OAKLEY.
BASINGSTOKE.

NQUIRE WITHIN FOR COMPANY'S TIME TABLES AND THOSE OF
HANTS & DORSET MOTOR SERVICES LTD AND VENTURE LTD.
Wilts & Dorset Motor Services Ltd
BUFFET & WAITING ROOM
PARCELS & ENQUIRY OFFICE
BUSES LEAVE HERE FOR
SEND YOUR PARCELS
WILTS & DORSET
W. SHIPSEY.
CATERER & CONFECTIONER.

Probably keeping an eye on the competition in the picture below – the crew of Sparrow & Vincent's Leyland Lion PLSC3 MW 2955 pose for a photograph while working a Wilton service.
DAVID PENNELS COLLECTION

Also on these pages are examples of a Road Service Licence dating from 1937 and PSV driving licence certificates.

When motor buses started to run on the roads of the United Kingdom there was no overall system of licensing or control of either bus operators or bus routes. This certainly allowed entrepreneurs to introduce bus services where they saw prospects of good returns, So, in this generally laissez-faire climate, a fairly extensive network of bus routes spread across the country over a relatively short period during the 1920s.

Local authorities could exercise some control over bus services under the provisions of the Town Police Clauses Acts 1847-89, but this legislation had been formulated with horse drawn vehicles in mind, and in any case was broadly permissive in nature and certainly not applied in a uniform way across the country. To quote local examples, Salisbury Police issued enamel licence plates which were required to be fitted to the vehicles in question; this was also the case in Bournemouth, but there was no such requirement in Andover.

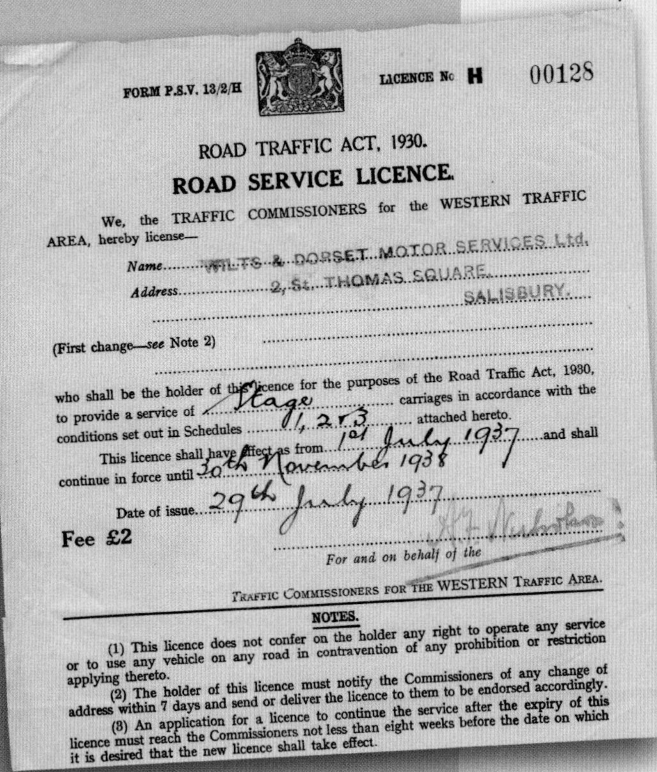
FORM P.S.V. 13/2/H LICENCE No H 00128

ROAD TRAFFIC ACT, 1930.

ROAD SERVICE LICENCE.

We, the TRAFFIC COMMISSIONERS for the WESTERN TRAFFIC AREA, hereby license—

Name WILTS & DORSET MOTOR SERVICES Ltd.

Address 2, St. THOMAS SQUARE. SALISBURY.

(First change—*see* Note 2)

who shall be the holder of this licence for the purposes of the Road Traffic Act, 1930, to provide a service of Stage carriages in accordance with the conditions set out in Schedules 1, 2 & 3 attached hereto.

This licence shall have effect as from 1st July 1937 and shall continue in force until 30th November 1938

Date of issue 29th July 1937

Fee £2

For and on behalf of the

TRAFFIC COMMISSIONERS FOR THE WESTERN TRAFFIC AREA.

NOTES.

(1) This licence does not confer on the holder any right to operate any service or to use any vehicle on any road in contravention of any prohibition or restriction applying thereto.

(2) The holder of this licence must notify the Commissioners of any change of address within 7 days and send or deliver the licence to them to be endorsed accordingly.

(3) An application for a licence to continue the service after the expiry of this licence must reach the Commissioners not less than eight weeks before the date on which it is desired that the new licence shall take effect.

This situation obviously allowed free competition between operators in providing services. Practices such as frequently changing timetables and fares to gain competitive advantage - or even running off schedule to get in front of the competitor's bus - were not really in the best interests of the public. Using small, relatively lightweight buses as 'chasers' to outwit competition was also common. No doubt always carried out with the best of intentions, there were occasionally unfortunate results - such as when a bus operated by Hants & Dorset ended its journey in Leigh Pond (fortunately shallow) while trying to get the better of a competing bus near Wimborne.

The 1930 Road Traffic Act introduced a system of quality and quantity licensing for bus and coach services that was to remain virtually unchanged for over 50 years.

CHAPTER 43. A.D. 1930.

An Act to make provision for the regulation of traffic on roads and of motor vehicles and otherwise with respect to roads and vehicles ... make provision for the protection ... risks arising out of the ... connection with

From now on a Road Service Licence would be required to operate every bus or coach route, excursion or tour. This licence set out in detail the route to followed, the timetable to be operated and the fares to be charged; permission had to be sought by the operator to vary any of these elements.

FORM P.S.V. 30/2/H
LICENCE No. Hbe 01078
BADGE No. HH 4815
ROAD TRAFFIC ACTS, 1930 to 1934.
LICENCE TO DRIVE A PUBLIC SERVICE VEHICLE.
THIS LICENCE is issued by the TRAFFIC COMMISSIONERS for the WESTERN TRAFFIC AREA and authorises—
Frederick Samuel Mitchell
'Chelmonds' Heath Rd.
Bemerton.
Salisbury Wilts.
*Strike out the words which follow if not appropriate.
to drive a public service vehicle* ~~of the type or types shown in the schedule below~~.
This licence shall have effect as from - 3 AUG 1935 and shall continue in force until 1st September 1937
Date of issue - 3 AUG 1935
Fee 2/-
Signature of licensee (see Note 1) F.S. Mitchell
SCHEDULE.
Type or types of public service vehicles which the licensee is licensed to drive.
NOTES.
(1) The licensee must sign this licence in the space provided above immediately on receiving it; but must not write anything else on it.
(2) The licensee must notify the Commissioners of any change of address within 7 days of such change.
(3) This licence does not absolve the licensee from the obligation to obtain a licence to drive under Part I of the Act of 1930. The latter licence has a stiff cover in which this licence when folded into six can conveniently be kept.
[OVER

Bus drivers and conductors now had to hold vocational licences and to wear numbered badges at all times when on duty. It was necessary to pass a medical and provide evidence of good character to gain such licences; drivers also now had to pass a special driving test to drive a bus, as well holding an ordinary driving licence.

All vehicles operated had to have a Certificate of Fitness to be legally used on bus or coach services, which had to be renewed regularly. As the vehicle became more elderly, so the Certificate of Fitness would be renewed for progressively shorter periods. As well as being regularly examined for Certificate of Fitness requirements, officials could make spot checks on the condition of any vehicle at any time. Finally, operators themselves had to hold licences to demonstrate that they were 'fit and proper persons' to provide transport services.

The country was divided into Traffic Areas - initially ten covering England & Wales plus one for Scotland within which the requirements of the Act were administered by Traffic Commissioners. In considering applications for Road Service Licences the Traffic Commissioners were required to consider the suitability of the route and the extent to which the area in question was already provided for by transport services.

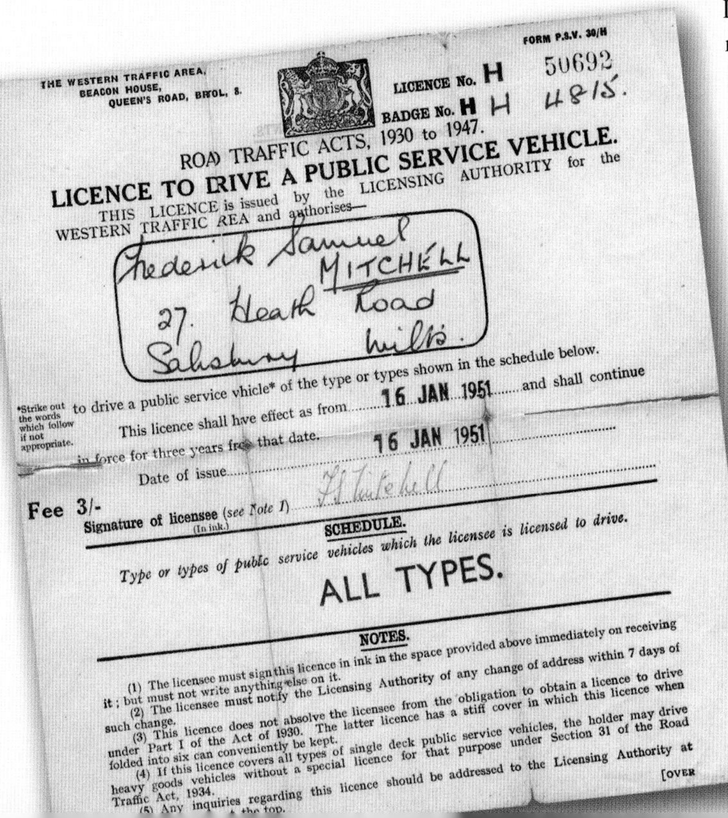
THE WESTERN TRAFFIC AREA,
BEACON HOUSE,
QUEEN'S ROAD, BRIOL, 8.
FORM P.S.V. 30/H
LICENCE No. H 50692
BADGE No. H H 4815.
ROAD TRAFFIC ACTS, 1930 to 1947.
LICENCE TO DRIVE A PUBLIC SERVICE VEHICLE.
THIS LICENCE is issued by the LICENSING AUTHORITY for the WESTERN TRAFFIC AREA and authorises—
Frederick Samuel MITCHELL
27. Heath Road
Salisbury Wilts.
*Strike out the words which follow if not appropriate.
to drive a public service vhicle* of the type or types shown in the schedule below.
This licence shall hve effect as from 16 JAN 1951 and shall continue in force for three years from that date.
Date of issue 16 JAN 1951
Fee 3/-
Signature of licensee (see Note 1) (In ink.) F.S. Mitchell
SCHEDULE.
Type or types of public service vehicles which the licensee is licensed to drive.
ALL TYPES.
NOTES.
(1) The licensee must sign this licence in ink in the space provided above immediately on receiving it; but must not write anything else on it.
(2) The licensee must notify the Licensing Authority of any change of address within 7 days of such change.
(3) This licence does not absolve the licensee from the obligation to obtain a licence to drive under Part I of the Act of 1930. The latter licence has a stiff cover in which this licence when folded into six can conveniently be kept.
(4) If this licence covers all types of single deck public service vehicles, the holder may drive heavy goods vehicles without a special licence for that purpose under Section 31 of the Road Traffic Act, 1934.
(5) Any inquiries regarding this licence should be addressed to the Licensing Authority at ... the top.
[OVER

Details of the applications were given in the regular publication *Notices and Proceedings*. Any operator likely to be affected by the route, and also local authorities and members of the public, could object to the new applications or applications for variations so listed.

The applications were then considered at public sittings of the Traffic Commissioners. These were sometimes referred to as traffic courts, although witnesses were not under oath and the general ambience was often quite informal. The onus was on the applicant to prove the need for the route.

Although it in effect protected established operators, the act was in many ways a sound item of legislation at that time and rightly or wrongly it did last until 1986.

With an eye on the coach hire market, competitor Victory bought this Dennis Arrow with a 32 seat Duple body in July 1931. It got to be part of the Wilts & Dorset fleet when Victory (Sparrow & Vincent) was taken over by Wilts & Dorset in 1933, and this coach remained in Wilts & Dorset's operational fleet until requisitioned for the war effort in 1941.

DAVID PENNELS COLLECTION

in 1931

The first issue of The Highway Code was published.

Deteriorating economic conditions resulted in salary cuts for some public sector employees, a reduction in unemployment benefit and the imposition of a means test.

A national coalition government was formed in August owing to the financial crisis; Ramsay MacDonald remained Prime Minister leading a national government after the general election in October.

London's Abbey Road Studios opened.

Popular music included Minnie the Moocher by Cab Calloway and Tiger Rag by the Mills Brothers.

1931

With effect from 1 July 1931 half of the shares in Wilts & Dorset were owned by the Southern Railway. It was agreed that the words 'In association with the Southern Railway' would appear after the name Wilts & Dorset on all publicity material produced by the Company. Wilts & Dorset were to send 21 copies of all timetable books to the Southern Railway, who in turn would supply eight copies of the SR timetable for use in Wilts & Dorset offices. Stocks of timetables were also exchanged on a sale or return basis to be sold at railway stations and bus company travel offices. Space was allocated in Wilts & Dorset timetables for details of principal train services, and Wilts & Dorset was given a free page in the railway's Hints for Holidays book.

The Traffic Commissioners held a public sitting on 29/30 June at which a substantial number of applications by the Company for Road Service Licences under the provisions of the 1930 Road Traffic Act were heard.

New garage premises came into use in Castle Street, built by C Collins and Sons.

At the end of the year a Christmas bonus was paid to staff, however notice was given that this should not be regarded as an annual bonus but could only be paid when the Company's trading position justified it.

Leyland Titan TD1 MW 9396 was brand new when it was involved in an unfortunate accident on 28 July 1931. Travelling from Amesbury towards Salisbury, the driver had descended White Railings Hill when he pulled onto the verge on the left to let another vehicle pass. The nearside wheels sank into the soft verge, causing the bus to fall onto its side and slip down a bank into a field. Sadly seven people were injured. The bus was recovered and repaired, and stayed in the fleet until November 1951.

DAVID PENNELS COLLECTION

Above is a line of Leyland Titan TD1 double decks, an impressive sight at Salisbury in 1931, with destination blinds set for city destinations and places further afield, too.

Prior to the construction of Amesbury bus station in 1933, Wilts & Dorset had a waiting room and booking office on the corner of Salisbury Street and Amesbury High Street, as seen on the left in 1931. This was on the site that had previously been used for Amesbury gaol.

New in May 1931, Leyland Tiger TS1 MW 8758 on the left here looks a very inviting and comfortable vehicle for a coach tour with its 32 seat Harrington coach body.

DAVID PENNELS COLLECTION

1932

Following complaints put forward through Salisbury City Council that fares were too high on some local bus routes, the Traffic Commissioners held a public sitting at Salisbury Guildhall on Friday 26 February. The Chairman of the Commissioners, Major General Sir Reginald Ford, observed *"It is human nature that the public want to get everything at as low a price as possible, whether they are buying meat or groceries at a shop, they want to get the best they can at the lowest price, which is not unnatural. In the same way, they want to be carried about from place to place at the lowest possible price, but as much as it is desired that they should be able to do so, that lowest possible price must be a remunerative one to the operators. No operator is going to run a service for the benefit of his health; he is going to run it to make a living for himself, and he is going to run it in the best interests of the public – to attract the public – giving an efficient service so as to make his business a paying one."* The outcome was that bus fares in Salisbury could remain unchanged for the time being.

Allegations of obstruction caused by buses in Salisbury Street, Amesbury, were received from Amesbury Parish Council. In response, the company announced it was considering plans to build a bus station which would alleviate this problem.

In the small picture below right and about to operate a journey to Wilton, the crew of MW 7048 posed for the photographer by the offside front of the bus, but the elderly gentleman carrying a pipe was obviously also determined to be in the picture. This bus was a Leyland Titan TD1 that had been new in June 1930 and would stay in service with Wilts & Dorset until January 1952.

DAVID PENNELS COLLECTION

in 1932

The first BBC radio broadcasts were made from the newly completed Broadcasting House in London.

Mars bars went on sale for the first time.

Book tokens were launched in the UK.

Using BBC radio, King George V delivered the first Royal Christmas Message.

Popular music included Night & Day by Fred Astaire and Brother, Can You Spare A Dime by Bing Crosby.

in 1933

The iconic London Underground diagram designed by Harry Beck was issued for the first time.

Adolf Hitler became German Chancellor.

The Oxford Union student debating society declared that *"this House will in no circumstances fight for King and Country."*

Popular music included Love is the Sweetest Thing by Ray Noble and Stormy Weather by Ethel Waters.

The conditions laid down by the 1930 Road Traffic Act were easier for larger operators to comply with, and Wilts & Dorset acquired the goodwill of 12 local operators during the year, including P C J Sawyer who ran between Netheravon and Salisbury. Sawyer was taken on by Wilts & Dorset as a driver, and later became Depot Inspector at Pewsey.

1933

The site for Amesbury bus station had been cleared by March 1933, and a contract for construction, including a passenger waiting room and local offices was awarded to James & Crockerell of Durrimgton for £1,958 - the lowest of nine tenders. The work was completed in June; a lock up shop that formed part of the new property was let to Mr E A Trend of Amesbury at a rental of £50 per year.

After long negotiations, the business of Wilts & Dorset's main competitor in Salisbury, Sparrow & Vincent, was acquired for £16,000. Competition had been serious and sustained, affecting not just bus services in Salisbury but also excursions and tours. The entire fleet of 16 vehicles was taken over. It was a varied selection. Nine had been withdrawn by the end of 1935 and most of the others disposed of during the 1940s, although two 1927 Leyland saloons were rebodied in 1945 and survived with Wilts & Dorset until July 1950.

In addition,six new Leyland double-deck buses joined the fleet in 1933. These remained in service until the mid 1950s, albeit with rebuilt or replacement bodies.

Entering service in January 1933, WV 2382 at the top of this page was one of six Leyland Titan TD2 lowbridge double deckers bought by Wilts & Dorset that year. In this batch, the front of the top deck was modernised, eliminating the 'piano-front' appearance of the previous all-Leyland double-deck buses. Notice also the concrete K3 telephone kiosk on the left.

DAVID PENNELS COLLECTION

One of the three buses bought with the Romsey-Andover route from Mr H Wolstenolme in 1930 was UK 8818. This was a 20-seat Guy ONDF, which by 1933 (and for several years thereafter) was a familiar sight on local routes in the Fordingbridge area. UK 8818 remained in service with Wilts & Dorset until January 1940.

A LACROIX / DAVID PENNELS COLLECTION

This impressive array of Wilts & Dorset vehicles was snapped in Salisbury Market Square on 14 July 1933. The numbers in the windscreens suggest it was a large private hire outing.

DAVID PENNELS COLLECTION

The new bus station at Amesbury had been completed in the summer of 1933, and looked very smart when Morris Commercial Viceroy MW 8761 was seen about to operate a journey to Larkhill early in 1934. Carrying a 24-seat body by Heaver of Durrington, this bus had been new in April 1931 and would remain in the fleet until May 1943

DAVID PENNELS COLLECTION

1934

Plans were approved for improvements to the garage at Junction Road, Andover, at an estimated cost of £1,240. The goodwill of the Primrose Bus Service route between Thruxton and Andover was also acquired.

Four new vehicles entered the fleet in 1934; two Leyland double decks with lowbridge Brush bodies (similar to some supplied to Hants & Dorset), and two coaches with Harrington 32-seat bodies.

1935

New heating apparatus was installed at the Castle Street works in Salisbury at a cost of £328; it was agreed that this work would be carried out during August.

Four vehicles joined the fleet in 1935. The first, delivered in April, were two Leyland KP3 Cub coaches, with Harrington bodywork seating 20 passengers. Then in July came the first diesel engined buses to be delivered to Wilts & Dorset. These were two Leyland TD4 double deck buses with 52 seat Leyland lowbridge bodies. They were in service with Wilts & Dorset until 1956-7.

in 1934

The National Council for Civil Liberties was established.

The first opera festival was held at Glyndebourne.

Dinky Toys were introduced.

Popular music included June in January by Bing Crosby and The Very Thought of You by Ray Noble.

in 1935

It was the Silver Jubilee of King George V.

Driving tests became compulsory.

Penguin Books was founded.

Stanley Baldwin succeeded Ramsay MacDonald as Prime Minister.

Clement Attlee became leader of the Labour Party.

Popular music included Cheek to Cheek by Fred Astair and Red Sails in the Sunset by Guy Lombardo.

The two Leyland Titan TD3 double-deck buses received in May 1934 were bodied by Brush, as exemplified by WV 4922 in a photograph taken for Brush before the bus was delivered to Wilts & Dorset, shown at the bottom of the opposite page. This particular bus stayed in service with Wilts & Dorset for almost 21 years.

In July 1934 two Leyland Tiger TS6 coaches bodied by Harrington were added to the fleet. The picture on the top of this page shows one of them, WV 5527, when new at Amesbury, where it spent most of its working life.

By mid 1934 WV 1274, one of the coaches taken over by Wilts & Dorset from Victory (Sparrow & Vincent) in December 1933, had been painted in Wilts & Dorset livery.

On the left you can see this coach having conveyed a party of ladies all in their best hats it would seem (plus a few children). It was an Albion PV70 with a 32-seat coach body by Heaver and had been new to Sparrow & Vincent in May 1932, and was requisitioned for the war effort in 1941.

On the left, photographed for Leyland prior to delivery, WV 7475 entered service with Wilts & Dorset in July 1935. This Leyland Titan TD4 with 52-seat Leyland lowbridge bodywork lasted in the fleet until November 1956.

DAVID PENNELS COLLECTION

July 1936 saw the delivery of two more Leyland Titan TD4 double deck buses. These had metal-framed Leyland lowbridge bodies with a more pleasing profile. They lasted until the spring of 1957. AHR 399 is seen on the right when new.

In October 1936 Wilts & Dorset acquired the business of W Rowland & Sons of Salisbury. Leyland charabanc MR 510, shown at the bottom of the page while still working for Rowland and with passengers bound for Weymouth, had been new in 1924. It was sold in July 1937 to Brighton Corporation, where it was converted into a tipper lorry that was in use until December 1947.

DAVID PENNELS COLLECTION

1936

It was decided to buy cottages and land adjoining the new Amesbury bus station so that a garage could be built. The company agreed to make reductions in the rents paid by the tenants provided they gave up sufficient of their gardens to allow construction of the garage.

Two Leyland Tiger TS7 coaches with Harrington 32-seat bodies joined the fleet in January, but didn't enter service until May owing to the seasonal nature of coach operations, and in July a further two Leyland Titan TD4 double-deck buses were delivered. These had more modern-looking, 52-seat Leyland lowbridge bodywork that was superior in passenger comfort. They remained in service until the spring of 1957.

In October Wilts & Dorset acquired the coach business of W Rowland & Sons of Salisbury. Of the seven vehicles in the fleet, five Leyland coaches were taken into stock. The other two were charabancs; these were quickly sold, notwithstanding the fact that one of them was based on a Rolls Royce Silver Ghost chassis.

1937

James & Crockerell of Durrington was contracted to build the new garage at Amesbury; once it came into use the garages at Larkhill and Bulford were relinquished from 29 September.

in 1936

King George V died, aged 70.

The first Butlins holiday camp opened, at Skegness.

Over 200 men marched from Jarrow to London in protest against unemployment and poverty.

King Edward VIII abdicated.

Popular music included Pennies from Heaven by Bing Crosby and Summertime by Billie Holiday.

in 1937

The coronation of King George VI took place at Westminster Abbey.

Prime Minister Stanley Baldwin retired. His place was taken by Neville Chamberlain, still leading the coalition National government.

The 999 emergency telephone number came into use.

The first issue of The Dandy comic appeared.

Popular music included Once in a While by Tommy Dorsey and September in the Rain by Guy Lombardo.

At the garage in Castle Street HR 74 was decorated in honour of the coronation, shown above. This lorry had started life as a Leyland charabanc and came to Wilts & Dorset when the company had acquired H R Bartley's Tidworth Motor Service in 1929. It was subsequently rebuilt as a lorry and known by the garage staff as 'Betsy'.

DAVID PENNELS COLLECTION

AMW 481 at Tidworth in the picture on the left was one of the two Leyland Lion LT7 saloons new in March 1937. Staff are standing proudly beside it. Note the elaborate bus shelter in the background.

ARTHUR BLAKE
DAVID PENNELS COLLECTION

Wilts & Dorset agreed to lease 45 Blue Boar Row in Salisbury for use as a booking office, as it was near the departure point for the company's excursions and tours.

More significantly, negotiations began to buy 10 Endless Street, 15 Rollestone Street and 17 Rollestone Street with a view to providing a coach station in Salisbury. Discussions began with the brewery Gibbs Mew & Co. to ascertain the terms on which they would exchange the Woolpack Inn (8 Endless Street) for the Wilts & Dorset offices that then occupied 6 Endless Street. The brewery proved willing to help - Wilts & Dorset must be one of the only bus operators that can claim to have been responsible for moving a public house.

Wilts & Dorset obtained the goodwill of the Silver Star (Shergold & White) route between Sling Camp at Bulford and Salisbury for £1,500, and attempted to negotiate terms for the purchase of the entire Silver Star operation but without success (Silver Star was eventually bought by Wilts & Dorset in 1963). Wilts & Dorset also bought the goodwill of R H & M Emm's bus route which ran between Woodminton (Bowerchalke) and Salisbury on Tuesdays and Saturdays.

Joining the fleet in March 1937 were two Leyland Lion LT7s with Harrington dual-purpose 32-seat bodies. Although built to coach standard, these were mostly used on bus work. Two new double-deckers came in October, Leyland Titan TD5s with 52-seat Park Royal bodies - there would be nine by June 1939.

Coachloads of people travelled to Southsea to see the ships taking part in the Coronation Fleet Review by King George VI in May 1937.

Suitably decorated with mini union flags on their radiators, MW 4594 (which had been rebodied by Harrington in 1936) and a Leyland Cub coach are ready to operate to Southsea from Salisbury Market Square.

W J HAYNES
DAVID PENNELS COLLECTION

Bound for Weymouth on the right in 1938, 1936 Leyland Titan TD4 AHR 399 awaits passengers in Chipper Lane, Salisbury, facing the junction with Endless Street. Work was beginning on the bus station in Endless Street that would open the following year.

The prestige of Wilts & Dorset's coach fleet was enhanced by two Leyland Tiger TS8s with Harrington 32-seat bodies that came in June 1938. BAM 800 below, photographed when new, exemplifies these superb vehicles.

DAVID PENNELS COLLECTION

1938

After consultations with architect H J Starkey, plans for what was now designated as a bus station in Endless Street were approved. Work began late in 1938, the contract for construction having been awarded to H & J Taylor Ltd. For temporary office accommodation during the work, Wilts & Dorset took a 12-month tenancy of 12 Endless Street which had previously been empty. Expansion at Castle Street for the garage was also agreed, the plans for this having been drawn up by Cogwell & Sons.

Gem Coaches (C J A Culley) held a licence for an express service between Salisbury Railway Station and the Race Plain in connection with race meetings. Wilts & Dorset bought the goodwill of this operation in September 1938 for £350.

Two more new dual-purpose Leyland saloons joined the fleet in March 1938, followed by a couple of Harrington bodied Leyland Tiger TS8 coaches in June. Four Leyland Titan TD5 double deckers arrived during June and July. These had Park Royal lowbridge bodies and remained in service until early 1956.

1939

In the spring of 1939 Germany occupied the whole of Czechoslovakia; the British government moved away from its previous policy of appeasement and began to rearm. War seemed inevitable, and this lead to a huge and very rapid expansion of Army facilities on Salisbury Plain, and the construction of a large army camp at Blandford. Wilts & Dorset gained contracts to provide transport for the construction workers engaged in building these camps; this was a massive exercise, the contract for Blandford Camp alone requiring no less than 119 vehicles. Secondhand buses were sourced from all over the country, including 58 from Southdown. Such was the haste that many stayed in their original liveries. Fitters often travelled from Salisbury to Blandford to work on the vehicles during the daytime before the evening return journey.

Salisbury bus station opened in August. The booking office at 45 Blue Boar Row was felt to be superfluous, especially in time of war, so the premises were loaned rent free to Salisbury Corporation for the duration of the war, to be used for Air Raid Precautions work, the Corporation agreeing to pay property rates.

in 1938

The Women's Voluntary Service (WVS) was founded.

The first issue of The Beano comic appeared.

War clouds were gathering, but Prime Minister Neville Chamberlain signed the Munich Agreement with German leader Adolf Hitler in September, and returned to Britain declaring 'peace for our time'.

Popular music included Begin the Beguine by Artie Shaw and A-Tisket, A-Tasket by Ella Fitzgerald.

in 1939

Distribution of Anderson air raid shelters to householders commenced in February.

Evacuation of children from major cities started on 30 August.

The fledgling BBC television service was closed; BBC radio was rationalised into one programme - the BBC Home Service - from 1 September.

On Sunday 3 September Prime Minister Neville Chamberlain announced that Britain was at war with Germany.

Popular music included Over the Rainbow by Judy Garland, Tea for Two by Art Tatum and Thanks for the Memory by Bob Hope and Shirley Ross.

With Wilts & Dorset staff being called up into the armed services, the company resolved that allowances may be paid to those staff who were now serving their country in this way. In general, these were paid only to married men, and each application was examined on its merits. By December 1939 the claims of 43 men had been received; allowances were made to 25, 12 were judged as not being entitled and the other six still under consideration.

Above is the last of a batch of nine Park Royal bodied Leyland Titan TD5s delivered 1937-39, BWV 664. This bus entered service in June 1939 and was photographed when brand new.

Pressed into service even before proper destination blinds could be fitted, UF 7430 was a former Southdown Leyland Titan TD1 with highbridge bodywork by Short which the company acquired in June 1939. Later rebodied by Eastern Coach Works in 1941, this particular bus was noted for its speed and remained in the Wilts & Dorset fleet until November 1952.

Wilts & Dorset busmen were photographed here with some of the company's recently acquired secondhand vehicles at Blandford Camp in 1939. Sometimes buses would take workmen to Blandford Camp in the morning and fitters would then work on the vehicles during the day at Blandford before coming back in the evening.

DAVID PENNELS COLLECTION

Oops – as you can see in the picture on the right, former Tyneside TY 6974 was somewhat incapacitated at Blandford Camp. New in 1930, this Leyland bodied Leyland Titan TD1 was one of four similar Tyneside vehicles acquired by Wilts & Dorset in July 1939 for the Blandford Camp contract.

This bus did not come to any serious harm in this incident, and survived to receive a new Duple lowbridge body in 1942, remaining in the Wilts & Dorset fleet until January 1952.

DAVID PENNELS COLLECTION

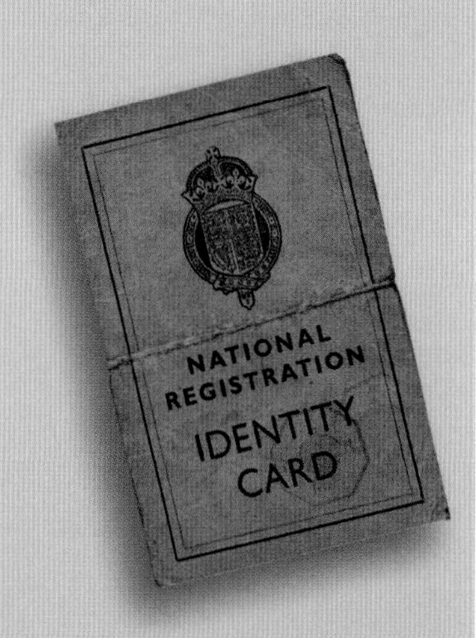

in 1940

Forces Programme began on BBC radio.

Food rationing began.

Neville Chamberlain resigned as Prime Minister, replaced by Winston Churchill.

Over 300,000 troops evacuated from Dunkirk to England.

Italy declared war on Britain and France.

The blitz began, with sustained bombing of London and other centres of population.

Popular music included We'll Meet Again by Vera Lynn, In The Mood by the Glenn Miller Orchestra, Maybe by the Ink Spots and When You Wish Upon A Star by Cliff Edwards.

1940

The establishment of Blandford Camp meant that the erstwhile arrangement to outstation two Wilts & Dorset buses in the yard of haulage contractor Stewart Best, near the railway viaduct in East Street, was no longer adequate. Plans for a garage to be built on the site of a nursery near the railway bridge in Salisbury Road were submitted to Blandford Town Council, who objected as the site was in a residential area. The company won an appeal against the Council's objection and construction began.

Wilts & Dorset was fortunate to receive a number of new vehicles by the end of March 1940 that were built to pre-war standards and specifications - they would soon be difficult to obtain with many bus factories given over to the war effort. Twelve new double deck buses (CHR 487-498) were the first for the company built by Bristol and had Eastern Coach Works bodies. This was a combination that was to become a standard for more than 35 years after the war. Powered by the economical and reliable Gardner 5LW diesel engine, these first examples were soon working very hard on heavily loaded services. The other new vehicles were dual-purpose Leyland Tiger TS8 single deckers which completed an order for 16 of the type; from December 1941 onwards all were converted to what was called a standee layout with perimeter seating - hardly dual-purpose any more.

The Government was keen to encourage everyone to contribute to the war effort by investing any spare cash into National Savings. Advertising slogans such as ***Hit Back with National Savings*** and later ***Fight in the Streets; Belong to your Savings Group*** were very effective. Wilts & Dorset supported this initiative, starting an Employees War Savings Scheme that made it easy for staff to save money regularly. On 1 August 1940 the Company Secretary reported that the scheme had been successfully inaugurated and had 98 subscribers.

A high proportion of bus conductors had joined the armed forces, their place being taken by women conductresses (often called clippies). An immediate result was the need to construct a conductresses' rest room at the east end of the new Salisbury bus station. As an occupation, bus work was made much more difficult by the blackout imposed during the hours of darkness.

Bombing of the Vickers Supermarine aircraft factory at Woolston in September 1940 led to around 50% of Wilts & Dorset's workshop and garage in Castle Street being requisitioned for Spitfire aircraft production. This resulted in a shortage of space for the overnight parking of the buses, which then had to be dispersed to various sites around Salisbury.

In January 1940 Wilts & Dorset received its first Eastern Coach Works bodied Bristol buses, a combination that was to become very familiar in the post-war years. The first of the batch of 12, CHR 487, was photographed leaving the coachbuilder at Lowestoft in the picture above. Smart, rugged and reliable, these buses were finished to peacetime standards and went on to give yeoman service for many years.

EASTERN COACH WORKS
DAVID PENNELS COLLECTION

More than 100 were killed in the air raid on the Supermarine Spitfire aircraft fighter factory at Woolston in Southampton, on 26 September 1940.

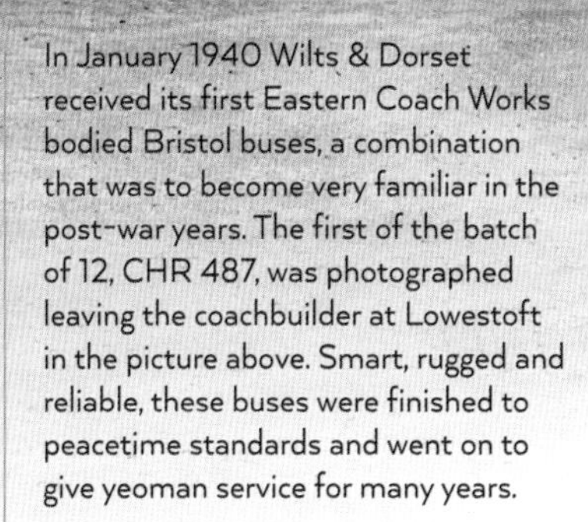

Within weeks 28 alternative sites had been found around Southampton as well as Reading, Hungerford, Newbury, Salisbury and Winchester, and aircraft were soon being produced again, right around the clock. Wilts & Dorset's Salisbury depot was partially commandeered to build wings and fuselages.

Many completed Spitfires were tested from the airfield at nearby High Post. There is a story that the Bishop of Salisbury complained to the Government about the noise from this test flying interrupting his sermons. He got a response which more or less outlined what Hitler would do if the Spitfires were not there!

Following the destruction of the Vickers Supermarine aircraft factories at Woolston by bombing, Wilts & Dorset's Castle Street depot in Salisbury was requisitioned for aircraft production.

Some buses, including a former Southdown Leyland double deck, were still in evidence when the photograph on the left was taken in late September 1940, but jigs for Vickers Supermarine had been delivered and are seen in the foreground, having recently been unloaded.

NORMAN PARKER COLLECTION
COURTESY DAVID PENNELS

It was quite unusual to see highbridge double deck buses in service with Wilts & Dorset, and care had to be taken that they were not allocated to routes that had restricted height clearances such as low bridges. There were no such problems on the Salisbury city route to Waters Road, and this is where former Chatham & District Leyland Titan TD1 KR 6530 was bound when photographed in Salisbury bus station.

New in 1930, this vehicle was acquired by Wilts & Dorset in July 1939; it would subsequently receive a new Willowbrook lowbridge body in 1944 and remained in the fleet until September 1952.

DAVID PENNELS COLLECTION

in 1941

The blitz continued.

Japan attacked the American fleet at Pearl Harbour; Britain and America declared war on Japan.

Germany declared war on America.

One of the highest selling records was Warsaw Concerto, a light classical piece especially written for 1941 British film Dangerous Moonlight by Richard Addinsell; popular for many years. Hits of 1941 included Chattanooga Choo Choo by Glenn Miller and Amapola by Jimmy Dorsey.

1941

Wilts & Dorset continued to encourage staff to take part in National Savings, adding the incentive of bonus certificates to subscribers. The company was now included in the provisions of the Essential Works Order 1941, which effectively meant that staff could not leave the company's employment or be dismissed except with the sanction of the Ministry of Labour.

When clothes rationing was introduced, everyone in the country was allotted an initial supply of 66 coupons to last for the year from 1 June 1941. Items of clothing required varying numbers of coupons - for example a man's overcoat required 16 coupons, a shirt eight. By a regulation of the Board of Trade, all members of Wilts & Dorset's uniformed staff were required to surrender 12 coupons for their uniform.

Now with headlamp masks to comply with blackout regulations, Leyland Titan TD5 BWV 663 was on the local service between Blandford and Blandford Camp in the picture on the left, with some of the camp buildings in the background.

DAVID PENNELS COLLECTION

In March 1941 Wilts & Dorset bought land at 35-39 Bridge Street in Andover, and plans were quickly made to provide a bus station here. It was agreed that 42 copies of each Wilts & Dorset timetable book would be delivered to the Southern Railway, which would distribute them to various stations and offices. Charges for emergency hire of buses to the Southern Railway were agreed at 1/3d (6p) per mile or 10/- (50p) per hour for a single deck, or 1/6d (7.5p) per mile or 12/6d (62.5p) per hour for a double deck vehicle, the higher of the two options to apply in all cases, but with a maximum charge for any vehicle of 30/- (£1.50).

It was also agreed that the company would buy Gardner 5LW diesel engines as and when such units were available, to replace less efficient and outworn petrol engines in as many buses as possible under the circumstances.

The existing contract with Salisbury Billposting Limited expired on 24 December 1941; advertising on the sides of Wilts & Dorset buses was then dealt with by the Publicity Department of Tilling's association.

In the picture at the bottom of the opposite page is what had been former Southdown Leyland Titan TD1 double deck UF 7407. It was acquired by Wilts & Dorset in June 1939, but in service as a bus with the company only until February 1940, at which point it was rebuilt as a breakdown lorry.

Here it is in that guise in the post-war period some years later. Remaining in the fleet until September 1961, UF 7407 had the distinction of being the last of the acquired Leylands in service with Wilts & Dorset, albeit not in bus form any more.

BRIAN JACKSON COLLECTION

As men employed by Wilts & Dorset joined the armed forces during the war, their place as bus conductors (or in some cases mechanics) was taken by women. The first snapshot on the right was taken in the then new Blandford garage late in 1941; the driver standing by the nearside front wheel is Stan Jay, who later became Depot Inspector at Blandford. Their bus is TK 2591, a former Hants & Dorset Leyland Titan TD1 that had been acquired in 1939.

DAVID PENNELS COLLECTION

Conductress Edith Rolf joined Wilts & Dorset in February 1941 and was based at Andover. Edith recalled the difficulties of operation during the war time blackout; on one very foggy night she had to walk along in front of the bus carrying a flag to help the driver because visibility was practically nil.

BARRY ROLF

Bus crews certainly performed a vital role in the war effort. The number of passengers needing to travel is illustrated by this photograph of queues at Salisbury bus station taken during 1942.

PHIL DAVIES COLLECTION

1942

Owing to heavy snowfall, the company had to cancel some Salisbury Plain services between 22 and 27 January; troops holding tickets issued by Wilts & Dorset were allowed to travel by train between Andover Junction and Salisbury and between Bulford and Salisbury.

By 1942 paper was in such short supply that even the minutes of board meetings had been typed onto the reverse of previously used sheets. In view of this, fewer Wilts & Dorset timetables were supplied to the Southern Railway. A letter in Modern Transport alleged that there was a lack of information at railway stations regarding the services of associated bus companies. Due to the arrangements to supply timetable books and display timetable sheets at Southern Railway stations, Wilts & Dorset felt this criticism could not be applied to itself, especially as company timetable sheets were also on display at the Great Western Railway Station in Westbury.

The goodwill of Mr L Sprackling's Blandford Camp to Blandford service was bought for £500; the remainder of Mr Sprackling's Ivory Coaches business passed to Bere Regis & District.Also in the year Mr R I H Longman was appointed General Manager of Wilts & Dorset; Mr R Herridge replaced him as Secretary.

in 1942

First broadcast of Desert Island Discs (on BBC Forces Programme) .

Singapore surrendered to Japanese.

German Army defeated by British 8th Army under General Montgomery at El Alamein.

Popular music included The White Cliffs of Dover by Vera Lynn, Kalamazoo by Glenn Miller and White Christmas by Bing Crosby.

1943

Wartime restrictions meant new buses were were scarce and operators had to accept whatever they were allocated by the Government. Wilts & Dorset obtained four Daimler double deckers in 1943 that entered service in a utility grey livery. They served the company well. After spending some years based at Blandford operating the Salisbury to Weymouth route, later they were often seen running between Salisbury and Southampton before ending their days on Salisbury city services in the mid-1950s.

Wilts & Dorset declined to buy Newbury & District Motor Services when it came up for sale, as the vendors wanted a substantial payment for the goodwill and it was considered inadvisable to spend such a large ammount in the present circumstances. A new staff canteen at Salisbury bus station was opened on 13 November..

in 1943

Allied forces invaded Italy.

Utility furniture became available; basic but sturdy, some lasted more than 50 years.

Total evacuation of Imber on Salisbury Plain and Tyneham in Dorset to provide more land for military training purposes. Both villages remain as unpopulated military training areas in the 21st century.

Popular music included You'll Never Know by Vera Lynn and Paper Doll by the Mills Brothers.

TK 2592 on the left was a Leyland Titan TD1 that originated with Hants & Dorset in 1929 and came to Wilts & Dorset ten years later. In September 1942 it was outshopped with a new Wilts & Dorset own-built 52-seat lowbridge body, which even in wartime austerity grey paint shows a pleasing aspect. It went on to serve a further ten years, mostly on Salisbury city services, and was finally withdrawn in 1952.

DAVID PENNELS COLLECTION

As at 31 December 1943 Wilts & Dorset employed 712 staff of whom 192 were drivers and 184 conductors. 189 vehicles were owned or hired, and the average mileage driven by a driver in a week was 446.

By now carrying a Park Royal lowbridge body fitted in August 1941, former Southdown Leyland Titan TD1 UF 7079 in the picture above was on an Andover service.

S L POOLE

DAVID PENNELS COLLECTION

CHR 477, at the top of the opposite page, was one of a batch of 16 Leyland Tiger TS8s with Harrington dual-purpose bodywork received in 1939-40. Starting in 1941, all were converted to standee layout with perimeter seating for 28 and standing room for 20, not returning to normal 32-seat layout until 1946.

With obligatory white-tipped mudguards and headlamp masks, CHR 477 was on the Salisbury to East Grimstead and Farley route with the driver standing by.

MALCOLM SCOTT

Sign of the times on the left! The masked headlamps were very noticeable when a driver and conductress from Blandford depot were photographed leaning on the front of their vehicle between trips in 1943.

BRIAN JACKSON COLLECTION

A strange sight during 1943 was eight London Transport buses usually to be found on Salisbury city routes or peak period country workings. They were loaned between December 1942 and May 1944.

GC 3976, an AEC Regent with LGOC 48-seat highbridge bodywork. appears to have a good load on a Wilton service, and is about to be overtaken by 1940 Bristol K5G CHR 492.

DAVID PENNELS COLLECTION

During 1943 the Ministry of War Transport allocated four new double-deck buses to Wilts & Dorset, Daimler CWG5s with 55-seat lowbridge Brush bodywork. CWV 779 is on the right, shortly after delivery in March 1943 and painted in utility wartime grey. You can see just how angular utility bodywork was with very little time-consuming and skilled panel beating being needed in its production.

S L POOLE
DAVID PENNELS COLLECTION

Leyland Titan UF 7396 had been new to Southdown in 1931, passing to Wilts & Dorset eight years later. But in March 1944 it was sent to Brush of Loughborough to have a new 55-seat lowbridge body put on it. At the bottom of the page is the coachbuilders' photograph, taken before fleetnames were applied and while the white edged mudguards, platform and guard rails were still pristine. This bus remained in service with Wilts & Dorset until March 1950.

BRIAN JACKSON COLLECTION

Towing its gas producer trailer, Leyland Titan TD1 UF 7415 was travelling eastwards along Blue Boar Row on a Salisbury city route in 1944. The conductress, with TIM ticket machine, looks out from the rear platform. Notice the ad for Everybody's magazine on the side of the bus exhorting readers to share their copy with friends – a reflection of wartime shortages.

J TAYLOR
DAVID PENNELS COLLECTION

Utility furniture, shown below, is mentioned on the 1943 page.

For the first few months of the Second World War output of new buses continued relatively unchanged, but the situation changed rapidly from the spring of 1940.

For a while, bus manufacture ceased altogether, as factories were turned over to production of essentials for war, but by 1941 it was evident that some sort of supply of new buses was essential. Accordingly, manufacturers were permitted to finish vehicles that had been in build at the time of the order to stop. These became known as 'unfrozen' buses.

The following year, production of utility buses started. At first the only types available were Guy Arab double-deck and Bedford OWB single-deck buses, but some other manufacturers were soon able to resume production - for example, Daimler in 1943 and Bristol in 1944. Buses were allocated by the Government to operators, with little regard to chassis make etc..

UTILITY FURNITURE

BEDROOM

WARDROBE: 4 ft. wide
First Section—Model 1
Price, in oak ... £15. 16. 6
Price, in mahogany, with dull finish (as shown) ... £17. 4. 9

WARDROBE: First Section—Model 1, open.

DRESSING CHEST: 3 ft. wide.
First Section—Model 3
(shown in mahogany)
Price, with mirror ... £10. 10. 0
" without mirror £9. 6. 9

TALLBOY:
First Section—Model 5
Price, in mahogany, with dull finish (as shown) ... £10. 2. 6

Their utility bodies were designed to cut down on the need for skilled manpower in production as well as materials; they were angular in appearance and had a limited number of opening windows.

In order to reduce dependence on imported oil, bus companies were required by the Government to convert 10% of their fleets to run on gas. Such vehicles towed trailers that produced the gas by burning anthracite, but the performance of these buses was very poor, especially on hills, and they tended to be expensive in maintenance. In general the 10% target for conversion was not reached, and the abandonment of the scheme towards the end of the war was widely welcomed.

I've got 9 lives
YOU haven't
LOOK OUT IN THE
BLACKOUT
There's danger on the roads

In the picture on the right an inspector checks to see if any more passengers can be packed into Bristol K5G CHR 497, waiting to leave Salisbury bus station for Blandford, Dorchester and Weymouth in March 1944. New in 1940, the bus is now in drab austerity grey. A number of the passengers appear to be servicemen, who will no doubt get off at Blandford.

W LAMBDEN
DAVID PENNELS COLLECTION

In March 1944 Leyland Titan TD2 WV 2382, new to Wilts & Dorset in January 1933, was given a new 48-seat lowbridge body built in Wilts & Dorset's own workshops. Painted in normal livery, the only concessions to wartime were masked headlights and white mudguard tips. Below, it was outside the works. This bus lasted with Wilts & Dorset until January 1955.

DAVID PENNELS COLLECTION

in 1944

Olympic Games cancelled, owing to the war.

PAYE system of income tax introduced.

D-Day landings as Allied forces invaded Normandy.

V1 flying bomb and V2 rocket attacks in Britain.

Popular music included Swinging on a Star by Bing Crosby and Mairzy Dotes by The Merry Macs.

in 1945

VE Day (8 May) celebrated the end of the war in Europe, with street parties across the country. VJ Day (August) marked the end of the war in the Far East.

General election resulted in a landslide victory for Labour, with Clement Attlee becoming prime minister.

The BBC Light Programme was launched on 29 July.

On 31 December Britain received a shipment of bananas, which had completely disappeared from the shops during the war.

Popular music included Rum & Coca Cola by The Andrews Sisters and Don't Fence Me In by Bing Crosby.

1944

General Manager Raymond Longman reported that the nine gas producer buses were in regular use, but it was not proposed to convert any more. The Salisbury to Wilton route was being operated entirely by these vehicles with a special rota of drivers, but it had been necessary to add in an extra five minutes per journey into the schedule. He reported that the company was slightly short of drivers and conductors, but no services had been lost on account of this. As at July 1944 applications were outstanding with the Ministry of Labour and National Service for an additional seven drivers and 11 conductors.

The Chief Engineer was still trying to get hold of Gardner 5LW diesel engines to replace outworn petrol units, but it required the consent of the Government's Regional Maintenance Officer, and this was not forthcoming.

In November Wilts & Dorset took over the services of Lampard's Garages of Pewsey. No vehicles were acquired, but six routes in the local area were transferred to Wilts & Dorset. An office in North Street was included, and Wilts & Dorset established a depot at Frog Meadow in Pewsey.

1945

By early 1945 a fuel tank had been installed and other work carried out at Frog Meadow in Pewsey to make the premises suitable for use. General Manager Raymond Longman reported that conditions there were now much more satisfactory and it had also been possible to concrete the floor inside the garage at Blandford, replacing the previous rolled gravel which had compacted with use and had proved a reasonably satisfactory temporary expedient.

The end of the war saw the end of gas powered buses; by advertising in the local press the company succeeded in selling off the trailers at £20 each.

At a board meeting on 17 July Mr Longman reported that the company was short of operating staff and in urgent of need of nine drivers and 28 conductors. He hoped the situation would improve as staff were released from the forces. He added that the opportunity was being taken to carry out necessary repairs and decoration to the company's properties, subject to the availability of licences, labour and materials.

The Ministry of Aircraft Production de-requisitioned the northern section of Salisbury Garage from 9 November. The following month the Chief Engineer expressed his satisfaction with the high quality workmanship on some Leyland single-deck buses whose bodies had been replaced by Beadle of Dartford, Kent (see picture on the right). He also announced that the 16 wartime 'standee' single-deck buses would be converted back to normal seating when these vehicles went through the workshops.

The photograph on the left was taken in June 1945 at the retirement of William Wells Graham (centre), founder of Hants & Dorset Motor Services Ltd. Raymond Longman, Managing Director of Wilts & Dorset, can be seen second from the right, while Douglas Morison, then Traffic Manager of Hants & Dorset and whose responsibilities as General Manager would expand to cover Wilts & Dorset between 1965 and 1972 is third from the left.

THE LATE HAROLD STEVENS COLLECTION

Acquired with the Sparrow & Vincent business in 1933, MW 2955 in the middle picture was a Leyland Lion PLSC3 dating from 1928. To give the by then ageing vehicle a further lease of life, it (together with a number of other Lions) was given a new 32-seat Beadle body in November 1945.

It carries the coach style script fleetname. For a while this newly rebodied vehicle was often used for short distance excursion work, and regularly appeared on trips to Southampton Football Club from Salisbury bus station.

Wilts & Dorset was justifiably proud of the bus at the bottom of this page when it was photographed in January 1945.

Leyland Titan TD1 MW 8753 had been new in 1931, but in December 1944 was given this new 48-seat lowbridge body built in the Wilts & Dorset workshop at Salisbury. Although rather upright, nonetheless it had a pleasing appearance. The new body incorporated such stylistic touches as outswept skirt panels.

DAVID PENNELS COLLECTION

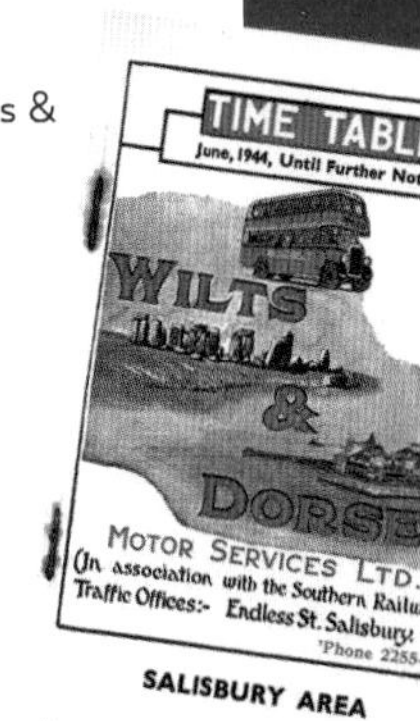

Full Wilts & Dorset livery was a great improvement on the wartime grey it had sported when delivered in 1943, Daimler CWG5 CWV 779 on the right had been rebuilt by the company in 1945, gaining sliding window vents and a more rounded rear dome with a glazed emergency door. Here it is in Salisbury on 2 July 1946, having recently arrived from Weymouth. Millers 'Dorsage' sausages and pies were made at a factory in Sterte Avenue, Poole, and were delicious.

The first new bus to be received by Wilts & Dorset after the Second World War was DMR 836, one of two Bristol K5Gs with a 55-seat Eastern Coach Works lowbridge bodies that entered service in March 1946.

Three more came in the early summer. DMR 840 below was brand new when photographed at Salisbury bus station loading passengers for Woodfalls on 2 July 1946. Notice the long queue of passengers and also the sign visible through the bus pointing towards the British Restaurant in Rollestone Street.

DAVID PENNELS COLLECTION

in 1946

The Bank of England was nationalised.

BBC television broadcasting, suspended for the war, resumed.

Bread rationing was imposed; it had not been rationed during the war, and this peacetime measure caused resentment.

BBC Third Programme launched.

Popular music included The Gypsy by The Ink Spots and Five Minutes More by Frank Sinatra.

in 1947

UK coal industry was nationalised.

Exceptionally severe winter weather during January & February, was exacerbated by a fuel shortage and extensive power cuts.

The school leaving age was raised to 15.

Princess Elizabeth and Philip Mountbatten were married in Westminster Abbey.

Popular music included La Mer by Charles Trenet and Smoke, Smoke, Smoke that Cigarette by Tex Williams.

1946

On 31 January General Manager Raymond Longman reported that the company now had an adequate number of drivers, but was still short of conductors - there were 172 (41 men, 131 women) but ideally another 30 were needed. The main difficulty of attracting the right calibre of man to the job was felt to be the comparatively low starting rate of 77/6d (£3.88) for a 48-hour week. A new pay scale was introduced from 30 November, giving a starting rate of 85/- (£4.25) for a 48-hour week, rising in due course to 94/- (£4.70).

The office at 45 Blue Boar Row, loaned to Salisbury City Corporation since 1939, was declared surplus to requirements, and put up for sale. The company negotiated to purchase Belle Vue House and 2.25 acres of land between Endless Street and its premises on the east side of Castle Street.

Most welcome were the urgently needed first new post-war buses, five new Bristol K5G double-deck buses with 55-seat lowbridge Eastern Coach Works bodies. These were quickly put to work on country services.

Passengers look out from the windows as Leyland Titan TD1 MW 7051 is extricated from a snowdrift during the severe conditions in February 1947. The efforts by staff to maintain services were very much appreciated by the company.

BRIAN JACKSON COLLECTION

1947

Managing Director Raymond Longman wrote on 31 January , *"This month marks the 32nd anniversary of the Company's incorporation, and I believe we are among the very few exceptional undertakings who have had no strikes or lost journeys on account of labour troubles throughout the whole of their existence."* These words soon came back to haunt him, because he reported on 21 April, *"I regret to place on record the fact that an unofficial one day strike took place on Saturday 15 March 1947. All depots were affected to a greater or lesser extent, the only place from which full services were operated was Blandford, although a small number of drivers and conductors reported for duty at Salisbury. By the use of other members of staff about 60 buses were operated, and reduced services were run on most roads."*

Staff who had worked during this dispute were later subjected to unpleasantness from their trade union officials and others. The happy atmosphere returned over time although there was a further unofficial strike at Andover on 1 November when staff refused to work with a driver who had worked during the earlier dispute. Fortunately, the situation was eventually resolved amicably.

Maintenance staff came in for special thanks for their hard work in repairing the damage caused to buses from the many minor mishaps that occurred during a period of very severe weather during January and February.

The revised pay rates agreed in 1946 appeared to have the desired effect; Mr Longman reported that staff numbers were satisfactory, with an ample number of applications for positions.

Received new by the company in 1940, CHR 482 was rebuilt by Wilts & Dorset in January 1946, having previously been converted to a standee layout with perimeter seating during the war.

Below it was posed for an official company photograph following the rebuild, and thereafter spent much of its time working from Bowerchalke outstation until withdrawal in October 1954.

DAVID PENNELS COLLECTION

Bought new by Wilts & Dorset in 1935, WV 7334 was a Leyland Cub coach with a 20-seat Harrington body. Photographed after the body had been rebuilt by Wilts & Dorset in October 1947, WV 7334 was sold to Empress Coaches of Stockbridge in 1950, and later operated from Emsworth for Hants & Sussex.

DAVID PENNELS COLLECTION

The line up of Leyland double decks on the right, each with slightly different bodywork, was in Salisbury's Salt Lane car park, Salisbury on 9 August 1948. A mere stone's throw from the bus station, this car park was used during the 1940s and 1950s as an overflow site for buses awaiting the call to duty.

JOHN SANTER
DAVID PENNELS COLLECTION

1948

Industrial relations problems reared their head again on Saturday 22 May when many drivers and conductors at Salisbury depot ceased work for about five hours as a protest about the appointment of a particular inspector. Around 3,000 miles of operation were lost, and it was threatened that the whole of the company's staff could come out on strike if the appointment was not cancelled. Management held firm, and in due course the feelings died down, with the staff and the inspector working normally together.

During the Royal Counties Agricultural Show, 23-26 June, Wilts & Dorset buses carried a total of 4,159 passengers between Salisbury railway station and the show ground; Traffic Manager Mr Bushrod commented that the public address announcements on Salisbury station about the bus service had been extremely helpful.

With the nationalisation of the railways from 1 January, Wilts & Dorset publications were now ***In association with British Railways*** rather than ***In association with the Southern Railway***, as previously. Moreover, in September 1948 Thomas Tilling Limited agreed to sell its transport interests to the British Transport Commission, thus Wilts & Dorset came into state ownership.

Much needed new buses continued to enter service; also received at the end of 1948 were the Company's first two new post-war coaches, which did not enter service until the following year.

On 13 June 1948 BWV 672, shown below, was one of the vehicles provided for a private hire from Salisbury to Swanage, where it is seen in the goods yard at the railway station.

This Leyland Tiger TS8 was new to Wilts & Dorset in June 1939. The 32-seat Harrington body had been rebuilt by Portsmouth Aviation two months previously, and this vehicle stayed in the fleet until October 1954.

J H ASTON
DAVID PENNELS COLLECTION

in 1948

The railways were nationalised.

The state of Israel came into being with the termination of the British Mandate of Palestine.

The National Health Service was launched.

Bread rationing ended.

Popular music included The Dream of Olwen by Mantovani & his Orchestra, So Tired by Russ Morgan and Buttons & Bows by Dinah Shore.

Very little traffic was evident on the main A345 road at Amesbury when 1940 Bristol K5G CHR 490 was photographed on the left, ready to depart on a short journey to Boscombe Down. Rugged and reliable, this batch of 12 similar buses did sterling service for Wilts & Dorset for more than 18 years.

DAVID PENNELS COLLECTION

Two-way traffic still flowed along Blue Boar Row in Salisbury when UF 7403 was photographed below operating on a Salisbury city route to Wilton beside Guildhall Square - notice the queue sign.

New to Southdown in 1930 and acquired by Wilts & Dorset in 1939, this bus had received a new Willowbrook 51-seat lowbridge body in 1944, but still had its original radiator when this view was taken. Later, it was given a more modern looking 'Cov-Rad' radiator. The bus was withdrawn in October 1953.

E SURFLEET
DAVID PENNELS COLLECTION

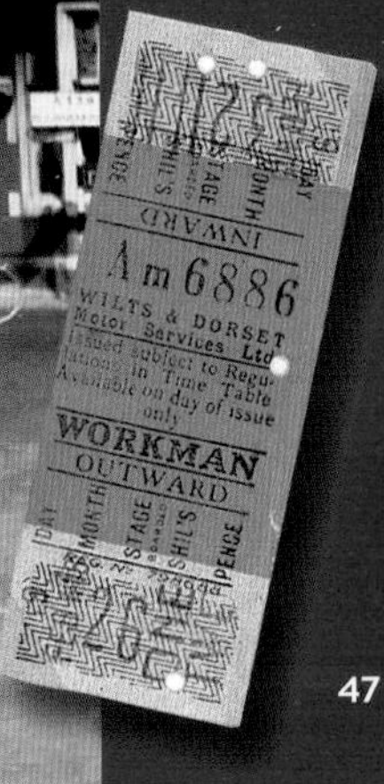

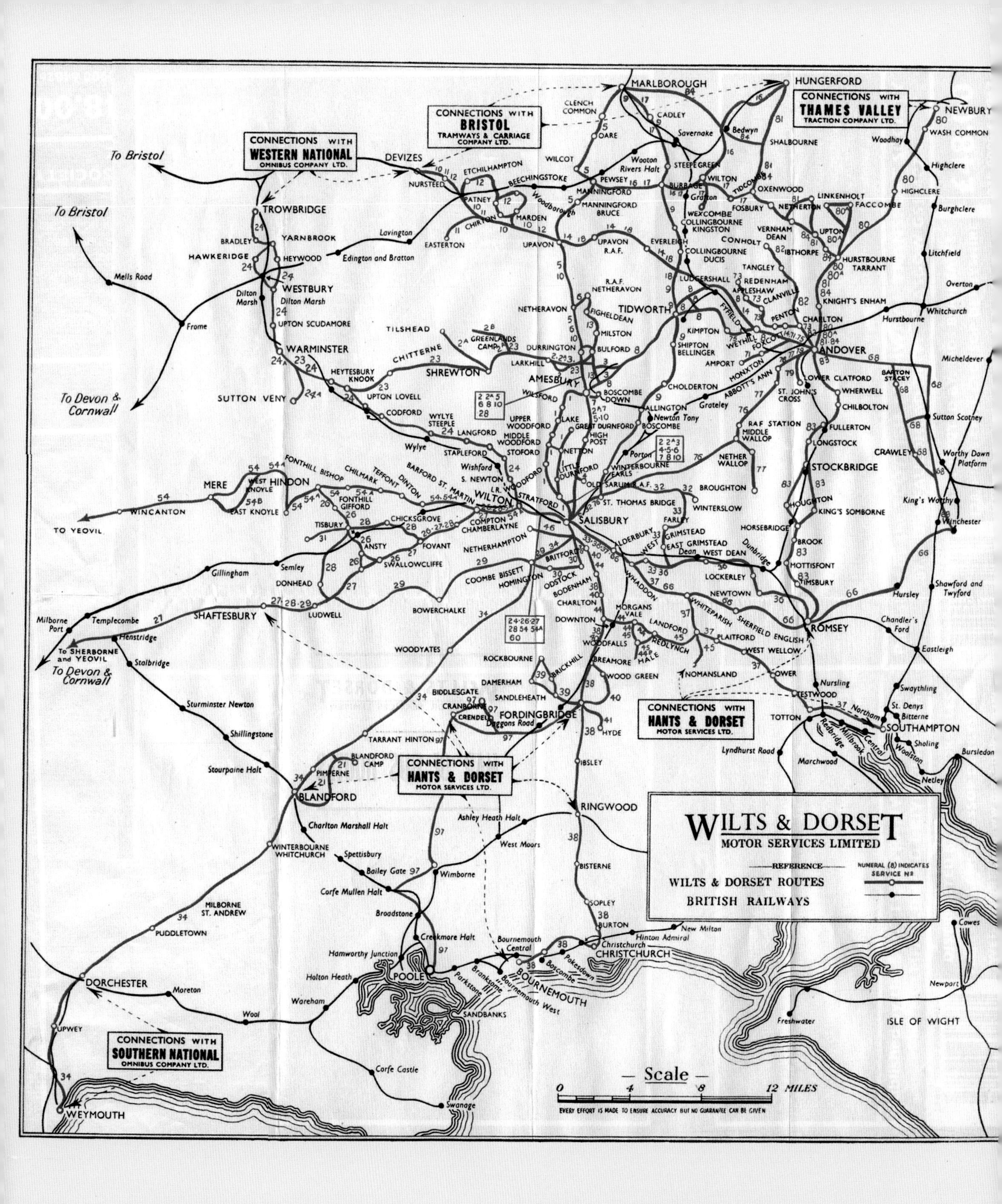
WILTS & DORSET
MOTOR SERVICES LIMITED
REFERENCE
NUMERAL (8) INDICATES SERVICE Nº
WILTS & DORSET ROUTES
BRITISH RAILWAYS
CONNECTIONS WITH WESTERN NATIONAL OMNIBUS COMPANY LTD.
CONNECTIONS WITH BRISTOL TRAMWAYS & CARRIAGE COMPANY LTD.
CONNECTIONS WITH THAMES VALLEY TRACTION COMPANY LTD.
CONNECTIONS WITH HANTS & DORSET MOTOR SERVICES LTD.
CONNECTIONS WITH HANTS & DORSET MOTOR SERVICES LTD.
CONNECTIONS WITH SOUTHERN NATIONAL OMNIBUS COMPANY LTD.
To Bristol
To Bristol
To Devon & Cornwall
TO YEOVIL
To SHERBORNE and YEOVIL
To Devon & Cornwall
MARLBOROUGH
HUNGERFORD
NEWBURY
WASH COMMON
CLENCH COMMON
CADLEY
Savernake
Bedwyn
SHALBOURNE
Woodhay
OARE
WILCOT
DEVIZES
NURSTEED
ETCHILHAMPTON
BEECHINGSTOKE
Wooton Rivers Halt
PEWSEY
STEEPE GREEN
BURBAGE
WILTON
Grafton
TIDCOMBE
OXENWOOD
Highclere
HIGHCLERE
Burghclere
TROWBRIDGE
PATNEY
CHIRTON
MARDEN
Woodborough
MANNINGFORD
MANNINGFORD BRUCE
WEXCOMBE
COLLINGBOURNE KINGSTON
FOSBURY
NETHERTON
LINKENHOLT
FACCOMBE
UPTON
BRADLEY
YARNBROOK
Lavington
EASTERTON
UPAVON
UPAVON R.A.F.
EVERLEIGH
COLLINGBOURNE DUCIS
CONHOLT
VERNHAM DEAN
IBTHORPE
HURSTBOURNE TARRANT
Litchfield
HAWKERIDGE
HEYWOOD
Edington and Bratton
TANGLEY
Mells Road
Dilton Marsh
WESTBURY
Dilton Marsh
R.A.F. NETHERAVON
LUDGERSHALL
REDENHAM
APPLESHAW
CLANVILLE
KNIGHT'S ENHAM
Overton
Frome
UPTON SCUDAMORE
NETHERAVON
FIGHELDEAN
TIDWORTH
FYFIELD
PENTON
CHARLTON
Hurstbourne
Whitchurch
TILSHEAD
GREENLANDS CAMP
DURRINGTON
MILSTON
KIMPTON
WEYHILL
FOXCOTT
ANDOVER
WARMINSTER
CHITTERNE
LARKHILL
BULFORD
SHIPTON BELLINGER
AMPORT
MONXTON
Micheldever
HEYTESBURY
KNOOK
SHREWTON
AMESBURY
ABBOTT'S ANN
LOWER CLATFORD
BARTON STACEY
SUTTON VENY
UPTON LOVELL
WILSFORD
BOSCOMBE DOWN
CHOLDERTON
ST. JOHN'S CROSS
WHERWELL
CODFORD
ALLINGTON
Grateley
CHILBOLTON
Newton Tony
BOSCOMBE
Sutton Scotney
WYLYE STEEPLE
LAKE
GREAT DURNFORD
RAF STATION
MIDDLE WALLOP
FULLERTON
UPPER WOODFORD
MIDDLE WOODFORD
HIGH POST
LONGSTOCK
Wylye
LANGFORD
STAPLEFORD
STOFORD
NETTON
Porton
NETHER WALLOP
CRAWLEY
Worthy Down Platform
Wishford
S. NEWTON
LITTLE DURNFORD
WINTERBOURNE EARLS
STOCKBRIDGE
FONTHILL BISHOP
CHILMARK
TEFFONT
DINTON
BARFORD ST. MARTIN
LR. WOODFORD
OLD SARUM R.A.F.
BROUGHTON
MERE
WEST KNOYLE
HINDON
FONTHILL GIFFORD
WILTON
STRATFORD
ST. THOMAS BRIDGE
WINTERSLOW
HOUGHTON
King's Worthy
KING'S SOMBORNE
EAST KNOYLE
WINCANTON
TISBURY
CHICKSGROVE
COMPTON CHAMBERLAYNE
SALISBURY
FARLEY
Winchester
HORSEBRIDGE
ANSTY
FOVANT
NETHERHAMPTON
ALDERBURY
WEST GRIMSTEAD
EAST GRIMSTEAD
Dean
WEST DEAN
BROOK
Gillingham
Semley
SWALLOWCLIFFE
BRITFORD
Dunbridge
MOTTISFONT
DONHEAD
COOMBE BISSETT
HOMINGTON
ODSTOCK
BODENHAM
WHADDON
LOCKERLEY
TIMSBURY
Shawford and Twyford
NEWTOWN
Hursley
CHARLTON
Milborne Port
Templecombe
SHAFTESBURY
LUDWELL
BOWERCHALKE
DOWNTON
MORGANS VALE
LANDFORD
WHITEPARISH
SHERFIELD ENGLISH
ROMSEY
Chandler's Ford
Henstridge
WOODFALLS
REDLYNCH
PLAITFORD
WEST WELLOW
Stalbridge
WOODYATES
ROCKBOURNE
BREAMORE
HALE
Eastleigh
BRICKHILL
WOOD GREEN
NOMANSLAND
OWER
Nursling
DAMERHAM
SANDLEHEATH
Swaythling
Sturminster Newton
BIDDLESGATE
CRANBORNE
CRENDELL
FORDINGBRIDGE
TESTWOOD
St. Denys
Bitterne
Daggons Road
HYDE
TOTTON
Northam
SOUTHAMPTON
Shillingstone
TARRANT HINTON
Redbridge
Millbrook
Central
Woolston
Sholing
Lyndhurst Road
Bursledon
BLANDFORD CAMP
IBSLEY
Marchwood
Netley
Stourpaine Halt
PIMPERNE
BLANDFORD
RINGWOOD
Charlton Marshall Halt
Ashley Heath Halt
West Moors
WINTERBOURNE WHITCHURCH
Spettisbury
Bailey Gate
Wimborne
BISTERNE
Corfe Mullen Halt
MILBORNE ST. ANDREW
Broadstone
SOPLEY
PUDDLETOWN
BURTON
New Milton
Cowes
Creekmore Halt
Bournemouth Central
Christchurch
Hinton Admiral
CHRISTCHURCH
Hamworthy Junction
POOLE
Pokesdown
Boscombe
Holton Heath
Branksome
Parkstone
BOURNEMOUTH
Bournemouth West
DORCHESTER
Moreton
Newport
Wareham
SANDBANKS
Wool
Freshwater
ISLE OF WIGHT
UPWEY
Corfe Castle
Swanage
WEYMOUTH
Scale
0
4
8
12 MILES
EVERY EFFORT IS MADE TO ENSURE ACCURACY BUT NO GUARANTEE CAN BE GIVEN

bus routes in 1949

This map from the 1949 Wilts & Dorset timetable book is of particular significance. As well as showing the extent of the company's routes immediately before the acquisition of Venture extended the network eastwards to the Basingstoke area, there are a number of other interesting things to note.

Route 97 is shown running on southwards from Cranborne via Wimborne, Corfe Mullen and Broadstone to Poole. This was a joint service with Hants & Dorset between Poole and Salisbury that had been introduced in 1948. It lasted only until May 1953; Wilts & Dorset then kept the Salisbury - Fordingbridge - Cranborne section renumbered as route 42, while Hants & Dorset operated separately from Poole to Cranborne, keeping 97 as the route number for this section.

The long route from Salisbury to Weymouth had been renumbered 34 from 1 January 1949; it had also become jointly operated with Southern National from that date. Route 27 will be seen extending west from Shaftesbury onwards to Sherborne and Yeovil. This route was introduced from 5 December 1948, also jointly operated by Wilts & Dorset and Southern National. This ceased from 3 October 1959, the 27 thereafter being a Wilts & Dorset only route between Salisbury and Shaftesbury via Fovant. Also shown is the joint Wilts & Dorset and Southern National 54 from Salisbury to Yeovil via Wincanton; this had started in 1949, but was destined to run only until 1952.

Notice also the extent of the British Railways network, with lines such as the branch to Tidworth still in use, although this did close to passengers in 1955, several years before the infamous Beeching cuts.

In the picture above a long queue is boarding WV 2384 for the journey north from Salisbury to Amesbury, Upavon and Marlborough on route 5 in September 1949.

This 1933 Leyland Titan TD2 now carries a Willowbrook lowbridge body dating from 1946, which prolonged the life of this vehicle until September 1954.

Parked beside it, 1939 Leyland Tiger TS8 BWV 670 will soon make the trip up the Woodford Valley to Lake and Amesbury.

A A TOWNSIN
DAVID PENNELS COLLECTION

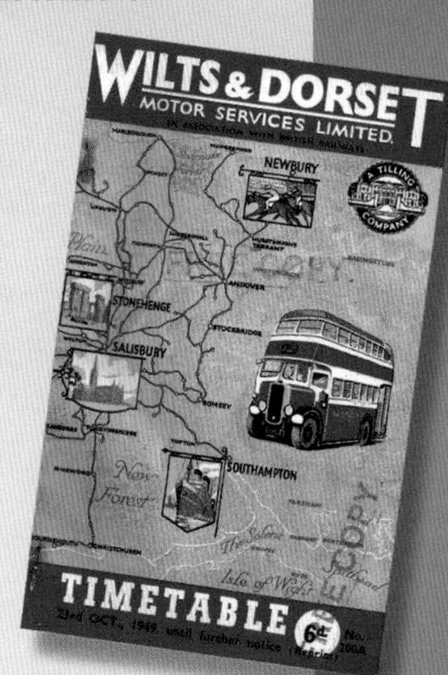

1929 Leyland Lion LT1 MW 4596 had had its earlier body damaged during an air raid at Trowbridge in 1942. It was given a new Eastern Coach Works 32-seat body in February 1943, which was partly to Ministry of Supply specification. This enabled it to remain in service until November 1952. On the right it was entering Salisbury bus station from Rollestone Street on 21 August 1949.

J H ASTON
DAVID PENNELS COLLECTION

1949

Arrangements for weekend forces leave services were publicised, based on servicemen travelling by bus from the military establishment to a railway station (normally Salisbury or Andover Junction) with onward travel by train to their final destination. Fuel, then still rationed, was no longer granted to certain independent operators who had begun coach services between Blandford Camp and London; as a result the number of passengers carried by bus from Blandford Camp to Salisbury increased by around 50%. In 1949 a combined road/rail ticket between Blandford Camp and London Waterloo cost 21/- (£1.05) return, from Larkhill Camp 16/4d (82p) and from Bulford Camp 15/10d (79p). 760 tickets had been issued between Blandford Camp and London Waterloo during the eight week period ending 21 May.

On 26 August an excursion ran from Salisbury to the Isle of Wight in conjunction with the British Railways steamer service between Portsmouth and Ryde and with Southern Vectis. This attracted 96 passengers, and plans were made to do the same during 1950.

All weekly paid staff were given a Christmas bonus, but it was stated that 1949 was likely to be the last year in which such a bonus would be paid.

1950

One event that had long lasting effects on the public transport industry, and indeed on the lives of everyone, was the ending of the rationing of motor fuel. For the past 11 years anyone who needed or wanted to travel beyond walking or cycling distance normally had no option other than to go by public transport.

Wilts & Dorset's first new post-war coaches didn't enter service until the beginning of the 1949 season. Nine new Bristol L6B coaches came into use that year, eight with Beadle 32-seat bodies, the comfortable interior of EMW 184 being shown below. The exterior view shows FAM 3, the ninth, which had a 32-seat Portsmouth Aviation body.

DAVID PENNELS COLLECTION

in 1949

Clothes rationing ended.

Longleat House opened to paying visitors; this was the first privately owned stately home to be opened to the public.

The pound was devalued by 30% against the dollar.

Popular music included Mule Train by Frankie Laine, La Vie En Rose by Edith Piaf and You're Breaking My Heart by the Ink Spots.

in 1950

Listen with Mother was first broadcast on the Light Programme.

The general election was won by Labour with a majority of five.

Rationing of motor fuel ended.

Conscripted National Service for young men was increased from 18 months to two years because of the Korean War.

Popular music included My Foolish Heart by Billy Eckstine, Music! Music! Music! by Teresa Brewer and The Harry Lime Theme by Anton Karas.

By the end of the year Wilts & Dorset had found that the end of fuel rationing had completely altered the whole situation in respect of weekend forces leave services inasmuch as independent operators were already making encroachments into this important traffic.

While Wilts & Dorset remained committed to try to make every success of the combined road/rail arrangements for forces leave journeys, the company felt that it could not sit back and let independent operators take away this traffic. Applications were therefore made to the Traffic Commissioners for authorisation to run express services from Boscombe Down and from Blandford Camp.

New buses were, of course, very much in evidence by 1950; GMR 27 was a Bristol K5G with a 55 -seat Eastern Coach Works lowbridge body, new in July. Looking splendid above, it would soon depart from Salisbury bus station for Trowbridge on route 24.

BRIAN JACKSON COLLECTION

Waiting at the Rollestone Street end of Salisbury bus station, having set down passengers from an afternoon excursion, BAM 800 had provided an attractive vehicle for a pleasure trip on 27 July 1950 immediately left. Carrying a 32-seat Harrington coach body, this Leyland Tiger TS8 was in the Wilts & Dorset fleet from June 1938 until August 1953.

DAVID PENNELS COLLECTION

A 1939 secondhand acquisition still on front line service in 1950 was TY 6972, which had started life with the Tyneside Tramways and Tramroads Company. It received a new 55-seat utility spec Duple lowbridge body in 1943, and this had been rebuilt by Wilts & Dorset in 1947. It's seen leaving Amesbury bus station on the final section of a Marlborough to Salisbury journey on route 5 on the left. This bus was withdrawn in January 1952.

JOHN SANTER
DAVID PENNELS COLLECTION

This former Venture highbridge Weymann bodied AEC Regent III had started life in the Newbury & District fleet. It's on what had been Venture's 11 route from Basingstoke to Winchester via Dummer, North Waltham and the A33. The route was soon renumbered 111 by Wilts & Dorset. It ran through a sparsely populated area and the end-to-end journey was duplicated by a faster rail service, so not surprisingly it was an early casualty of rationalisation in the early 1970s.

JOHN SANTER
DAVID PENNELS COLLECTION

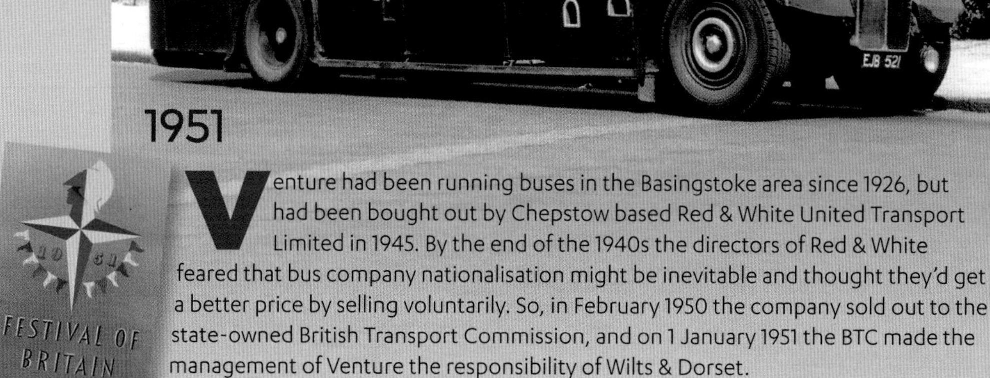

in 1951

The Goon Show was first broadcast on BBC radio.

The Festival of Britain took place on the South Bank, London.

General Certificate of Education (GCE) O levels and A levels replaced School Certificate examinations.

The general election was won by the Conservative Party with a majority of 17.

Popular music included Too Young by Jimmy Young and My Resistance is Low by Hoagy Carmichael.

1951

Venture had been running buses in the Basingstoke area since 1926, but had been bought out by Chepstow based Red & White United Transport Limited in 1945. By the end of the 1940s the directors of Red & White feared that bus company nationalisation might be inevitable and thought they'd get a better price by selling voluntarily. So, in February 1950 the company sold out to the state-owned British Transport Commission, and on 1 January 1951 the BTC made the management of Venture the responsibility of Wilts & Dorset.

The Venture fleet of more than 40 vehicles soon began to display Wilts & Dorset livery and fleetnames (although some of the earliest repaints still carried the Venture fleetname). One of the former Venture routes taken over ran to Park Prewett Hospital on the north western fringe of Basingstoke; combined rail and road tickets were made available for hospital visitors from distant locations - for example from Bournemouth Central for 9/1 (46p) return or Southampton Central for 5/1 (26p) return.

Following the applications made to the Traffic Commissioners late in 1950, weekend forces leave express services started running between Boscombe Down and London from 27 January and between Blandford Camp and London from 3 February.

Owing to the reduction in the number of train services on the branch between Ludgershall and Tidworth, it was agreed that passengers holding through rail tickets to and from Tidworth could travel between Ludgershall and Tidworth by bus at times when there was no suitable train service.

Also acquired with the Venture fleet in Basingstoke, ECG 646 was an 1942 AEC Regent. The utility origins of the highbridge body are clear. This was one of two similar vehicles that had been allocated by the Ministry of War Transport to Venture. In the picture on the left it is wearing Wilts & Dorset livery and was operating a Basingstoke local service.

JOHN SANTER
DAVID PENNELS COLLECTION

WILTS & DORSET
MOTOR SERVICES LIMITED

ARMY MANOEUVRES

The Public will be aware of notices which have been given over the radio and in the press that some modification in operation of 'bus services will arise in this area during the period 9th October to the 18th October inclusive.

Every effort will be made by this Company to maintain services although these may be subject to alteration, and in certain extreme cases, to curtailment without notice. In particular the public are hereby advised that revised and reduced services will be operated between Amesbury and Devizes, and between Amesbury and Marlborough, from the 12th to 16th October inclusive, details of which are given overleaf.

Although every effort will be made to give accurate information of times throughout the Company's system, it must be emphasised that developments hour by hour in the manoeuvres situation may make it impossible for information to be given by this Company's Enquiry Offices, and to this extent, therefore, the Public are asked wherever possible not to telephone the Enquiry Offices for advice as to whether a particular service is running or not as it is not anticipated that information can be given substantially in advance of the departure of the journey or journeys concerned.

You may, however, rest assured that we will, as always, do our very best to ensure that you will arrive at your destination.

Traffic Manager's Office,
Salisbury.

P.T.O.

28th September, 1951.

66780

The Salisbury Press Ltd., Salisbury.

EMERGENCY SERVICE
October 12th—16th, 1951, inclusive

Light figures denote a.m. times. Dark figures denote p.m. times.

Service 5 — SALISBURY—UPAVON—MARLBOROUGH — Service 5

		* NSu	* NSu	*	* NSu	Su	*	*	*	*	*
Salisbury, Bus Station	dep	6-45	8-45	10-45	12-45		2-45	4-45	6-45	8-45	9-45
Amesbury, Bus Station	arr	7-5	9-5	11-5	1-5		3-5	5-5	7-5	9-5	10-5
Amesbury, Bus Station	dep	7-10	9-10	11-10	1-10		3-10	5-10	7-10	9-10	10-10
Stonehenge Inn	..	7-16	9-16	11-16	1-16		3-16	5-16	7-16	9-16	10-16
Durrington, Post Office	..	7-21	9-21	11-21	1-21		3-21	5-21	7-21	9-21	10-21
Netheravon, Post Office	..	7-30	9-30	11-30	1-30		3-30	5-30	7-30	9-30	10-30
Enford, Bus Shelter	..	7-37	9-37	11-37	1-37		3-37	5-37	7-37	9-37	10-37
Upavon, Ship Inn	..	7-45	9-45	11-45	1-45		3-45	5-45	7-45	9-45	10-45
Woodbridge Inn	..	7-49	9-49	11-49	1-49		3-49	5-49	7-49	9-49	10-49
Manningford Bohune	..	7-52	9-52	11-52	1-52		3-52	5-52	7-52	9-52	10-52
Pewsey, Bus Office	..	7-59	9-59	11-59	1-59	1-59	3-59	5-59	7-59	9-59	10-59
Oare, White Hart	..	8-6	10-6	12-6	2-6	2-6	4-6	6-6	8-6	—	—
Clench Common	..	8-11	10-11	12-11	2-11	2-11	4-11	6-11	8-11		
Marlborough, High Street	arr	8-20	10-20	12-20	2-20	2-20	4-20	6-20	8-20		

		* NSu	* NSu	NSu *	NSu *	* Su	NSu *	*	*	*	*
Marlborough, High Street	dep			9-0	11-0		1-0	3-0	5-0	7-0	9-0
Clench Common	..			9-9	11-9		1-9	3-9	5-9	7-9	9-9
Oare, White Hart	..	—	—	9-14	11-14	—	1-14	3-14	5-14	7-14	9-14
Pewsey, Bus Office	..	7-1	7-31	9-21	11-21	1-1	1-21	3-21	5-21	7-21	9-21
Manningford Bohune	..	7-8	7-38	9-28	11-28	1-8	1-28	3-28	5-28	7-28	9-28
Woodbridge Inn	..	7-11	7-41	9-31	11-31	1-11	1-31	3-31	5-31	7-31	9-31
Upavon, Ship Inn	..	7-15	7-45	9-35	11-35	1-15	1-35	3-35	5-35	7-35	9-35
Enford, Bus Shelter	..	7-23	7-53	9-43	11-43	1-23	1-43	3-43	5-43	7-43	9-43
Netheravon, Post Office	..	7-30	8-0	9-50	11-50	1-30	1-50	3-50	5-50	7-50	9-50
Durrington, Post Office	..	7-39	8-9	9-59	11-59	1-39	1-59	3-59	5-59	7-59	9-59
Stonehenge Inn	..	7-44	8-14	10-4	12-4	1-44	2-4	4-4	6-4	8-4	10-4
Amesbury, Bus Station	arr	7-50	8-20	10-10	12-10	1-50	2-10	4-10	6-10	8-10	10-10
Amesbury, Bus Station	dep	7-57	8-30	10-17	12-17	1-57	2-17	4-17	6-17	8-17	10-17
Salisbury, Bus Station	arr	8-17	8-50	10-37	12-37	2-17	2-37	4-37	6-37	8-37	10-37

*—Change at Amesbury (Connections cannot be guaranteed). NSu—Not Sundays. Su—Sundays only.

t figures denote a.m. times. Dark figures denote p.m. times.

vice 10 — SALISBURY—UPAVON—DEVIZES — Service 10

		* NSu	* C	NSu	*	*	*	*	*	*
bury, Bus Station	dep	6-5	7-45	9-45	11-45	1-45	3-45	5-45	7-45	9-45
bury, Bus Station	arr	6-25	8-5	10-5	12-5	2-5	4-5	6-5	8-5	10-5
ıury, Bus Station	dep	6-25	8-10	10-10	12-10	2-10	4-10	6-10	8-10	10-10
ıenge Inn	..	6-31	8-16	10-16	12-16	2-16	4-16	6-16	8-16	10-16
gton, Post Office	..	6-36	8-21	10-21	12-21	2-21	4-21	6-21	8-21	10-21
avon, Post Office	..	6-45	8-30	10-30	12-30	2-30	4-30	6-30	8-30	10-30
Bus Shelter	..	6-52	8-37	10-37	12-37	2-37	4-37	6-37	8-37	10-37
Ship Inn	..	7-0	8-45	10-45	12-45	2-45	4-45	6-45	8-45	10-45
ı, Cat Inn	..	7-5	8-50	10-50	12-50	2-50	4-50	6-50	8-50	—
Turning	..	7-9	8-54	10-54	12-54	2-54	4-54	6-54	8-54	
New Inn	..	7-15	9-0	11-0	1-0	3-0	5-0	7-0	9-0	
Foxley Corner	..	7-20	9-5	11-5	1-5	3-5	5-5	7-5	9-5	
..	..	7-29	9-14	11-14	1-14	3-14	5-14	7-14	9-14	
Market	arr	7-35	9-20	11-20	1-20	3-20	5-20	7-20	9-20	

		NSu *	*	* NSu	*	*	*	*	†	*
ıarket	dep	8-0	10-0	12-0	2-0	4-0	6-0	8-0	10-0	
..	..	8-6	10-6	12-6	2-6	4-6	6-6	8-6	10-6	
›xley Corner	..	8-15	10-15	12-15	2-15	4-15	6-15	8-15	10-15	
w Inn	..	8-20	10-20	12-20	2-20	4-20	6-20	8-20	10-20	
·ning	..	8-26	10-26	12-26	2-26	4-26	6-26	8-26	10-26	
t Inn	..	8-30	10-30	12-30	2-30	4-30	6-30	8-30	10-30	—
Inn	..	8-35	10-35	12-35	2-35	4-35	6-35	8-35	10-35	11-0
ıelter	..	8-43	10-43	12-43	2-43	4-43	6-43	8-43	—	11-8
’ost Office	..	8-50	10-50	12-50	2-50	4-50	6-50	8-50		11-15
›st Office	..	8-59	10-59	12-59	2-59	4-59	6-59	8-59		11-24
ı	..	9-4	11-4	1-4	3-4	5-4	7-4	9-4		11-29
Station	arr	9-10	11-10	1-10	3-10	5-10	7-10	9-10		11-35
Station	dep	9-17	11-17	1-17	3-17	5-17	7-17	9-17		11-37
Station	arr	9-37	11-37	1-37	3-37	5-37	7-37	9-37		11-57

Amesbury (Connections cannot be guaranteed). NSu—Not Sundays.
ımences from Amesbury only at 8–10 a.m. on Sunday. †—Change at Upavon.

ısbury,
8th September, 1951.

The military establishments on Salisbury Plain brought in good business for Wilts & Dorset (especially with weekend leave services) during the 1950s, but during the autumn of 1951 military operations caused temporary changes to be made to the bus services between Amesbury and Marlborough and Devizes.

Arthur Spreadbury was a conductor at Pewsey depot for 31 years. The Royal Society for the Prevention of Accidents awarded this certificate to him to recognise his freedom from blameworthy accidents during 1951. The Road Operators Safety Council was subsequently formed in 1955 and assumed responsibility for issuing annual certificates and badges to bus drivers and conductors who have avoided blameworthy accidents. The scheme for drivers was still operating when this book was published in 2015.

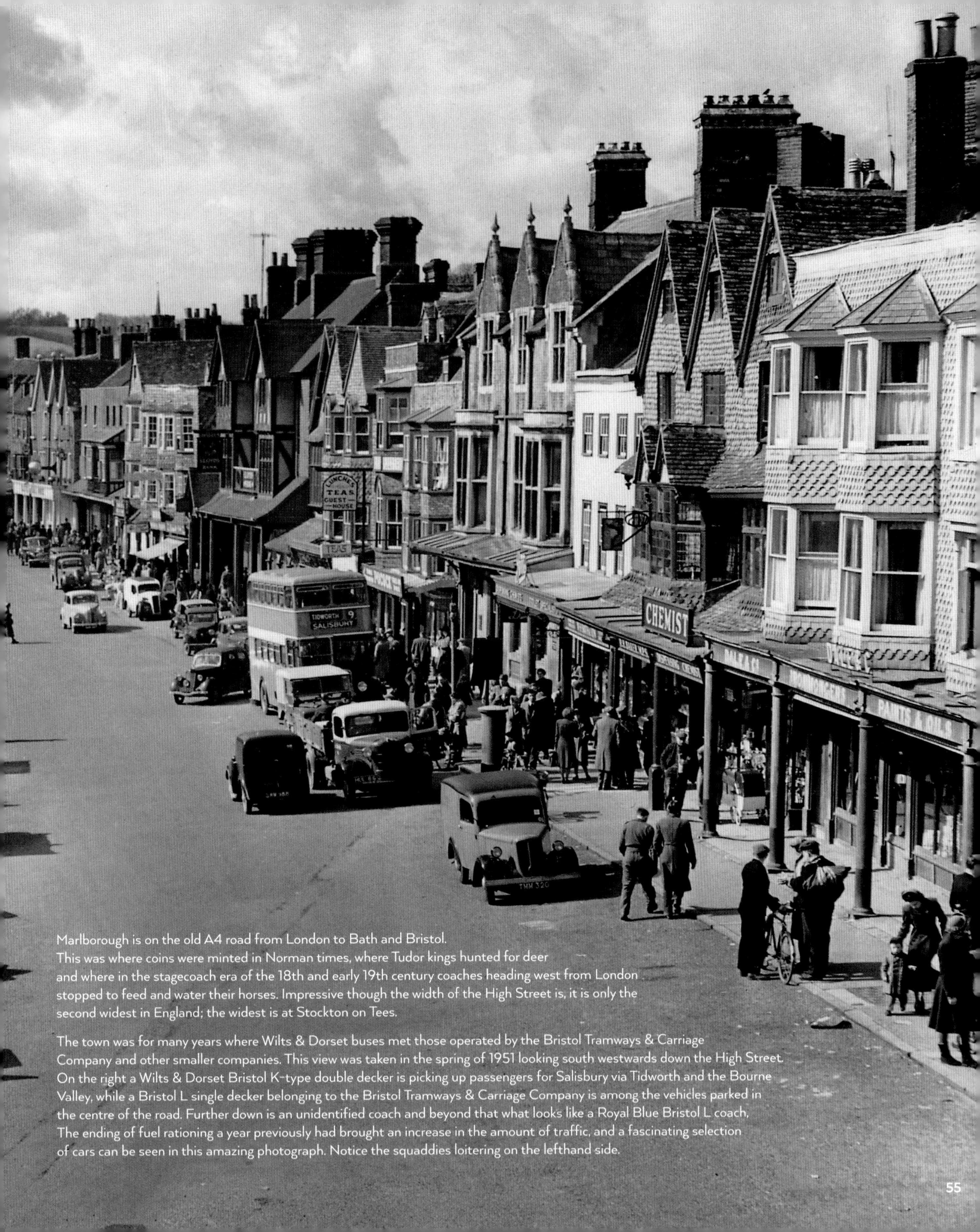

Marlborough is on the old A4 road from London to Bath and Bristol.
This was where coins were minted in Norman times, where Tudor kings hunted for deer and where in the stagecoach era of the 18th and early 19th century coaches heading west from London stopped to feed and water their horses. Impressive though the width of the High Street is, it is only the second widest in England; the widest is at Stockton on Tees.

The town was for many years where Wilts & Dorset buses met those operated by the Bristol Tramways & Carriage Company and other smaller companies. This view was taken in the spring of 1951 looking south westwards down the High Street. On the right a Wilts & Dorset Bristol K-type double decker is picking up passengers for Salisbury via Tidworth and the Bourne Valley, while a Bristol L single decker belonging to the Bristol Tramways & Carriage Company is among the vehicles parked in the centre of the road. Further down is an unidentified coach and beyond that what looks like a Royal Blue Bristol L coach. The ending of fuel rationing a year previously had brought an increase in the amount of traffic, and a fascinating selection of cars can be seen in this amazing photograph. Notice the squaddies loitering on the lefthand side.

1952

Early in the year Wilts & Dorset needed to boost the single deck fleet and bought five such vehicles from Hants & Dorset, and also exchanged ten double deck buses with Crosville for ten single deck buses.

A scheme was prepared for rebuilding the canteen block at Salisbury bus station and providing additional office accommodation, while work started on the new Andover bus station in June. The goodwill of the bus services of Huntley & Son of East Oakley was bought for £1,500.

In November, delivery began of Wilts & Dorset's first underfloor-engined single deckers, Bristol LS6Gs with dual-purpose 39-seat bodywork by Eastern Coach Works. In coach livery, these vehicles started to enter service in December, initially used on a variety of duties, including weekend forces leave express services.

1953

Following on from the 1952 plans, agreement was reached with James & Crockerell Ltd for demolition of part of the existing buildings and the erection of a new two storey extension at Salisbury bus station at a cost of £7,459.

Traffic Manager Mr R Bushrod was awarded an MBE, but resigned on 31 March to take up an appointment with an associated company. Mr H W Mills became Traffic Manager from 1 April.

Delivery of underfloor-engined dual-purpose saloons continued; by April Wilts & Dorset had 28 such vehicles, and a further eight were taken into stock between June and October.

Also during the year, 22 new double-deck buses entered the fleet, the final lowbridge type buses with a sunken side gangway on the upper deck to be bought new by Wilts & Dorset. On the last 19 of these, the upper-deck bench seats were divided into four slightly staggered individual seats, thus ensuring that people sat four across at times of peak loading rather than each bench seating three very well spaced passengers as was sometimes the case with earlier vehicles of this type. Some of these, intended for country routes, were the first Wilts & Dorset double decks to have manually operated platform doors.

in 1952

King George VI died aged 56 as a result of lung cancer.

Compulsory identity cards, which had been imposed by National Registration Act 1939, were discontinued.

A devastating flood at Lynmouth, Devon, resulted in 34 deaths.

Tea rationing ended.

A railway accident at Harrow & Wealdstone claimed the lives of 108 people.

Popular music included Unforgettable by Nat King Cole and Here In My Heart by Al Martino.

in 1953

A catastrophic flood caused many deaths in coastal areas bordering the North Sea.

Sweet rationing ended.

Conquest of Mount Everest by Edmund Hillary and Tenzing Norgay.

Coronation of Queen Elizabeth II at Westminster Abbey.

No.1 hits included I Believe by Frankie Laine and She Wears Red Feathers by Guy Mitchell.

Former Venture AEC Regent III highbridge double decker HAD 745 was on a local journey to Picket Piece when photographed in Andover bus station on 9 October 1952 on the left.

BFM 181 in the background was a Leyland Tiger TS7 with a 32-seat Eastern Coach Works body, one of ten acquired from Crosville during April 1952 in exchange for ten Leyland Tiitan TD1 double decks. All of these ex-Crosville single decks were withdrawn during 1954.

DAVID PENNELS

The summer and autumn of 1953 saw the last lowbridge double deck buses join the fleet, a batch of 15 Bristol KSW6Bs intended for the longer distance routes. They had manually operated platform doors, the first Wilts & Dorset double deck buses to be so fitted. Allocated to Blandford depot when new, JWV 381 is seen at the top of the opposite page leaving Weymouth at the start of the long run to Salisbury on route 35.

BRIAN JACKSON COLLECTION

Wilts & Dorset's first underfloor-engined single deckers had started to enter service in December 1952. These Bristol LS6Gs with dual-purpose Eastern Coach Works bodywork had doorways at the front and rear.

No less than 36 of this type had entered the fleet by October 1953 and, painted in the coach livery, they were used on weekend forces leave services, excursions, and ordinary bus work, too. JMW 413, new in July 1953, is seen on the left on an excursion.

R H G SIMPSON
BRIAN JACKSON COLLECTION

These interior views illustrate that Wilts & Dorset's final batch of Bristol KSWs solved one of the problems associated with lowbridge buses.

The staggered seating on the upper deck ensured that passengers sat four across. Of course, the intrusion of the gangway into the lower deck ceiling remained - often causing bumped heads for people sitting downstairs on the offside.

On the plus side, the leg room in the upper deck seats was excellent. Lowbridge buses remained in the fleet until April 1974.

These photographs were taken in the early 1970s - the vehicle is still in fine condition after many years service.

1954

Restricted height clearances on a number of routes meant that most double deckers used by Wilts & Dorset had been of the lowbridge type, with a sunken side gangway on the upper deck. In the early 1950s Bristol and Eastern Coach Works developed the Bristol Lodekka, a double deck bus with a centre gangway on both decks that was no higher than the old lowbridge type. Wilts & Dorset switched to the Lodekka for its new double deck buses in 1954; seven were taken into stock between March and October of that year and were initially put to work on Salisbury city routes.

More surprising was the batch of single deck buses received during October and November. Two years after switching to underfloor-engined saloons, Wilts & Dorset took delivery of 15 traditional front-engined half-cab single-deck buses, with rear entrance bodies seating 39 passengers. Meanwhile the underfloor-engined dual purpose saloons now covered the majority of the weekend forces leave express services - destinations had been widened to include Birmingham, Liverpool, Preston, Manchester and Leeds.

The new bus station and garage in Bridge Street in Andover opened on 6 October. The first journey to use it was the 1235 journey on route 8 to Salisbury.

WILTS & DORSET
MOTOR SERVICES LIMITED

OPENING OF NEW BUS STATION, BRIDGE STREET, ANDOVER

ON WEDNESDAY, 6th OCTOBER, 1954
Service 8, Andover-Amesbury-Salisbury will be operated from the New Bus Station, Bridge Street, Andover as from the 12-35 p.m. departure and will follow the normal time-tabled route. No other services will be operated from the new Bus Station on this day.

On and from Thursday, 7th October, 1954, all services time-tabled to start from the Bus Station will commence and terminate at that point in lieu of Andover Junction Railway Station.

TRAFFIC MANAGER'S OFFICE, 8 ENDLESS STREET, SALISBURY.

in 1954

Roger Bannister became the first person to run a mile in under 4 minutes.

Rationing finally ended with meat no longer rationed.

Britain's first purpose-built comprehensive school opened at Kidbrooke in South East London.

The first UK Wimpy Bar opened in London.

No 1 hits included Cara Mia by David Whitfield and Secret Love by Doris Day.

1955

Eight underfloor-engined 41-seat Bristol LS5G single deck buses were new in May. They were equipped for driver only operation, and negotiations proceeded to agree a rate of pay for this type of work. A further five to this specification were delivered in December. Meanwhile, ten more Bristol Lodekka double deck buses entered service during the year.

Managing Director Raymond Longman summed up: *"The year 1955 has been a busy and successful one. The fine summer helped a lot, and more passengers were carried than last year. With the cooperation of staff we have extended the use of driver only operated buses, and more will come in the future; this is the only way to continue some services where loadings and receipts are consistently light. However, an unofficial strike at Basingstoke in October caused considerable inconvenience and annoyance to the public and loss to the Company."*

in 1955

Prime Minister Winston Churchill resigned owing to ill health; his place was taken by Anthony Eden, previously Foreign Secretary.

The general election was won by the Conservative Party with a majority of 31.

Independent Television (ITV) transmissions began, ending the monopoly of the BBC.

Clement Attlee resigned as leader of the Labour Party, replaced by Hugh Gaitskell.

No 1 hits included Rose Marie by Slim Whitman and Rock Around the Clock by Bill Haley & His Comets.

Still with full side and front destination displays when photographed at Weymouth on 23 June 1955 and shown on the left, 1949 Bristol K6B FAM 4 was soon to leave for Salisbury on route 34 via Dorchester and Blandford.
By now it rare to see side displays over the platform in use; they were not fitted to vehicles built from 1950, and in due course were panelled over on older stock.

DAVID PENNELS COLLECTION

The new bus station at Andover opened on 6 October 1954, a great improvement on the previous cramped premises. The first journey was the 1235 to Salisbury on route 8, seen opposite top ready at the stand 35 minutes before departure.

PETER COOK COLLECTION

Photographed in September 1954 was one of two particularly unusual single deckers that had been taken over from Venture at Basingstoke. These were AEC Regals dating from May 1938 with 31-seat open back bodies by Park Royal. Both remained in service with Wilts & Dorset until February 1956.On the left is the interior of one of them, COT 547.

DAVID PENNELS

The Bedford OB shown below, dating from 1947, was one of two that came to Wilts & Dorset from Venture in 1951. Transferred from Basingstoke to Pewsey depot, FOR 634 looks very smart here in Wilts & Dorset's coach livery on 4 July 1954, and was soon to leave for Hungerford.

DAVID PENNELS

Dual-purpose Bristol LS6G saloon KHR 654 was new in February 1954, and only four months old when photographed as an express coach on hire to Royal Blue on 5 June. It's seen at the bottom of the opposite page at the Swan Hotel, Hartley Wintney, a regular refreshment halt for Royal Blue coaches between London and the West Country. Notice a good load and both doorways in use. Like other vehicles in the batch it was converted to just front door layout early in 1955.

D T SHARWOOD
DAVID PENNELS COLLECTION

Spring 1954 saw the arrival of Wilts & Dorset's first seven Bristol Lodekka double deckers. Ten more came in 1955. Most were used on city routes in Salisbury.

On the left is LD6B-type LMR 741, which entered service in January 1955. Compare the long radiator grille fitted to these early Lodekkas to later models with a neater short one.

BRISTOL VINTAGE BUS GROUP
DAVID PENNELS COLLECTION

Following the Wilts & Dorset debut of the type on Salisbury city services two years earlier, three Bristol Lodekkas were ordered for the Salisbury to Weymouth route, where they entered service in May 1956. NHR 844 on the right was photographed in Dorchester when travelling from Weymouth to Salisbury. Note the Dorchester slip-board carried on the radiator.

This batch of three LD6B-type Lodekkas ran on this route until the autumn of 1959, when it was converted to single-deck driver only operation. The Lodekkas then moved to other routes.

BRIAN JACKSON COLLECTION

Below is the view from the lower-deck front seat of a Bristol K returning from Bournemouth to Salisbury on 10 March 1956. Bristol K5G EMW 285, new in 1947 but later modified by Wilts & Dorset with a T-shape front destination display, is approaching from the opposite direction on a route 44 journey to Woodfalls. The location is north of Downton on the A338 road.

DAVID PENNELS

1956

With the new bus station and garage in Andover, opened in 1954, the company no longer needed the site in Junction Road, which was sold for £10,450. Three more driver only single-deck buses entered service in February, then a further nine between August and December.

The three Bristol Lodekka double deckers that were new in April went to Blandford depot for the Salisbury-Blandford-Weymouth route. With ten more coming between October and December, the type was now being seen quite widely across the network.

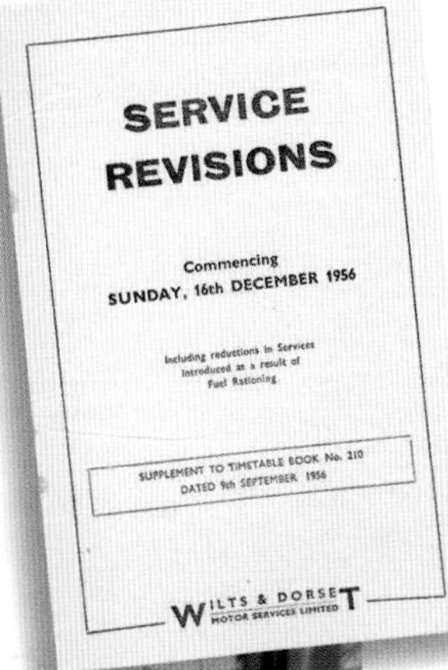

SERVICE REVISIONS

Commencing SUNDAY, 16th DECEMBER 1956

Including reductions in Services introduced as a result of Fuel Rationing

SUPPLEMENT TO TIMETABLE BOOK No. 210 DATED 9th SEPTEMBER 1956

WILTS & DORSET MOTOR SERVICES LIMITED

The Suez Campaign by the British and French governments during 1956 had detrimental effects for both Wilts & Dorset and its passengers. With fewer service personnel, both National Service and regular, based at the camps served by the company ,demand for bus services to and from these camps fell. Bus passengers were hit by a government imposed surcharge on bus fares under the provisions of the Hydrocarbon Oil Duties (Temporary Increase) Act, 1956.

in 1956

Third class in British Railways trains was redesignated as second class.

Corgi Toys first appeared.

Petrol rationing was imposed owing to blockades from the Middle East as a result of the Suez Crisis.

Premium Bonds went on sale for the first time in November.

British and French troops withdrew from Suez in December.

No 1 hits included Memories are Made of This by Dean Martin and The Poor People of Paris by Winifred Atwell.

By the time this photograph was taken on 1 February 1956, the dual-purpose Harrington body on BWV 666 had been rebuilt twice by Wilts & Dorset - in 1947 and 1952. Dating from 1939, this Leyland Lion LT8 would remain in service until August 1957, when the last pre-war Leylands were withdrawn from the passenger carrying fleet.

DAVID PENNELS

The British Transport Commission had a series of generic posters produced in the 1950s, which BTC bus operators could overprint with their individual company names. Here are two of them that Wilts & Dorset had on display in its travel offices and bus stations.

courtesy of KEN WIGMORE

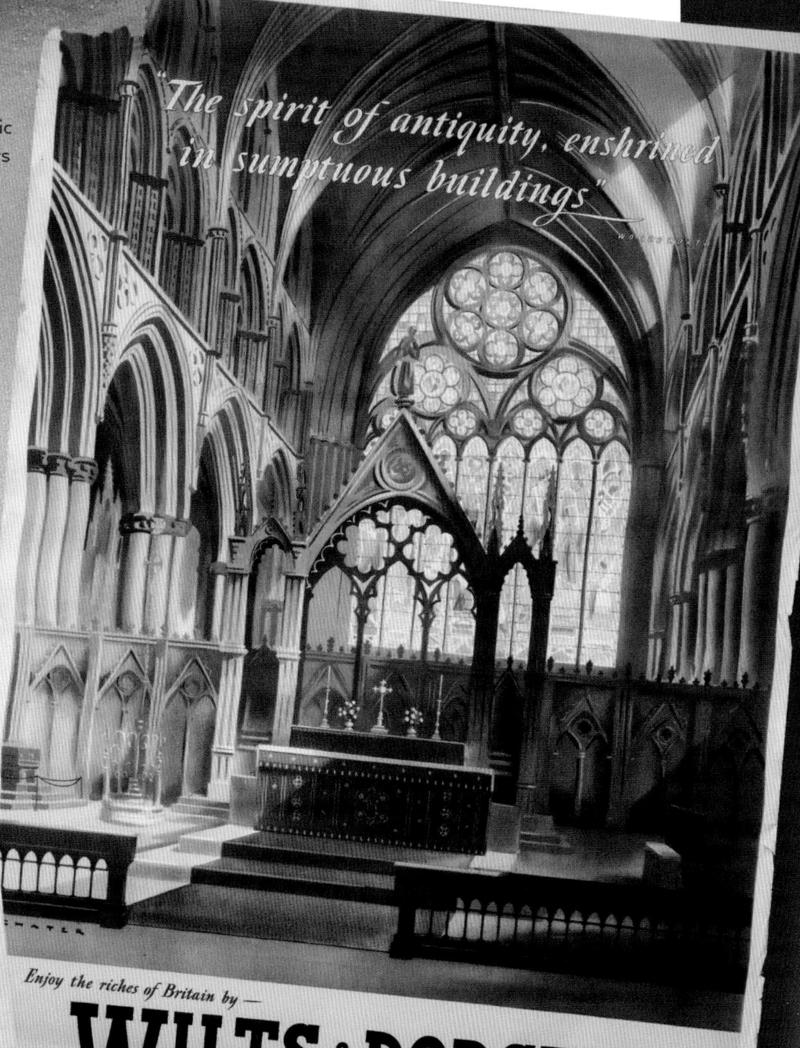

Unfortunately, strike action afflicted the bus industry during the summer of 1957. This picture shows pickets on duty at Castle Street. The gentleman standing in front of the group wearing a cap and glasses is Leslie Smith who worked for Wilts & Dorset as a driver for many years.

THE LATE AUSTIN UNDERWOOD

The weather was unseasonably wet and cool on 18 May 1957, as the partly steamed up windows of GHR 364 below show. This 1950 Bristol K5G with 55-seat Eastern Coach Works lowbridge body was often seen on the 30 mile route 5 between Marlborough and Salisbury. Here it is at Figheldean.

DAVID PENNELS

1957

The temporary surcharge imposed on bus fares at the end of 1956 was removed from 23 April 1957, but local bus passengers greeted this news with little enthusiasm, as it was also announced there'd be a general increase in Wilts & Dorset bus fares from the same date.

The summer of 1957 was a time of industrial unrest in the bus industry. From midnight on 19 July busmen in most areas of the country came out on strike in support of a claim for a £1 per week increase in wages; the companies had offered 3/- (15p). The deadlock was referred to the Industrial Disputes Tribunal for arbitration. On 26 July the tribunal recommended an increase of 11/- (65p) per week. This was accepted and the strike called off.

It was notified that the company's chief officers would normally retire at 65, but may, subject to the approval of the Board, remain in office until the age of 68.

November saw the entry into service of two Bristol Lodekka double deck buses with much improved semi-coach seating upholstered in green hide. This became a standard for the company's double deck buses for the next six years.

in 1957

Prime Minister Anthony Eden resigned due to ill health, replaced by Harold Macmillan.

Petrol rationing, introduced because of the Suez crisis, ceased.

A fire in the nuclear reactor at Windscale, Cumbria, released radio-active contamination.

A rail crash in dense fog at Lewisham resulted in 90 deaths.

No 1 hits included Young Love by Tab Hunter, All Shook Up by Elvis Presley and Diana by Paul Anka.

in 1958

The chartered plane bringing the Manchester United football team back from a European Cup match in Belgrade crashed on take off after a refuelling stop at Munich.

The Campaign for Nuclear Disarmament was launched.

There were riots at Notting Hill, London.

Preston by-pass, the first stretch of motorway in Britain, opened.

No 1 hits included Magic Moments by Perry Como, All I Have to Do is Dream by the Everly Brothers and Carolina Moon by Connie Francis.

On the left several passengers are boarding GAM 11 at Tidworth on the busy 8 route between Andover and Salisbury on 12 September 1958, the ladies very fashionable for the day. New in February 1950, this Bristol K5G had its front destination screen modified to the T-shape in 1957. This was one of the company's first Ks to have flexible, rather than rigid, engine mountings. Passengers would notice the reduction in noise and vibration.

The 76 via Middle Wallop was a more direct route between Salisbury and Andover, but carried fewer passengers than the 8 which ran through more centres of population along the way.

1958

The summer of 1958 saw six new luxury coaches join the fleet, the first new pure coaches for eight years. These 39-seat Eastern Coach Works bodied Bristol MW vehicles were delivered in Wilts & Dorset's then new coach livery of red below the waistline and cream.

Coach excursions from Salisbury in July included Clovelly for 18/9d (94p), Chichester, Guildford & Winchester for 13/- (65p), Lynton and Lynmouth for 14/9 (74p) and Lyme Regis for 10/- (50p). You could have had a conducted tour of London Airport on Sunday 20 July for 10/6 (52.5p), leaving Salisbury bus station at 9am and due back at 8pm.

At the Pavilion Theatre in Bournemouth 'The Big Show of 1958' starred Bob Monkhouse, Denis Goodwin and the Beverley Sisters; on Wednesday 9 July and Wednesday 23 July Wilts & Dorset ran a coach trip leaving Salisbury at 7pm for 11/- (55p) which included a 6/- (30p) admission ticket.

The year ended with the delivery of three more Bristol LD6G Lodekkas with semi-coach seating; these were put to work on the Salisbury-Bournemouth route.

At the beginning of 1958, dual purpose saloon JMR 639 was repainted in an experimental livery - largely cream but with maroon window surrounds, roof and mudguards.

This was an attempt to brighten up the company's coach livery, but the result, as seen on the photograph above, taken on 24 June, was not considered a success and no more vehicles were so treated.

On the left, nearing journey's end on the 115 minute trip from Basingstoke to Salisbury on the 76 route, 1956 built LD6G-type Bristol Lodekka OHR 123 was photographed at St Thomas's Bridge on 29 April 1958.

DAVID PENNELS

As late as October and November 1954 - two years after the delivery of the company's first underfloor engined saloons - Wilts & Dorset received 15 Bristol LWL5G single-deck buses with traditional rear-entrance 39-seat Eastern Coach Works bodies. These were a special order, as by then the half-cab single-deck bus was considered obsolete, but the company felt that these simple, rugged buses would have lower maintenance costs, given the condition of many rural roads its buses ran on.

One of these buses, LAM 744, shown on the left, was photographed by David Pennels at Salisbury bus station on 4 April 1956, having just come in from Shaftesbury via Bowerchalke and Broad Chalke on route 29.

However, by 1958 it was recognised that these vehicles had been a costly mistake, as they needed a crew of driver and conductor. So, in July of that year one of the batch was returned to Eastern Coach Works to be rebuilt with a forward entrance to make it suitable for driver only operation. This conversion kept its half cab and bulkhead, but drivers found the layout unworkable.

Therefore the rest of them were rebuilt in Wilts & Dorset's own workshops. They were given a full width front designed by the company, and the bulkhead between the driver and seating area was removed. The initial Eastern Coach Works modification was subsequently rebuilt to conform to this specification.

Rebuilding by Wilts & Dorset started in November 1958, with all the buses completed by the spring of 1960. These rebuilt buses were soon nicknamed 'conkerboxes' by staff, and were used quite widely across the company's network during the 1960s.

KWV 933 above, modified in January 1959, was photographed by David Pennels at Upavon on 27 May that year while working the 18 route which linked the village and RAF Upavon with a journey time of seven minutes.

KWV 934, in the picture at the top of the opposite page from Brian Jackson's collection, was converted in November 1959. Here it was about to leave Salisbury bus station for Shaftesbury on route 28 via Tisbury and Donhead St Andrew early in 1960.The three smaller fixed windows at the rear of the nearside offer a good clue of the original design of the bus.

Below is a passenger's view of a conkerbox after conversion taken by David Pennels, in this case LAM 278. The removal of the majority of the front bulkhead gave travellers the full benefit of the melodic(?) sounds from the 5-cylinder Gardner engine. These were certainly among the company's more noisy vehicles on which to make a journey. Note the Clayton heater, which at least ensured that the bus was reasonably warm during the winter.

Some journeys from Larkhill to Amesbury on route 2 continued onwards to Salisbury, mainly Saturday afternoons. This was clearly required on 10 September 1960 when Bristol Lodekka LD6B NHR 909 on the right was photographed well loaded with happy passengers near Old Sarum on the outskirts of Salisbury.

DAVID PENNELS

In the warm summer sun on 15 August 1959, Bristol LS5G bus NHR 128 was photographed below at Burbage, Seymour Pond, having stopped to pick up some youngsters while on the way from Pewsey to Hungerford on route 16. It epitomises Wilts & Dorset's rural routes in those days. This bus was new in February 1956. Notice the bus stop, complete with shaped timetable case.

DAVID PENNELS COLLECTION

1959

The summer of 1959 was very warm and sunny, and Wilts & Dorset was able to make good use of two more 39-seat Eastern Coach Works bodied Bristol MW coaches that were delivered during April in time for the coaching season.

In June Wilts & Dorset route 9 (Salisbury-Tidworth-Marlborough) was linked with Bristol Omnibus Company route 70 to provide a new jointly-operated through service between Salisbury and Swindon without the need to change buses at Marlborough. Two new Bristol Lodekkas, again with semi-coach seating, joined the fleet towards the end of the year and were normally allocated to this route, which was given route number 709.

The Wiltshire branch of the Rural District Councils Association debated whether school contract journeys in rural areas should be made available to adult fare paying passengers; snags were pointed out, including that such journeys would then have to be operated as stage services and would require Road Service Licences. It was decided on a majority vote not to approach the Traffic Commissioners on this issue.

in 1959

Post codes were first used in the UK, initially as an experiment in Norwich.

The first BMC Mini went on sale.

The general election was won by the Conservative Party with a majority of 100.

The first section of the M1 motorway opened.

No 1 hits included Side Saddle by Russ Conway and It Doesn't Matter Any More by Buddy Holly.

in 1960

The News Chronicle ceased publication.

Public services began on the Bluebell Railway in Sussex, the first standard gauge line in Britain to be operated by preservationists.

The soap opera Coronation Street began on ITV.

Farthings ceased to be legal tender.

No 1 hits included Cathy's Clown by the Everly Brothers, My Old Man's a Dustman by Lonnie Donegan and Apache by the Shadows.

Bristol LS6G dual purpose on the left, JHR 605, had been painted in the new simpler red and cream coach livery, and here on 6 June 1960 about to act as a relief Royal Blue coach to London. Wilts & Dorset vehicles were often hired by Royal Blue at busy periods, to the extent that 'On hire to Royal Blue' was included on the destination blind. Royal Blue was, of course, synonymous with express coach travel in the South West until the early 1970s.

The weather on 9 June 1960 was clearly inclement in the picture below, when sister vehicle JMR 324 had just arrived from Blandford and Weymouth. This 1953 dual purpose Bristol LS6G was still in the former coach livery but had been converted to single doorway layout for driver only operation, and provided very comfortable travel for passengers on this long route.

DAVID PENNELS

1960

Mr R Wigmore resigned as Wilts & Dorset's Secretary on 31 January, having taken up an appointment with Western and Southern National. His place was taken by Mr D G Finley, whose career in transport had started with the Great Western Railway before the Second World War. Since 1954 he had been Secretary of Cumberland Motor Services in North West England. Mr E F Phillips was appointed Assistant Secretary.

Mr M J Richardson, Assistant Traffic Manager, resigned with effect from 31 July, replaced by Mr B Hewkin. Traffic Manager Mr H W Mills resigned on 30 November to take up an appointment with Southern Vectis, with Mr G Carruthers replacing him from 1 December.

Construction of a new bus station and depot at Basingstoke at an estimated cost of £93,150 had been approved by the British Transport Commission, and tenders were invited for its construction. The contract was awarded to H N Edwards & Partners of Basingstoke for £112,000; the lowest of the nine tenders received. No new vehicles were added to the fleet in 1960.

On the left you can just see the comfortable camel back semi-coach seats in Bristol LD6G-type Lodekka SHR 441, just pulling out of the recently renovated Bournemouth bus station, bound for Salisbury on the 38, a route operated jointly with Hants & Dorset. The Hants & Dorset vehicle on the left carrying the advertisement for Olivier cigarettes was an AEC Regent III with Northern Counties lowbridge bodywork, one of six similar buses originally intended for Western SMT in Scotland but diverted to Hants & Dorset in 1949.

DAVID PENNELS COLLECTION

1961 ended on a wintry note as you can see on the right, but 1947 Bristol K6B EAM 614 was making steady progress along the snow and ice covered road towards Amesbury and Salisbury when photographed on 31 December.

However, 1962 was worse, with a snowfall on Boxing Day. This was a foretaste of what was to come, for during the early hours of Sunday 30 December a blizzard blanketed southern England in deep snow, with strong winds causing considerable drifting.

DAVID PENNELS

Based on the novel The Lost Country by J R Salamanca, the film Wild in the Country starring Elvis Presley went on release in June 1961 and was showing at the Gaumont in Swindon when passengers were getting off Bristol LD6B NHR 845 at the conveniently located bus stop directly outside the cinema in the picture below. Note the wonderful 1961 hairstyles and fashions.

R H G SIMPSON
BRIAN JACKSON COLLECTION

1961

The coal fired heating in Salisbury workshops was at the end of its useful life, so Hamworthy Engineering was contracted to convert the existing boiler for oil firing, and to fit wiring and supply Dimplex equipment for office heating, at an estimated cost of £1,700.

Salisbury breakdown lorry UF 7407 was taken out of service in March. This had originally been a Leyland Titan TD1 double-deck bus with Southdown and was one of the many secondhand buses acquired by Wilts & Dorset in 1939. Conversion into a breakdown lorry in 1940 meant that UF 7407 was the last remaining survivor of this huge influx of vehicles, albeit not in bus form. UF 7407 was sold for £88 in September 1961 and subsequently acquired by a preservationist.

Mr W H Tryhorn, Chief Engineer, died on 1 June, and his place was taken by Mr W L F Henderson from 1 September.

Work was proceeding on the new premises at Basingstoke, and approval was given for the purchase of 102 conductors box lockers, 120 clothes lockers, a night safe, time clocks and office furniture for the new depot.

A further six new luxury coaches, plus five new single deck buses entered the fleet in 1961.

in 1961

Betting shops were legalised.

The birth control pill became available on the National Health.

The first Private Eye was published.

No 1 hits included Wooden Heart by Elvis Presley and Walking Back to Happiness by Helen Shapiro.

in 1962

The world held its breath over the Cuban missiles crisis.

The first James Bond film, Dr No, came out.

BBC television started the satirical show That Was The Week That Was.

Fog in early December was followed from Christmas by a spell of exceptionally cold weather across the country.

No 1 hits included I Remember You by Frank Ifield, Come Outside by Mike Sarne & Wendy Richard and Telstar by the Tornadoes.

Early in 1962 the company revised the coach livery again to be all-over cream with maroon mudguards, wheel trims and radiator grille. This new style was rapidly applied to the 1958-61 deliveries of Bristol MW coaches, and on 22 February 1962 David Pennels was asked to take a photograph of 1959 MW6G SWV 688 in the new livery. For several years afterwards this photograph was used on the rear cover of Wilts & Dorset's timetable books to advertise coach hire.

DAVID PENNELS

1962

A major event this year was the opening of the new bus station, depot and workshop at Basingstoke on 28 June. Used by eight Basingstoke town routes and 13 country routes run by Wilts & Dorset and others, the bus station had the capacity to deal with 180,000 bus departures per year.

Another significant event was the retirement of Managing Director Raymond Longman on 30 June. He'd joined Wilts & Dorset in 1919, becoming Secretary in 1924, General Manager from 1942 and Managing Director from 1946. The new General Manager was David Deacon.

Eastern Coach Works had developed a new design for its luxury coach bodies, and three of this type were delivered to Wilts & Dorset in May 1962. They were the first for the company to include public address equipment, and were initially used on long distance private hires and excursions. They came in a new Wilts & Dorset coach livery of cream with maroon mudguards, and this started to be applied to the other coaches in the fleet.

Between September and December 13 Bristol FS-type Lodekka double deckers with semi-coach seats were brought into service. Delivery of the first five enabled the withdrawal, at the end of September, of the last of the former Venture AEC Regent double deckers at Basingstoke.

Three more new coaches, similar to those that came in May, were taken into stock in November, but did not enter service until April 1963.

WILTS & DORSET
MOTOR SERVICES LIMITED
OFFICIAL
TIMETABLE
PRICE 1/-
HEAD OFFICE:
ENDLESS STREET, SALISBURY
TELEPHONE 3255
No. 216
6th MAY 1962, until further notice.

The new bus station at Basingstoke was opened on 28 June 1962. In the picture below invited guests and staff are looking on as Managing Director Raymond Longman (standing by the microphone) invites the Mayor of Basingstoke to cut the ribbon and declare the new bus station open. This was Mr Longman's last event as Managing Director, as he retired two days later. Is that why none of them are smiling?

THE LATE C J BURT COLLECTION

New vehicles received by Wilts & Dorset in 1963 included a pair of dual purpose Eastern Coach Works bodied Bristol MW6G saloons, the first of which you can see on the right after arrival at Salisbury garage when new.

CHARLIE HARDY COLLECTION

Also new in 1963 were Wilts & Dorset's first two forward-entrance double-deck buses. Bristol Lodekka FLF6G 467 BMR is at Salisbury bus station in the picture at the bottom of this page, having recently arrived from Bournemouth on route 38. These were the last new double-deck buses to feature the comfortable camel back semi-coach seating.

R H G SIMPSON
BRIAN JACKSON COLLECTION

1963

On 5 June 1963 the bus routes and express services operated by Silver Star of Porton were taken over by Wilts & Dorset. Silver Star had been started by Eddie Shergold and Ben White in 1923, and operated a bus service through the Bourne Valley to Salisbury as well as forces weekend leave services from the Salisbury Plain camps to various parts of the country. The principal routes run immediately before the takeover are shown on the map on the opposite page.

Eddie Shergold had died in October 1962 and Ben White wished to retire, so Silver Star was sold to Wilts & Dorset. Silver Star had a fleet of 23 vehicles at the time of the sale; Wilts & Dorset kept nine of them, and most of others were transferred to either Western National or the Bristol Omnibus Company.

New vehicles in 1963 included Wilts & Dorset's first two forward-entrance Bristol FLF-type Lodekka double-deck buses and seven more Bristol Lodekka FS-types following on from those delivered in 1962, plus two dual purpose Eastern Coach Works bodied Bristol MWs.

in 1963

The year began with record low temperatures and lying snow remained until early March.

Labour Party leader Hugh Gaitskell died; his place was taken by Harold Wilson.

The Beeching Report, advocating significant cuts in the railway network, was published.

BRITISH RAILWAYS BOARD
The Reshaping of British Railways
PART 1: REPORT
LONDON

The requirement for National Service having been ended, the last conscripted serviceman was demobbed.

Prime Minister Harold Macmillan resigned; he was succeeded by Sir Alec Douglas Home.

John F Kennedy, President of the USA, was assassinated in Dallas, Texas.

No 1 hits included From Me to You and She Loves You by the Beatles, and I Like It by Gerry & The Pacemakers.

photo Allan Warren

THE GUARDIAN
President Kennedy assassinated
Police arrest suspect

1963

SALISBURY — BISHOPDOWN — WINTERBOURNE — PORTON — ALLINGTON

The big news for 1963 was, of course, the acquisition of Silver Star of Porton from 5 June. The Silver Star fleet had included modern rear-engined Leyland Atlantean double deckers, which didn't enter service with Wilts & Dorset but were transferred to Bristol Omnibus Company.

The newest, 1013 MW, was only a year old when photographed above on 11 May 1963, seen passing the former home of Silver Star co-founder Eddie Shergold. This bus has been preserved and is in its original Silver Star condition.

On the right is the setting of the Silver Star - the emblem on the front of Leyland Tiger Cub PMW 386 is being painted over so that this vehicle can immediately start work with Wilts & Dorset on 5 June.

DAVID PENNELS

When this map from the 1964 Wilts & Dorset timetable book is compared with the 1949 map shown on page 48, the most noticeable difference is the significant expansion of the company's territory eastwards. Acquiring Venture in 1951 had given Wilts & Dorset a base in Basingstoke so, as you can see, now Wilts & Dorset buses could be found in such places as Aldermaston, Alton and Cheriton running on routes that at no point entered either of the two counties in the company's title.

Intending passengers in 1964 no doubt found the map useful when planning both local and longer distance journeys. Places where the bus routes linked up with the railway network were apparent, while towns where connections could be made with services run by other operators were clearly shown. A nice detailed touch is the use of a heritage typeface to show Stonehenge.

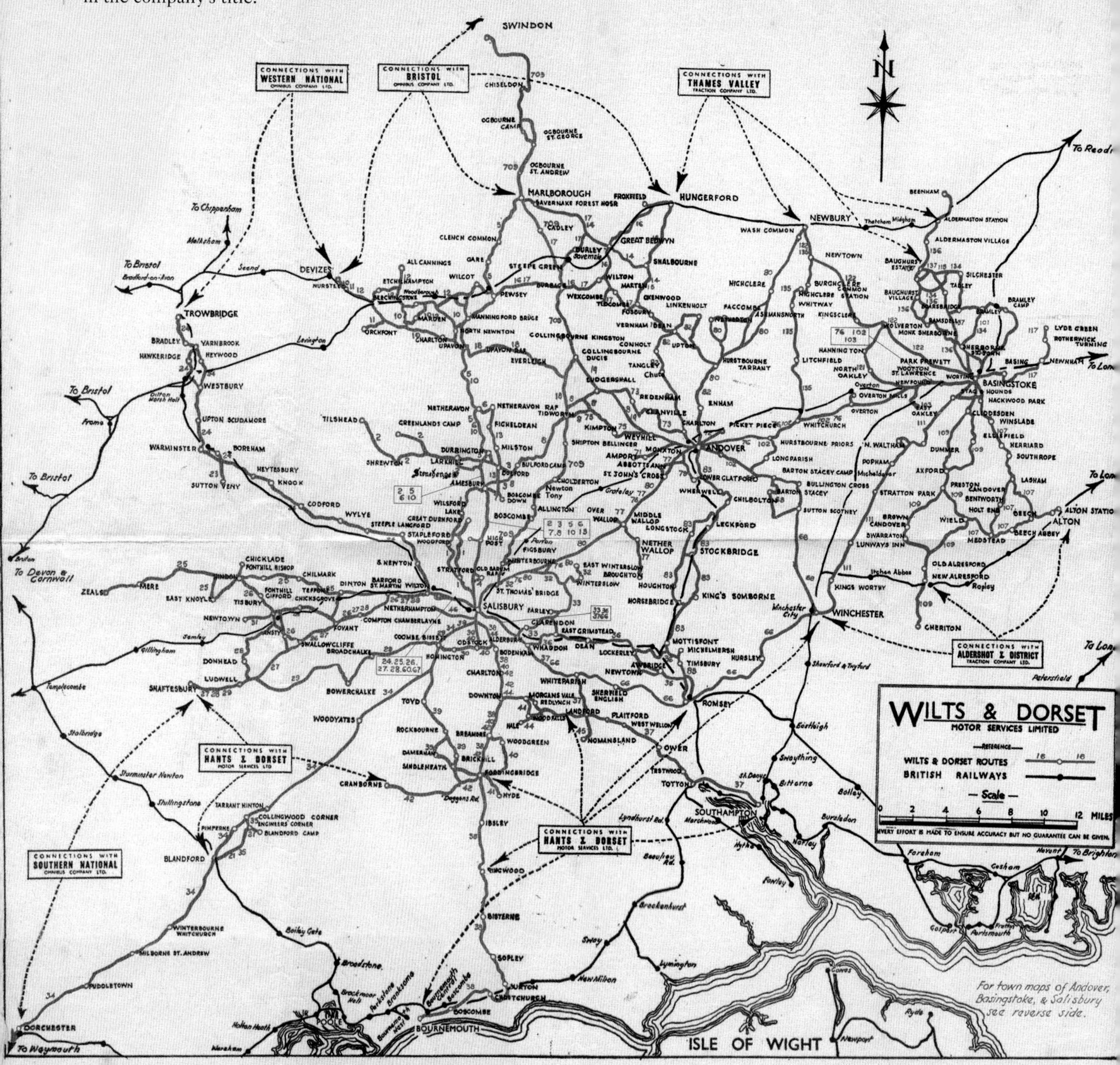

This map also shows the extent of the Wilts & Dorset network when the management of the company was merged with that of Hants & Dorset, and therefore is of particular interest. Timetable books issued from 1965 onwards would include a map showing the routes of both companies combined onto one fold-out map.

Of significance is the extent to which the railway network has contracted since the 1949 map. There are no longer railway lines from Broadstone to Brockenhurst and from West Moors to Salisbury, which closed in May 1964.

The railway line from Andover to Romsey via Stockbridge is correctly still shown on the map, but by then its days were numbered, as it closed in September 1964. The next few years would see further closures as the Beeching proposals continued to be implemented.

On the right are the local maps that appeared on the back of the main fold-out map showing the Salisbury city network and Basingstoke town network. By this time Basingstoke had been scheduled as a London overspill town, and would see much further development from the late 1960s onwards.

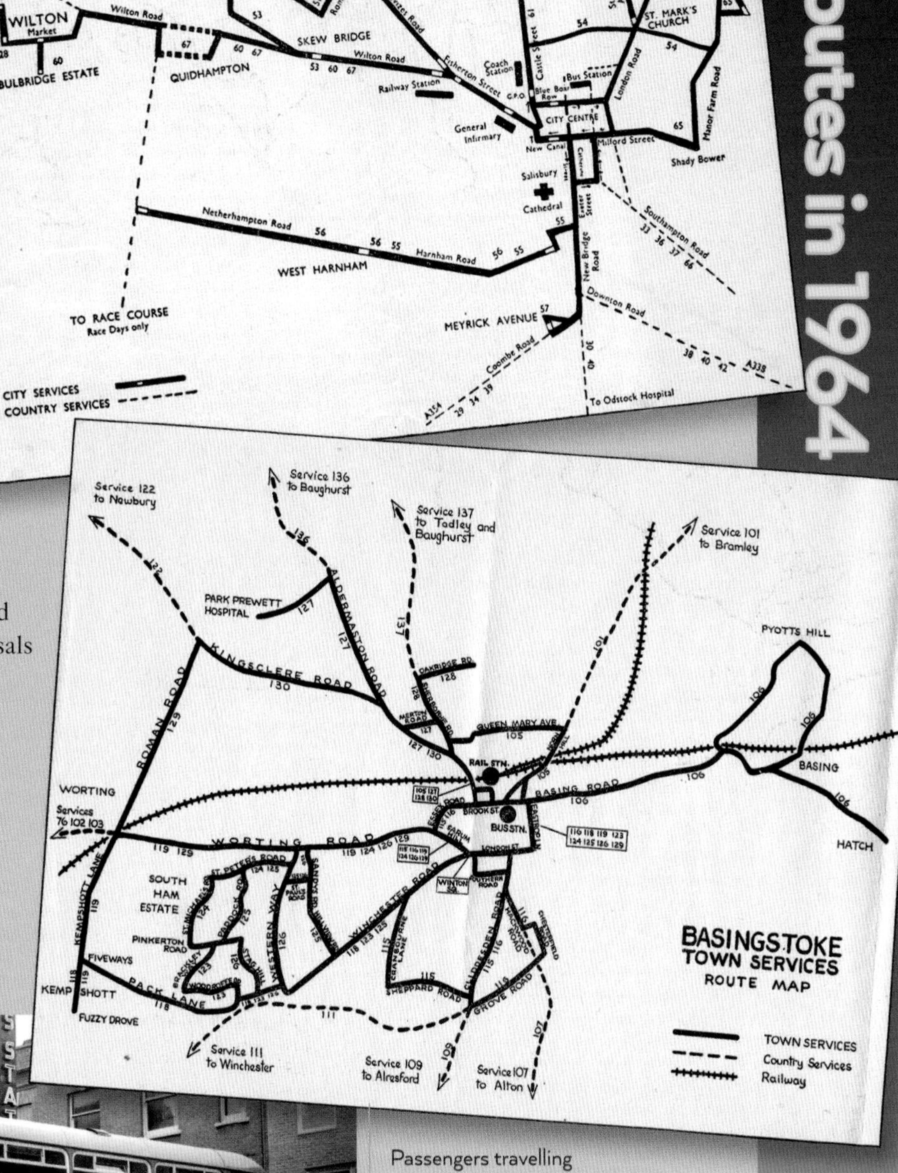

Passengers travelling to Ringwood, Christchurch and Bournemouth on 18 April 1963 are assured of a comfortable journey on 1962 Bristol FS6B Lodekka 688 AAM, which had camel back semi-coach seats.

Notice the large vertical bus station sign, part of which is visible on the Endless Street corner of the building.

DAVID PENNELS

Salisbury Racecourse is located on downland to the south west of the city, and excursions to race meetings provided good business for Wilts & Dorset. On the right is a line up of four former Silver Star Leyland coaches provided to take racegoers from Salisbury bus station to the course on 1 July 1964. The weather that day was ideal for a day at the races

1964

This was an important year in the history of Wilts & Dorset, as from 1 April the company's management was merged with that of Hants & Dorset Motor Services in Bournemouth. General Manager David Deacon relinquished his role but became Chairman of Wilts & Dorset the following year, with Douglas Morison, General Manager of Hants & Dorset now undertaking this role for both companies. Wilts & Dorset's Traffic Manager, George Carruthers, became Assistant General Manager.

New vehicles in 1964 included four more forward-entrance Bristol FLF double deckers and another eight Bristol FS double deckers, but the new vehicles were now fitted with standard bus seats and not the very comfortable semi-coach seating that had been specified between 1957 and 1963.

It was agreed that all clerical and supervisory staff would be entitled to 18 days holiday after 12 months service with the Company.

Below market day crowds were boarding former Silver Star Leyland Tiger Cub PMW 386 on city route 54 to Laverstock on 15 August 1964. No route number was carried on the front of the bus, but the wording St Mark's Church shows that this is a 54 rather than a 65, which ran to Laverstock via Milford Hill. The Cadena Cafe in Blue Boar Row was for many years a popular eating place for visitors to Salisbury

DAVID PENNELS

in 1964

Pirate station Radio Caroline began broadcasting.

BBC 2 began, but the opening night for the new television channel was completely disrupted by a power cut.

The Daily Herald newspaper ceased publication.

The general election was won by Labour, with a majority of five.

No 1 hits included You're My World by Cilla Black, Have I the Right to Hold You by the Honeycombes and Always Something There to Remind Me by Sandie Shaw.

in 1965

Revised style traffic signs started to come into use on the roads.

Cigarette advertising was banned on British television.

Capital punishment was suspended in England, Scotland and Wales.

A 70mph overall speed limit was imposed on the roads.

No 1 hits included Help by the Beatles, Tears by Ken Dodd and The Carnival is Over by the Seekers.

70

1965

The process of management integration with Hants & Dorset continued. The Secretary of Wilts & Dorset, Mr D Finley, became the Secretary of Hants & Dorset as well from 1 April. The registered office of Wilts & Dorset Motor Services was transferred from 8 Endless Street, Salisbury to The Square, Bournemouth, the registered office of Hants & Dorset, on 10 May.

Wilts & Dorset's Assistant Secretary, Mr E F Phillips, resigned on 31 May to take up an appointment with Southern Vectis.

The only new vehicles in 1965 were five Bedford SB13 coaches with Leyland engines and Duple Bella Vega bodies. This was a type of vehicle more associated with independent operators than the state owned sector, but Wilts & Dorset used these Bedfords extensively on both excursions and express work.

Timetables changed to the 24-hour clock format in 1965 and explanatory leaflets were provided for passengers, like the one shown on the left.

On 1 July 1965 Wilts & Dorset ran a large private hire contract to take military families from Bulford for a day on the coast. 20 coaches were required, with half going to Bognor Regis and half to Southsea. Freeland Noyce, seen on the left in the photograph on the left, was the Wilts & Dorset official in charge of this operation, which was managed with great efficiency.

Royal Blue passengers heading for Paignton on the relief coach on 14 August 1965 were treated to one of Wilts & Dorset's newest vehicles, when BMW 136C, a Bedford SB13 with Duple Bella Vega body, was used, as shown above.

The 68 route between Andover and Winchester was operated jointly by Wilts & Dorset and Hants & Dorset. Representing Wilts & Dorset on 30 July 1965 on the left was 686 AAM, a Bristol FS6B new in 1962. It was photographed in the Hants & Dorset bus station in Winchester.

DAVID PENNELS

Starting from 31 January 1966, the new 38A route provided a faster limited stop service between Salisbury and Bournemouth, with timings very suitable for people commuting to Bournemouth or making day visits to Salisbury.

The regular bus operating all journeys on the 38A in 1966 was 1962 Bristol Lodekka FS6G 684 AAM, which was painted cream with maroon mudguards for this role and had comfortable semi-coach seats.

HANTS AND DORSET MOTOR SERVICES LIMITED
WILTS AND DORSET MOTOR SERVICES LIMITED

38A A new limited stop service commencing 31st January, 1966 Bournemouth to Salisbury via Ferndown, Ringwood and Fordingbridge.

Picking up and setting down at the following stops.

Weekdays

SALISBURY (Bus Station)	0730	1600
St. Osmund's School	0733	1603
Coombe Road Junction	0734	1604
Britford (Bus Shelter)	0736	1606
Nunton Lane End	0739	1609
Charlton (Stag)	0742	1612
Downton (Bull Hotel)	0745	1615
Breamore (Post Office)	0750	1620
Burgate (Hour Glass)	0753	1623
Fordingbridge (Riverside Cafe)	0756	1626
North Gorley Turning	0759	1629
Ibsley Church	0803	1633
Blashford (Snails Lane)	0806	1636
Poulner Turning	0807	1637
Ringwood (Bus Station)	0810	1640
St. Ives (Post Office)	0814	1644
St. Leonard's (Post Office)	0816	1646
St. Leonard's Hospital	0818	1648
Dear's Garage	0819	1649
Tricketts Cross	0821	1651
Ferndown (Penny's Hill)	0823	1653
Dormy Hotel	0825	1655
Parley Cross Roads	0828	1658
New Road Corner	0831	1701
Horse and Jockey	0834	1704
Banks, Winton	0838	1708
Cemetery Junction	0842	1712
Lansdowne (Post Office)	0845	1715
BOURNEMOUTH (Bus Station)	0848	1718

BOURNEMOUTH (Bus Station)	0915	1735
Lansdowne (Post Office)	0918	1738
Cemetery Junction	0921	1741
Banks, Winton	0925	1745
Horse and Jockey	0929	1749
New Road Corner	0932	1752
Parley Cross Roads	0935	1755
Dormy Hotel	0938	1758
Ferndown (Penny's Hill)	0940	1800
Tricketts Cross	0942	1802
Dear's Garage	0944	1804
St. Leonard's Hospital	0945	1805
St. Leonard's (Post Office)	0947	1807
St. Ives (Post Office)	0949	1809
Ringwood (Bus Station)	0953	1813
Poulner Turning	0956	1816
Blashford (Snails Lane)	0957	1817
Ibsley Church	1000	1820
North Gorley Turning	1004	1824
Fordingbridge (Riverside Cafe)	1007	1827
Burgate (Hour Glass)	1010	1830
Breamore (Post Office)	1013	1833
Downton (Bull Hotel)	1018	1838
Charlton (Stag)	1021	1841
Nunton Lane End	1024	1844
Britford (Bus Shelter)	1027	1847
Coombe Road Junction	1029	1849
St. Osmund's School	1030	1850
SALISBURY (Bus Station)	1033	1853

PRINCIPAL FARES

From Bournemouth (Bus Station) to:	Single	Return
Ringwood (Bus Station)	2/9	4/6
Fordingbridge (Riverside Cafe)	3/6	5/9
Breamore (Post Office)	3/9	6/6
Downton (Bull Hotel)	4/-	6/6
Salisbury (Bus Station)	4/6	7/-

From Salisbury (Bus Station) to:	Single	Return
Ringwood (Bus Station)	3/-	5/-
Ferndown (Penny's Hill)	3/9	6/-
Parley Cross Roads	4/-	6/3
Banks, Winton	4/3	6/6
Bournemouth (Bus Station)	4/6	7/-

NOTE:
Return tickets issued on this service, or on Service 38, and Hants and Dorset services 12, 13, 13A and 27 are interavailable between common points. The same passenger may not be both picked up and set down between Bournemouth Bus Station and Longfield Drive. A 1/- minimum fare will apply over the following sections: (*a*) Bournemouth Bus Station and Penny's Hill, Ferndown, and (*b*) Salisbury Bus Station and Britford.

Issued subject to the Companies Published Regulations and Conditions *Head Office: The Square, Bournemouth.*

1966

Mr Henderson, Chief Engineer of Wilts & Dorset, became Chief Engineer of Hants & Dorset too from 1 April.

There had been discussions about the possibility of extending Wilts & Dorset's workshops in Salisbury to create a main central works for both Wilts & Dorset and Hants & Dorset. Hants & Dorset facilities in Southampton, considered outdated, would then be closed. In the event this didn't happen.

New vehicles received in 1966 were 10 forward-entrance double-deck buses, two Bristol MW single-deck buses and five dual-purpose Bristol MW saloons - the latter were often used on Royal Blue relief work.

1967

Management integration was taken a step further on 1 May when Mr B Hewkin also became Assistant Traffic Manager of Hants & Dorset.

New buses included more Bristol Lodekka FLF forward-entrance double deckers, and an innovation for this batch was semi-automatic transmission. This was readily apparent to passengers, as these buses had a particularly high (and noisy) engine note that is perhaps best described as a scream.

This year there were also five new coaches, Bedford VAM14s with Leyland engines and Duple Viscount bodies, plus two two single-deck Bedford buses, again with Leyland engines. Both had dual-door bodywork - one by Strachans and the other by Willowbrook.

in 1966

The general election was won by Labour with a majority of 96.

Longleat Safari Park opened.

Barclaycard, the first British credit card, was introduced.

The England football team won the World Cup, beating West Germany at Wembley.

The collapse of a coal tip at Aberfan, South Wales, resulted in 144 deaths, 116 of them children.

No 1 hits included Pretty Flamingo by Manfred Mann, Sunny Afternoon by the Kinks and Green, Green Grass of Home by Tom Jones.

in 1967

Supertanker Torrey Canyon ran aground between Lands End and the Scilly Isles.

BBC2 became the first British television channel to transmit programmes in colour.

BBC radio was reorganised, with new Radio 1, and Radio 2, Radio 3 and Radio 4 replacing the familiar Light Programme, Third Network and Home Service.

No 1 hits included Puppet on a String by Sandie Shaw, A Whiter Shade of Pale by Procul Harum, All You Need is Love by the Beatles and The Last Waltz by Englebert Humperdink.

A different style of vehicle was introduced to the Wilts & Dorset fleet in 1967 with the arrival of two Bedford single deck buses with what was sometimes called standee type bodywork. HHR 943E, shown on the opposite page, was bodied by Strachans of Hamble and could carry 33 seated passengers plus another 25 standing - close to the capacity of a lowbridge double deck bus, but in far less comfort.

The other one, shown at the top of this page, HWV 326E, had a Willowbrook body. It looks like the seating and standing capacity was used to the full to ensure that all of these girls got to school from Salisbury bus station on 16 June 1967. The interior view, taken when the bus was empty, looks to the rear of the vehicle and clearly shows the large standing area at the back, complete with vertical stanchions and ceiling mounted grab rails.

DAVID PENNELS

Standee single deck buses were clearly something of a fad in 1967, as this slightly bizarre conversion illustrates. It was unfortunate that Eastern Coach Works bodied 1958 Bristol MW6G coach RMR 992 was damaged in a road traffic accident, but instead of repairing the nine year old vehicle as a coach Wilts & Dorset decided to rebuild it as a standee single deck bus in the company's own workshops.

These photographs were taken by David Pennels in Salisbury bus station on 3 July 1967 and you can just about make out the single seats in the rear section through the windows of the exterior view.

The interior view is also of interest, showing the unusual mixture of coach and bus features within the vehicle. Standee single deck buses were understandably less than popular with the travelling public and the company's experiment with this fashion was, luckily, short lived.

Parked at Wilts & Dorset's depot at Frog Meadow in Pewsey on the right, 1952-built Bristol KSW5G HWV 293 had come in on route 12 from Devizes via Patney and Woodborough when photographed on 19 June 1968. Note the irony of a bus carrying advertisements for car dealers. The space was sold on the company's behalf by British Transport Advertising but it does seem strange that no objection was raised.

1968

At the start of the year came the death of Mr D Spencer, Operating Superintendent at Basingstoke, on 6 January. His place was taken by Mr A Duffin, who was appointed as Depot Superintendent, Basingstoke, from 1 March. Later in the year Chief Engineer Mr W Henderson also died, so Reg Smith carried out these duties until Mr A Gurley was appointed Chief Engineer from 1 December. Then in the autumn Mr A C Postlethwaite, Workshop Superintendent, and Mr J W Clay, Operating Superintendent, at Salisbury both died suddenly. The new Operating Superintendent from 1 November was Mr P T Fairweather.

New vehicles during 1968 included the last two new-front engined double deckers that needed both driver and conductor, forward-entrance Bristol FLF Lodekkas with semi-automatic transmission. They entered service in January. There were four new Bedford coaches with Duple Viceroy bodies and five Bedford single-deck buses with Willowbrook bodies, this time with just one door at the front and no centre exit door.

1969

On 1 January, the National Bus Company came into being, bringing into one organisation all the former Tilling Group companies and what had been the BET companies in the UK. At first there were few changes, but in due course many changes were to occur.

In addition to Frog Meadow, Wilts & Dorset also had a small enquiry office next to Lampard's garage in Pewsey. When photographed below on 19 June 1968, time was running out for this; it was closed a couple of years later. For some years Pewsey (Bus Office) had been a timing point; following closure the designation in the timetables was changed to Pewsey (North Street).

DAVID PENNELS

in 1968

The I'm Backing Britain campaign spread across the country.

A gas explosion caused the partial collapse of the Ronan Point tower block in East London.

Use of steam locomotives by British Rail ceased.

First and second class post was introduced.

No 1 hits included Cinderella Rockefella by Esther & Abi Ofarim, What a Wonderful World by Louis Armstrong, and Those Were the Days by Mary Hopkin..

in 1969

Prince Charles was invested as the Prince of Wales.

Neil Armstrong, leading the Apollo 11 mission, became the first man to walk on the moon.

The 50p coin replaced the 10/- note in preparation for future decimalisation of the UK 's currency.

Regular colour television broadcasts began on BBC1 and ITV.

No 1 hits included Blackberry Way by the Move and Bad Moon Rising by Creedence Clearwater Revival.

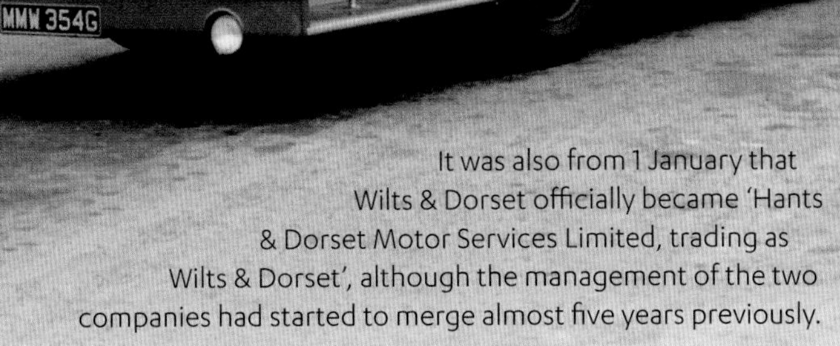

It was also from 1 January that Wilts & Dorset officially became 'Hants & Dorset Motor Services Limited, trading as Wilts & Dorset', although the management of the two companies had started to merge almost five years previously.

The closure of Wilts & Dorset's account with Lloyds Bank in Salisbury was also in its way symbolic. In the early 20th century Lloyds had taken over the Wilts & Dorset Bank, and the loss of that name in local banking is said to have been an inspiration for the name of the bus company back in 1915. From April 1969 banking for Wilts & Dorset was handled through the Hants & Dorset account with the National Provincial Bank.

Maps were included in timetable books issued by Hants & Dorset and Wilts & Dorset showing the routes operated by both companies. The observant traveller would also have noticed that the registrations of new Wilts & Dorset buses after April 1969 were allocated from Bournemouth instead of the familiar Wiltshire registrations that had graced such vehicles for many years previously.

The first of Wilts & Dorset's Bristol RE single deck buses arrived in 1969, and the initial batch of seven were the last new vehicles for the company to carry Wiltshire registrations.

Seen above at Upavon, MMW 354G exemplifies this batch of vehicles. Henceforward, new Wilts & Dorset buses would carry Bournemouth registrations. Notice the Wilts & Dorset Parcel Agent sign on the wall directly above the pillar box on the left of the photograph.

DAVID PENNELS

Wilts & Dorset Social Club darts team won the Salisbury & District Inter Clubs League Division 1 and the Knockout Cup in 1969, and the winning team was photographed:

back row (left to right)

Maurice Engelbretson (Salisbury Works)
Ken Hartley (conductor)
Les Thornton (conductor)

front row (left to right)

Harry Palmer (Salisbury Works)
Bill Donthwaite (Salisbury Works)
Wilf Martin (conductor)
Ivor West (schedules office)
Eric Lynch (driver)

IVOR WEST COLLECTION

An important customer service role is maintaining bus stops and making sure displays in timetable cases are up to date. For a number of years the unsung hero who carried out this task for Wilts & Dorset was Sid Kerley. On the left he had been photographed standing beside his Bedford CA van during a visit to Pewsey depot at Frog Meadow.

ROGER KERLEY COLLECTION

1970

When, on 1 January, the National Bus Company took over the Gosport & Fareham Omnibus Company, based at Hoeford and which traded as Provincial, management was assigned to Hants & Dorset. Mr T D McQuade was transferred from Ringwood to take charge of the operation.

Hants & Dorset's seal was affixed to the deed of exchange for the new bus station at Poole; departures had moved from the former Kingland Crescent site in the spring of 1967 to allow building of the Arndale (now Dolphin) shopping centre.

The company signed an agreement with the NUR on 16 June 1970 for consolidated rates of pay. At the same time, as agreed by the National Council for the Omnibus Industry, holiday entitlement and overtime pay was improved.

1971

Six new Daimler Fleetline double-deck buses, originally intended for the Gosport & Fareham fleet, would instead be delivered to Hants & Dorset and Gosport & Fareham would get six Bristol RE single deckers in their place. This brought the first driver-only operated double deckers into the Hants & Dorset fleet. Initially, four were allocated to Poole and the other two to Southampton.

A complete Wilts & Dorset/Hants & Dorset fleet renumbering took place in September. Vehicles were allocated numbers in blocks by type rather than on the basis of age or acquisition.

Engineering was rationalised by closing the Wilts & Dorset central works in Salisbury. In future the garage there would handle day to day work, but major overhauls would be dealt with at Southampton. A running shed would be provided at the Belle Vue site in Salisbury, the tender of £49,807 from James Drewitt & Sons to construct this having been accepted.

General Manager Douglas Morison was retired early by the National Bus Company in December 1971; he was 63 years old and had joined Hants & Dorset in 1936.

in 1970

The age of majority in the UK was reduced from 21 to 18.

Half Crowns and 10/- notes ceased to be legal tender.

General election was won by the Conservatives with a majority of 31.

The Beatles split up.

No 1 hits included Wand'rin Star by Lee Marvin, Yellow River by Christie and In the Summertime by Mungo Jerry.

in 1971

Decimal currency was introduced in the UK.

BBC Open University broadcasts began.

Postal workers were on strike for 47 days.

The Daily Sketch ceased publication.

No1 hits included Knock Three Times by Dawn, Maggie May by Rod Stewart and Ernie (The Fastest Milkman in the West) by Benny Hill.

Former Silver Star Harrington Wayfarer IV bodied Leyland Leopard coach WAM 441 had been painted into dual-purpose livery by 1970 and was seen below on route 34 from Salisbury to Weymouth.

Not quite at the half way point on this long journey, this coach is swinging onto the forecourt of Wilts & Dorset's Blandford Depot in Salisbury Road in the picture below. Over the years the depot was here, Blandford staff found the fish & chip shop next door to be a useful source of sustenance.

BRIAN JACKSON

By 1971 the 38 route between Salisbury and Bournemouth had been converted to driver only operation. Above, loading in Christchurch High Street on a sunny July day, was new dual-purpose Bristol RELL6G TRU 948J, providing a quiet, smooth and comfortable journey to Salisbury.

W T CANSICK
DAVID PENNELS COLLECTION

It was unfortunate that a vehicle ran into the rear of Harrington Cavalier bodied Leyland Leopard coach WWV 564 in 1970, but Wilts & Dorset's skilled engineering staff rebuilt this vehicle into a useful driver-only operated bus. The remodelled interior looking towards the rear is on the left.

From the outside that new rear wasn't the prettiest, however, as you can see. Wilts & Dorset and Hants & Dorset fleets were renumbered in September 1971, and here a member of Salisbury garage staff is seen changing the fleetnumber of WWV 564 on 4 September.

DAVID PENNELS

15 February was when decimal currency was introduced in the UK, and Wilts & Dorset's fares changed on the Sunday afterwards.

1972

Peter Hunt was appointed General Manager of Hants & Dorset and Wilts & Dorset from 1 February and Mr R A Luxton Assistant Chief Engineer in May. It was announced this year that the entire operation would in future trade as Hants & Dorset; the Wilts & Dorset name would effectively disappear.

By now the National Bus Company was imposing a corporate identity on the operating companies, with prescribed liveries of leaf green or poppy red. Wilts & Dorset buses had been red for many years, while those operated by Hants & Dorset had traditionally been green. It was decided that from October 1972 onwards the buses operated by the now enlarged Hants & Dorset would be painted in poppy red. So although buses in the former Wilts & Dorset area remained red (albeit a different shade), they would have a new name, and bus users in Poole, Bournemouth, Lymington, Southampton and surrounding areas would have red instead of green buses but keep the Hants & Dorset name.

in 1972

A seven week strike by the National Union of Mineworkers led to the declaration of a state of emergency by the Government.

A BEA flight from London to Brussels crashed at Staines shortly after take off from Heathrow, resulting in the deaths of all 188 people on board.

School leaving age was raised from 15 to 16.

Restrictions on broadcasting hours were lifted, allowing the growth of daytime television.

No 1 hits included Vincent by Don McLean and Mouldy Old Dough by Lieutenant Pigeon. Heard everywhere during the summer was Seaside Shuffle by Terry Dactyl & the Dinosaurs which reached number two in August and was in the chart for 12 weeks.

Newcastle upon Tyne, Manchester and Leeds are among the destinations that will be served by these coaches at the top of this page, all awaiting departure on forces leave express services from Aliwal Barracks at Tidworth in the summer of 1972

There's an ECW bodied Bristol MW in the background on the right, but the other three coaches are all Duple Viceroy bodied Bedford VALs. LMR 734F in the foreground dates from 1968, while the other two were new in 1971; notice how the styling of the bodywork has been sharpened up on the two newer coaches. This was done by Carl Olsen.

The Bedford VAL model was introduced in 1962 and stayed in production until 1972. It had twin-steer front axles, allowing for smaller wheels and a lower floor. However, the engine was still at the front ahead of the axles, alongside the driver in an upright position, so there was still a high level of engine noise inside the coach.

DAVID PENNELS

Top left is a portrait of Mr Peter Hunt, who became General Manager from 1 February 1972.

Bristol LS5G saloon SRU 973 had been new to Hants & Dorset in July 1956. At the beginning of September 1972 it was transferred to the Wilts & Dorset fleet, having been give a full repaint from Tilling green into Tilling red livery, and Wilts & Dorset fleetnames. Within days of arriving at its new home, it was photographed at Salisbury bus station on route 9 for Porton.

The ad on the bus extols the virtues of the company's parcel service, but in reality the its usage was in decline by the 1970s, and conversion to 100% driver only operation would lead to the final demise of the parcels service some years later.

DAVID PENNELS

New to Maidstone & District over in Kent in 1967, Willowbrook bodied Leyland Panther JKK 198E on the left was one of a number that was transferred to the Wilts & Dorset and Hants & Dorset fleets in 1972. As Maidstone & District was also part of the National Bus Company, such transfers were easy. It was picking up a good load for Southampton on the 37 route at Salisbury bus station on 2 August. A notice on the concourse reminds conductors that they must call at the window for parcels 'within 10 minutes of every departure'

DAVID PENNELS

Below is sister Panther JKK 208E in Salisbury depot and behind it, with its rear just in view, another still in Maidstone & District green and cream.

DENIS STRANGE

On the right is Eastern Coach Works bodied Bristol LH6L XEL 838K, new to Wilts & Dorset in 1972, and had taken on passengers in Salisbury bus station ready to leave for Winterslow via the Grimsteads and Farley when photographed on 31 March 1973.

DENIS STRANGE

Two vehicles that had started life in the green Hants & Dorset fleet during the 1950s were operating in Salisbury during 1974 in the picture below. Bristol LS5G saloon SRU 974, new in July 1956 and picking up passengers for Laverstock in Blue Boar Row is overtaken by Bristol Lodekka LD6G NEL 23, new in October 1954 and bound for Harnham.

'Part of the National Bus Company, Together we're really going places' said the advertisement on the side of NEL 23; a number of elderly but reliable buses most certainly did.

DAVID PENNELS

1973

Hants & Dorset's first six one-man-operated, rear-engined Eastern Coach Works bodied 74-seat Bristol VR double deckers entered service on 1 January at Basingstoke, although one had been used for a couple of weeks at Poole during December 1972.

By the 1970s vehicle maintenance and staff shortages were causing considerable problems for King Alfred, (owned by the Chisnell family), which ran local bus services in and around Winchester. Moreover, the Chisnell brothers wished to retire, so decided to sell out to Hants & Dorset for £68,500. The last day of King Alfred was Saturday 28 April 1973, and most of the King Alfred staff transferred to Hants & Dorset's Winchester depot.

The vehicles acquired from King Alfred were very non-standard compared with the Hants & Dorset fleet. Then more non-standard vehicles came later in the year in the shape of four Leyland Leopard coaches with distinctive Weymann Castillian bodywork that had been new to Southdown in 1962-3.

Difficulties in obtaining new vehicles meant that many 'old faithfuls' had to continue in service. The bus fleet was supplemented by six 1960 Leyland Atlantean double deckers from Maidstone & District and two Bristol Lodekkas (with 5-cylinder Gardner engines) dating from 1954-5 that had previously been in the Eastern National fleet.

It was a time of staff shortages, and on occasions bus journeys had to be cancelled at short notice because there simply was not a crew available to cover the journey, despite many staff working considerable amounts of overtime. It was also a time of staff unrest, largely attributable to the vehicle problems.

in 1973

The UK entered the Common Market (EEC).

A Middle East oil crisis led to fuel shortages and the imposition of a temporary overall maximum speed limit of 50mph.

Industrial action by miners let to coal shortages and to electricity power cuts.

No 1 hits included Tie a Yellow Ribbon round the Old Oak Tree by Dawn and Merry Christmas Everybody by Slade.

in 1974

For the first time, New Year's Day was a public holiday.

To conserve energy, a three day working week was imposed on industry; this lasted from 1 January until 7 March, the miners' strike having ended on 6 March.

A general election in February resulted in a hung parliament; Harold Wilson formed a minority Labour government. A further general election in October was won by Labour with a majority of three seats.

McDonald's opened its first UK restaurant - in Woolwich.

No 1 hits included Seasons in the Sun by Terry Jacks and Waterloo by Abba.

1974

From 1 January the Western National bus operations and garage at Swanage passed to Hants & Dorset. Included were five Bristol LS5G saloons dating from 1954-6 and a 1968 Bristol RE single-deck bus. The LS saloons were soon withdrawn, but the RE was kept and got painted into NBC poppy red before the year was out.

The vehicle situation remained critical, with stock having to be borrowed from other operators to keep services running. During 1974 these included AEC Swift single deck buses from Southampton Corporation, Leyland double-deck and Daimler single-deck buses from Bournemouth Corporation and AEC double-decks from Devon General. All these ran in their home company's liveries, and with the Hants & Dorset fleet in the process of being repainted from green to red it was often anybody's guess what colour the bus would be on a given journey.

A further six 1956 Bristol Lodekka LD5G double decks were bought from Eastern National, and four 1962 Bristol FS Lodekkas that had started life with Brighton Hove & District. Serious fires at Basingstoke depot in September and December did nothing to help the vehicle situation.

New buses coming into the fleet included no less than 25 Ford single deckers with Eastern Coach Works bodies, which allowed many of the Bristol LS saloons from the 1950s to be withdrawn. The delivery of further driver-only operated Bristol VR double deckers also enabled the last of the Bristol KSW double deckers, then over 20 years old, to be withdrawn.

Bristol FLF Lodekka JMR 821F is about to leave Salisbury bus station for Andover on 31 March 1973 in the picture above. It was the final bus bought new by Wilts & Dorset that needed a crew of a driver and a conductor..

Behind is one of the Willowbrook bodied Bedford VAMs bought in 1968.

Old coaches didn't die - they were adapted for driver-only bus work. Bristol MW6G XMR 944 on the left in the picture below, also taken on 31 March 1973, had been new as a coach in 1961. It was heading for Hindon on route 26. Similar RHR 852 was new in 1958. Showing the rather unhelpful destination 'Service' it was in fact operating a route 4 journey to Old Sarum.

DENIS STRANGE

WILTS & DORSET MOTOR SERVICES LTD.

EASTER EXCURSIONS

PROGRAMME 1933

WILTS & DORSET MOTOR SERVICES LIMITED

Good Friday, April 14th, 1933

Time	Destination	Fare
a.m. 9-30.	BOURNEMOUTH	3/6
9-30.	SANDBANKS	3/6
p.m. 2-30.	STONEHENGE	2/6
2-30.	SURPRISE TOUR	3/6
2-30.	BOURNEMOUTH	3/6

Easter Sunday, April 16th, 1933

Time	Destination	Fare
a.m. 9-30.	SOUTHSEA	5/6
9-30.	CHEDDAR CAVES (Via Bath and Wells)	6/6
9-30.	BOURNEMOUTH	3/6
9-30.	SANDBANKS	3/6
p.m. 2-30.	STONEHENGE	2/6
2-30.	SURPRISE TOUR	3/6
2-30.	BOURNEMOUTH	3/6
2-30.	SANDBANKS	3/6
6-30.	SURPRISE TOUR	2/6

Easter Monday, April 17th, 1933

Time	Destination	Fare
a.m. 9-30.	SOUTHSEA	5/6
9-30.	CHEDDAR CAVES (Via Bath and Wells)	6/6
9-30.	WEYMOUTH	6/-
9-30.	BOURNEMOUTH	3/6
9-30.	SANDBANKS	3/6
p.m. 2-30.	BEAULIEU ABBEY (New Forest)	3/6
2-30.	SURPRISE TOUR	2/6
6-30.	SOUTHAMPTON (Empire Theatre)	2/6

DAILY AT 9-30 A.M.

BOURNEMOUTH .. .. 3/6 Return

RESERVE SEATS EARLY AT Wilts and Dorset Booking Office, 31 Market Place, Salisbury; Wilts and Dorset Enquiry Office, 6 Endless Street, Salisbury; or any of the Company's Agents.

THE PAST—

ARRANGE YOUR OUTINGS ON THE QUIET DAYS OF THE WEEK — MONDAY, TUESDAY, THURSDAY, FRIDAY — THE COST WILL BE LESS —

WILTS & DORSET MOTOR SERVICES LIMITED

AS IN THE PAST — SO IN THE FUTURE — WE ARE AT YOUR SERVICE — ALWAYS

YOUR OUTING — OUR CONCERN

THE PRESENT—

On going there... and coming back!

FOCUS ON PLANNING PARTY TRAVEL

Brighton has always been a popular destination for coach excursions, and regularly featured in the trips operated by Venture from Basingstoke.

Wilts & Dorset kept this tradition up, and on August Bank Holiday Monday 4 August 1952 former Venture Duple bodied AEC Regal III coach GCG 816, repainted into Wilts & Dorset coach livery, was at Brighton. In the picture on the right, as the coach went to pick up passengers for the return journey, you can see that the driver has set the other blind to read Venture – perhaps old habits (or loyalties) died hard.

DAVID PENNELS

As well as running local bus services, Wilts & Dorset was quick to exploit the market for pleasure travel by charabanc and coach. Private hire of vehicles to cater for groups such as works or social club outings always were a feature of the company's operations, and Wilts & Dorset could organise bespoke days out for groups including, arranging meals, booking theatre seats etc., thus making things very easy for the party organiser.

By the early 1930s, regular programmes of day excursions by luxury coach were being advertised to the general public. During the Easter weekend of 1933, for example, Southsea, Cheddar Caves, Sandbanks and Beaulieu Abbey were among destinations on offer from Salisbury. Particularly popular during the 1930s were excursions to Southampton Docks to view the ocean liners. You could even go aboard ships berthed in the docks to see at first hand the luxurious accommodation that first class passengers would enjoy. Southampton Docks were operated by the Southern Railway then, so it would provide Wilts & Dorset with advance information about ships due.

The outbreak of the Second World War in September 1939 put a stop to coach excursions. After the war, at Easter time 1946, a limited programme of excursions was introduced, increased for the summer months. By 1950 3-day coach tour holidays were being offered; for example you could take a 3-day tour to North Devon leaving on Mondays 24 July and 28 August that year for just 6 guineas (£6.30).

From 1953 fully inclusive holiday tours were advertised, including Aberystwith and the Elan Valley (3 days), Blackpool and the English Lakes (8 days) and Llandudno and North Wales (8 days).

However, by the 1960s Wilts & Dorset had become an agent for Hants & Dorset's extensive programme of luxury coach touring holidays, which offered pick-ups in the Wilts & Dorset area, so its own programme was wound down.

3-DAY TOUR TO ABERYSTWYTH VIA THE ELAN VALLEY

If you have previously enjoyed a well conducted motor coach holiday then you will need very little persuasion to become interested in our tour to Aberystwyth. If you have not yet availed yourself of this ever increasingly popular mode of travel then we suggest that our 3-day Tour may serve as a pleasant introduction to all the pleasures of holidays by coach. The tour is described briefly below.

1st Day—TUESDAY: The outward bound route of our 200-mile journey is via Warminster and the Roman City of Gloucester to Ross-on-Wye which is situated in a high position and overlooking one of the most delightful stretches of the River Wye. Here, we stop for lunch and then proceed via Hereford, Kington and Rhayader (" Falls of the Wye ") to the lovely Elan Valley and Welsh Lakes (famous for the great Birmingham Waterworks), where we break for tea. We are now within less than 40 miles of Aberystwyth where we will be welcomed at the Talbot Hotel or the Prince Albert Hotel for dinner.

2nd Day—WEDNESDAY: The morning is completely free to spend at will in Aberystwyth, which has been described as the " Biarritz of Wales." It is a delightful progressive seaside resort, situated on the West coast of Wales in the perfect sweep of Cardigan Bay, with a hinterland of mountains and ravines.

...fter lunch an afternoon tour has been arranged to Talyllyn Lake ...ing via Towyn and Aberdovey. Stretching ...mmands considerable

WHOLE DAY TOUR TO THE EXE VALLEY BY WILTS & DORSET

SHAFTESBURY
Built on an escarpment overlooking cosy Dorset meadows, Shaftesbury is historically one of the more romantic places in Britain being closely associated with the early Kings of Wessex. The town is very quaint with its steep little streets running down into the vale below.

SHERBORNE
Another former stronghold of ancient Wessex lies close to the border between Dorset and Somerset. It was at Sherborne that Sir Walter Raleigh first smoked a pipe of tobacco in the Castle grounds. The town is quite unspoilt and is a beautiful example of historical England.

CREWKERNE
Is a compact little market town in the valley of the River Parret just inside Somerset. Dating back to Saxon times Crewkerne is rich historically and possesses some interesting old buildings, some of which were erected as far back as the 15th century.

CHARD
Consisting principally of a long, wide street on a gentle slope, the character of Chard is mainly 19th century but several interesting old buildings, such as the 16th century Grammar School, testify to its antiquity. The town is the centre for a prosperous trade in the manufacture of agricultural implements and machinery.

HONITON
Nestles in the valley of the River Otter in a country-side of beautiful orchards. Its main street has some charming thatched buildings and is dominated by the Parish Church on Dumpdon Hill. Honiton has been famed since the reign of Elizabeth for its pillow lace.

EXETER (L)
The county town and ecclesiastical centre of Devon, Exeter suffered severely from aerial bombardment during the war. Many of its picturesque old buildings however, including the 800 years old Cathedral, and the Guild Hall still remain to charm the eye of the visitor.

TIVERTON
Mentioned in Alfred the Great's will and in the Domesday Book, Tiverton is one of the older towns in Devon. Originally the centre of the woollen industry its burghers turned to lace making when the Yorkshire mills stole the market.

DUNSTER
Is the story book town complete to the last detail. Its 17th century Yarn Market stands in the centre of a very wide street of mediaeval aspect and the whole is presided over by Dunster Castle. One almost expects to see a cavalcade of knights and men-at-arms cantering up the slope.

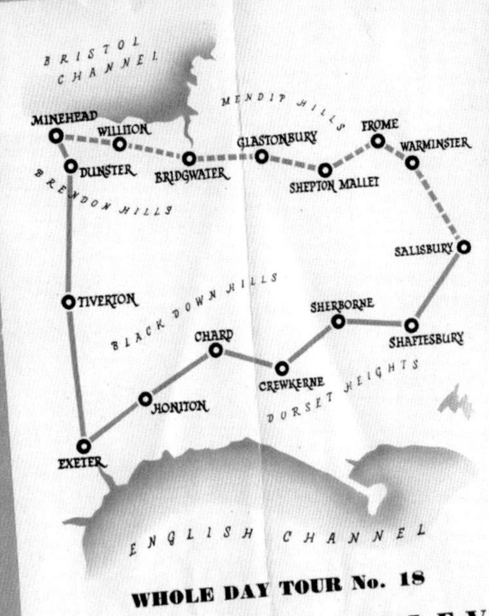

WHOLE DAY TOUR No. 18

THE EXE VALLEY

KEY: L—Stop for Lunch, T—Stop for Tea, B—Short Break

MINEHEAD (T)
Has grown from a small fishing port to the largest and most popular seaside resort in West Somerset. The more picturesque part of Minehead is clustered around the harbour, and the old fourteenth century parish church is considered to be one of the most beautiful in the country.

WILLITON
Set in the mouth of a valley between the lovely Quantock and Brendon Hills, this small and charming town is typical of unspoilt Somerset. Its chief claim to historical fame is that it was the birthplace of Reginald Fitzurse, one of the four Knights who murdered Thomas a' Beckett.

BRIDGWATER
Is situated on the River Parret some eight miles from its outlet into Bridgwater Bay. It is a prosperous market town which in spite of its tranquil atmosphere has known stirring times. It was here that the ill-fated Duke of Monmouth was proclaimed King and made his headquarters in 1685 before the battle of Sedgemoor.

GLASTONBURY (B)
The Avalon of King Arthur, is a very ancient market town at the foot of the 500 feet Glastonbury Tor. It is a veritable treasure house of antiquity with a romantic and stirring history dating from the times of St. Dunstan who founded the Abbey.

SHEPTON MALLET
Is a small market town sited just off the Roman Fosse Way on the southern outskirts of the Mendip Hills. Its famous 15th century hexagonal market cross is still in a remarkable state of preservation and many priceless examples of ancient coins and jewellery have been unearthed in the immediate neighbourhood.

FROME
Nowadays a prosperous town, Frome's commercial history has been somewhat chequered. Once it was a woollen manufacturing town but, like so many of the southern centres in the woollen trade, all the business passed to Yorkshire and the inhabitants had to find other outlets for their industry.

WARMINSTER (B)
At the upper end of the Wylye Valley, Warminster is about 400 feet above sea level and lies under the shadow of Salisbury Plain. Its wonderful situation and proximity to the downs make it an attractive town with many historic buildings to give it added interest.

A TOUR THROUGH MANY HISTORIC TOWNS AND PICTURESQUE VILLAGES

The 1950s and 1960s were the halcyon period for Wilts & Dorset coach day excursions. Destinations included the Isle of Wight, Clovelly, the Vale of Evesham and Dartmoor. Passengers on an excursion were given attractive leaflets detailing the route that would be followed - normally different for the outward and return - and points of interest both along the way and at the destination. During the early 1960s special day excursions to the Channel Islands and Cherbourg were popular.

Extensive programmes of day excursions continued to operate into the 1970s, when the company was subsumed into Hants & Dorset. However, towards the end of that decade increasing car ownership, changing habits and even such factors as colour television had diluted the demand for the traditional day excursion by coach.

The Wilts & Dorset Bus Company reborn in 1983 did not run coach excursions as such, but for several years operated Summertime Specials that offered days out using double deck buses at bargain Explorer Ticket prices. Visiting places such as Longleat House or Thorpe Park, these trips were so popular that on occasions several vehicles had to be provided for each departure.

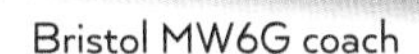

Bristol MW6G coach 673 AAM , at the top of this page, was on a day excursion to Brighton on 4 May 1969 when photographed during a refreshment stop at Chichester. When new in 1962 this was the first Wilts & Dorset coach to have this new style of 39-seat bodywork by Eastern Coach Works; and above is the interior.

Smile, you're going for a day out on a new coach! - opposite, some of the young occupants of Duple Bella Vega bodied Bedford SB13 BMW 135C are posing for the camera at Picton Barracks in Bulford on 1 July 1965.

DAVID PENNELS

1975

Hants & Dorset began the new year still waiting for the delivery of over 60 new vehicles from its 1973 and 1974 orders. Four 1962 Bristol FSF6B Lodekkas from Brighton Hove & District were pressed into service to help, but some of the new vehicles started arriving in January. This enabled withdrawals of the Bristol LD Lodekkas to begin, some of which were over 20 years old.

Consideration was being given to acquiring workshop premises at Barton Park, Eastleigh, on the former railway carriage works.

1976

After a break of several years, open top buses were again used in Bournemouth and Poole on the routes to Sandbanks and Rockley Sands, with four convertible open-top buses that had been new to Brighton Hove & District in 1959. The hot, dry summer of 1976 was to prove ideal for a ride on an open top bus.

The major event of 1976 was the destruction of Bournemouth bus and coach station by fire during the early hours of Sunday 25 July. Fortunately, buses parked overnight on the upper level were quickly driven to safety in nearby streets, in some cases by people who happened to be passing while on their way home from a Saturday night out. Company staff later had to walk round the town to find some of them.

Improvised arrangements, including using Bournemouth Town Hall forecourt, were made to ensure that all scheduled journeys ran on the Sunday morning. By Monday 26 July The Triangle had been established as a terminal point in Bournemouth. Premises at 31 The Triangle were leased for three years for use as a travel shop and a small canteen for staff was set up in the basement.

The former Hants & Dorset garage at Norwich Avenue, which had been closed when the bus station was rebuilt in 1959, was repurchased. The office block at the bus station was largely unaffected by the fire, and continued in use as Hants & Dorset's head office for a further five years.

Having lost a bus station in Bournemouth, the company gained one in Swanage when the terminal point for buses serving the town was moved from the pier approach to the former railway station forecourt (the station had been closed in 1972). Eastleigh bus station was also moved from Blenheim Road to Upper Market Street, where portacabin offices provided accommodation for several years.

Plans were prepared to set up a new central engineering works facility at Barton Park, Eastleigh; this would involve the closure of the existing central works at Shirley Road, Southampton and the body shop at Winchester Road, Southampton. It was also decided that the Western Area Engineering Works at 315 Ashley Road, Upper Parkstone would be closed.

The 10 dual-purpose Leyland Nationals delivered to the company early in 1975 were very comfortable vehicles, with seating virtually to full coach specification, as the interior photograph below shows. GLJ 682N was entered by Salisbury Bus Enthusiasts for a transport rally in Bristol on 31 August 1975, and driver George Hackett was standing proudly beside the vehicle.

DAVID PENNELS

in 1975

Margaret Thatcher became leader of the Conservative Party, having defeated Edward Heath in a leadership election.

A London Underground train ran into a tunnel end wall at Moorgate station, resulting in the deaths of 43 people.

The comedy series Fawlty Towers was seen on television for the first time.

The National Railway Museum in York was opened by HRH The Duke of Edinburgh.

No 1 hits included Bye Bye Baby by the Bay City Rollers, Oh Boy by Mud, Sailing by Rod Stewart and Bohemian Rhapsody by Queen.

in 1976

Prime Minster Harold Wilson resigned – his place was taken by James Callaghan.

A very warm, dry summer saw temperatures reach 90 degrees fahrenheit on many days between mid June and late August, while the absence of rainfall led to serious water shortages.

British Rail introduced the first Inter City 125 high speed trains – on the route from London to Bristol and Swansea.

Chancellor of the Exchequer Denis Healey negotiated a £2.3billion loan from the International Monetary Fund, and announced public expenditure cuts.

No 1 hits included Save Your Kisses For Me by Brotherhood of Man and Dancing Queen by Abba.

It was good to see open top buses back in service with Hants & Dorset. OPN 803 was a Bristol Lodekka LDS6B that began life with Brighton Hove & District, and had come to Hants & Dorset via Southdown.

On the left it's in Avenue Road, Bournemouth during July 1976.

BRIAN JACKSON

In the black and white picture the Mayor of Swanage welcomes Hants & Dorset General Manager Peter Hunt to the company's new terminal at the town's former railway station. Bob Smith, Depot Inspector at Swanage, stands second from right, arms folded.

ARTHUR GRANT

The 276 route ran from Basingstoke to Salisbury via Whitchuch, Andover and Middle Wallop. In the picture below, taken on 30 April 1976 Leyland National MLJ 920P was running through rolling, open countryside on the A30, on the last stage of the journey towards Salisbury.

DENIS STRANGE

By January 1977, Bristol VR double deckers were coming into use on Salisbury city services. On the left JJT 441N on route 260 to Wilton leads the way at New Canal on a particularly wet winter day. Note the illuminated 'Please pay as you enter' signs on both buses.

A batch of Bristol LH single deck buses that had been delivered in 1974 had their lower front panelling cut away to avoid grounding, especially at low tide, while driving on to or off the Sandbanks chain ferry which operated across the mouth of Poole Harbour. ORU 531M demonstrates this below in 1977 leaving the ferry on the route between Swanage and Bournemouth.
DAVID PIKE

1977

The whole of the Andover town bus network was converted to driver-only operation on Sunday 3 April. New routes and timetables were introduced to reflect the great changes the town had seen during recent years, bringing bus services to several new areas.

The Western Area Workshops at 315 Ashley Road, Upper Parkstone, were closed during May; the travel shop, opposite St John's Church, remained open. Meanwhile plans for the new central works at Barton Park were proceeding well.

Freeland Noyce, Operating Superintendent at Salisbury, retired on 1 November. He had joined the bus industry in 1929 as a conductor, becoming an inspector in 1940, promoted to Depot Inspector at Amesbury in 1964 and had become Operating Superintendent at Salisbury in 1972.

POOLE'S NEW BUS NETWORK

Starting Sunday 26th February 1978

- New routes
- New numbers
- More buses for Broadstone, Canford Heath, Corfe Mullen, Creekmoor, Merley, Waterloo Estate and Wimborne
- New links from Poole to Kinson, West Howe, Winton, Moordown and Boscombe
- Many services to Bournemouth extended from The Square to The Lansdowne

AMENDMENT LEAFLET No. 3 to Poole Area Timetable dated June 197
Minor changes to services in the Bere Regis, Swanage and Wareham area are contained in Amendment Leaflet No. 4.

HANTS & DORSET
a NATIONAL bus company

Issued free of charge and subject to the Company's Published Regulations Conditions and the approval of the Traffic Commissioners. Feb.

1978

Severe blizzards struck Dorset and South West Hampshire late on Saturday 18 February. Unusually, conditions were especially bad close to the south coast, with snowdrifts up to four feet even in the towns of Poole and Bournemouth. Neither Hants & Dorset nor Bournemouth Transport ran any services in the conurbation on Sunday 19 February.

in 1977

Foreign Secretary Anthony Crossland died after suffering a stroke; his place was taken by David Owen.

Tuesday 7 June was granted as an additional public holiday to mark the Silver Jubilee; street parties and other celebrations were enjoyed up and down the land.

A new style smaller pound note came in.

British Airways began a regular supersonic Concorde service between London and New York.

No 1 hits included Don't Cry For Me, Argentina by Julie Covington, Yes Sir, I Can Boogie by Baccara and Mull of Kintire by Wings.

in 1978

The May Day bank holiday was introduced.

Anna Ford became the first female news reader on ITV.

A fire on a night sleeper train at Taunton resulted in 11 deaths.

Strike action by bakers caused panic buying and shortages of bread.

No 1 hits included Wuthering Heights by Kate Bush, Rivers of Babylon by Boney M and Summer Nights by John Travolta & Olivia Newton John.

In 1978 almost all of the remaining crew-operated double deck buses at Basingstoke were Bristol Lodekka FLFs, as shown above by JMR 812F, a FLF6B that had been new in September 1967, on route 315 to Oakridge on 5 April 1978.

DAVID PIKE

Fortunately, a thaw came fairly quickly; limited town services were able to run from mid morning on the Monday and services in the urban area were close to normal by Tuesday, although there was some disruption in country areas until Thursday.

The blizzard disrupted the final stages in the distribution of more than 180,000 leaflets produced to explain the largest reorganisation in the Poole area bus network since 1954. A special publicity bus toured the town, with staff handing out timetables and answering questions from customers. Notwithstanding the weather, the new network was introduced very smoothly from Sunday 26 February.

Matching the supply of bus services to customer demand is key to the success of any operation. Working in conjunction with independent consultants Colin Buchanan & Partners, the National Bus Company developed a method of identifying, area by area in special studies, bus networks that could be maintained in the long term at acceptable levels of fares. Initially called the Viable Network Project (VNP) and trialled in several parts of Midland Red's area, the study was rolled out across all of the National Bus Company as the Market Analysis Project (MAP).

During 1978 MAP surveys were carried out on all of Hants & Dorset's bus routes, the company's area being divided into a number of study areas for this purpose. Locally recruited teams recorded all passenger journeys, and this information was supplemented by a number of house-to-house surveys to include opinions from people who were not currently using public transport. The huge amount of data collected was processed and tabulated on a central computer at Birmingham, and the results were used by Hants & Dorset's schedules teams to plan revised networks over the next couple of years. It was noted that customer participation in Hants & Dorset's MAP surveys was around 80%; this was better than in similar surveys elsewhere, but just as well as the outcome of MAP was to have a significant effect on the future of the company.

To spread the word about the largest change in Poole's bus network for over 23 years, dual doorway Bristol LH6L REL 745H was converted into a publicity bus which toured the area during the period leading up to the change. This bus had been new to Hants & Dorset in 1969.

The new network introduced in the Poole area from 26 February 1978 made changes to all bus routes, with new timetables and route numbers.

Although the information booklet was described on the cover as 'Amendment leaflet no. 3 to Poole area timetable dated June 1977', it was in fact a substantial 48-page booklet in its own right, and in effect replaced the previous timetable book for journeys being made entirely within the urban area.

November 1979 saw the launch of the Antonbus MAP network in Andover. This line up of eight Leyland Nationals on the right, each carrying Antonbus vinyls, was photographed at Andover garage to the rear of the Bridge Street bus station.

BRIAN JACKSON

Below is Bristol LH GLJ 491N passing through Corfe Castle village with the craggy outline of Corfe Castle towering above in 1980. The bus would continue along the valley road via Harman's Cross.

DAVID PIKE

330|331
Buses from Oakley
To
Bus Station
Rail Station
Daneshill
Basing
Venturebus

1979

Severe winter weather during January and February meant temperatures were so low that in some instances ice packed the underside of the chassis frame of buses, causing air and sometimes fuel systems to freeze. Salt and grit from the roads also took its toll, and the Chief Engineer reported that 350 buses had sustained damage.

Good news was that work was progressing well at the Barton Park site; the transfer of the body shop from Winchester Road in Southampton was completed by 21 May, with work continuing on the engineering offices and central repair works.

There was concern about delays in processing MAP surveys at the Birmingham computer centre, which meant revised bus networks would happen later than planned. The Regional Director got on the case, and the survey results for Basingstoke were delivered in late Spring. Commercial Manager Jim Heasman said these surveys had given a much clearer picture than the company had ever had before of people's travel needs, which would help to deliver the best possible service.

Venturebus, the Basingstoke area MAP network, was launched on Sunday 2 September 1979. The publicity bus had been used to spread the word around the town, and advertising spots had been taken on local commercial radio. The Andover MAP network, marketed as Antonbus, was introduced on 4 November.

in 1979

At the beginning of the year a series of strikes across the country caused serious disruption, exacerbated by the very cold weather and gave rise to the press headline 'The Winter of Discontent'.

The government lost a motion of confidence by one vote, leading Prime Minister James Callaghan to announce that a general election would be held on 3 May. This was won by the Conservatives with a majority of 43 seats.

A strike by technicians caused the shut down of ITV from August until October.

Lord Mountbatten of Burma (shown below) was assassinated by an IRA bomb while on holiday in the Republic of Ireland.

No 1 hits included Heart of Glass by Blondie and Bright Eyes by Art Garfunkel.

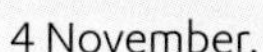

in 1980

The 'tanner' (pre-decimal sixpence) was finally withdrawn from circulation.

Council tenants in England and Wales of at least three years' standing were given the right to buy their homes at a discount.

Express coach services were deregulated.

Former Beatle John Lennon was shot dead in New York.

No 1 hits included Another Brick in the Wall by Pink Floyd, Crying by Don McLean and Super Trouper by Abba.

photo Allan Warren

1980

The Wiltsway MAP network was introduced in Salisbury and Wiltshire on Sunday 6 January 1980. 80,000 timetables and maps were distributed, a 4-page tabloid size news sheet produced and there were discounted fares for the first fortnight. Writing in May, Hants & Dorset Commercial Manager Jim Heasman commented that so far the results of the MAP networks had been encouraging, with previous deficits at Basingstoke and Andover having been eliminated. Although it was too early to judge the results at Salisbury, initial indications looked good.

He added that the introduction of the MAP networks had led to a reduction in the number of buses needed at Basingstoke from 52 to 40, at Andover from 28 to 21 and at Salisbury & Pewsey from 96 to 78. The exercise would continue, with further MAP networks being introduced at Winchester, Eastleigh, Southampton, Fareham and Bournemouth/Poole during the year.

Company Secretary Desmond Finley retired; his place was taken by Mr G J Mayhew from 1 July. The optimism in the spring had largely dissipated by the autumn; the country had gone into a recession and this was starting to have a serious effect on Hants & Dorset's finances, with a possible loss of approaching £2.5million feared. In October the General Manager issued a nine-point programme indicating measures to be taken to secure the future of the company.

The MAP network in Bournemouth and Poole came into operation on Sunday 30 November, called South Wessex. It included the closure of Bournemouth as an operational depot, with staff transferring to Poole, Ringwood and Blandford. The garage at Norwich Avenue acquired after the 1976 fire was relinquished during the summer, and the old Royal Blue garage at Rutland Road, Bournemouth, was used for the last few months. Saturday 29 November was also the last day of crew-operated buses by Hants & Dorset; the final journey was by a 70-seat rear-loading double decker dating from 1962 that was suitably decorated for the occasion.

This 227 from Salisbury, above, operated by Bristol VR GEL 681V new in February 1980, would run direct via Whitesand Cross and Ludwell to Shaftesbury. A connection on route 226 ran from Swallowcliffe Corner via Tisbury and Fonthill Gifford, provided here by 1978 Leyland National VFX 983S. Passengers are changing buses at Swallowcliffe Corner on 1 September 1980.

DAVID PIKE

The final MAP network in Bournemouth and Poole led to the end of crew working on Hants & Dorset. The last journey of all, from Wimborne to Bournemouth, was run by 1962 Bristol Lodekka 7685 LJ. Many in the photo below on that last run were staff. The inspector is the late Ron Coat.

the late C J BURT collection

Upavon is the location for this picture on the right of two Bristol VRs that were allocated to Pewsey depot in 1981, both carrying Wiltsway local identity.
On the left ELJ 220V, new in January 1980, will shortly depart for Devizes on the 210 route, while 1979 BFX 666T has recently arrived on route 212.

DAVID PIKE

The weather was appalling on 9 January 1982, but every effort was made to keep the buses running. In the picture below Leyland National PJT 266R, normally based at Andover depot, hence the Antonbus branding, had been pressed into use on Salisbury route 233, where it was photographed in a snowstorm on Milford Hill.

JOHN WEAGER

in 1981

Roy Jenkins, David Owen, William Rodgers and Shirley Williams formed the Social Democratic Party.

The first London Marathon was held.

Prince Charles married Lady Diana Spencer at St Paul's Cathedral.

Rioting broke out in a number of inner city areas during the summer.

No 1 hits included Making Your Mind Up by Bucks Fizz and Prince Charming by Adam and the Ants.

in 1982

Argentina invaded the Falkland Islands, precipitating the Falklands War.

Pope John Paul II visited the UK.

Roy Jenkins became leader of the Social Democratic Party.

Channel 4 television began broadcasting.

No 1 hits included Seven Tears by the Goombay Dance Band, House of Fun by Madness and Come On Eileen by Dexys Midnight Runners.

1981

A most significant event was the launch, in April, of Explorer round trip tickets by the National Bus Company. At the same time a paperback book England by Bus, written by Elizabeth Gundrey and published by NBC and Hamlyn, showed it was very practical and enjoyable to explore almost anywhere in the country by bus. Explorer tickets quickly became recognised and Hants & Dorset allowed ticket holders to go anywhere they wished with no restrictions on times or distances travelled. A novel feature of Explorer tickets was that they could be bought in advance and subsequently dated for use by the customer. Tickets were sold in local newsagents and post offices as well as in the company's travel shops. Hants & Dorset sold 100 Explorer tickets during the first week they were available and by the peak holiday season weekly sales were averaging 5,000 tickets.

The new central repair works at Barton Park was officially opened by Eastleigh MP Sir David Price on 29 May 1981, replacing the engineering functions previously carried out at Shirley Road and at Winchester Road in Southampton.

The National Bus Company urged that the fire damaged bus station at Bournemouth Square, where the largely intact office block was still being used as Hants & Dorset's head office, should be disposed of. In June the company took the tenancy of The House of Travel, 21-23 Oxford Road, Bournemouth and this became the registered office.

THE Sun

HUGE BATTLES ARE RAGING FOR THE FALKLANDS

WAR

- Troops storm the islands
- 5 Navy ships damaged
- 14 Argy planes downe

1982

Company Secretary Graham Mayhew resigned on 4 April, replaced by Mr Hugh Malone. Dawson Williams also resigned as Chief Engineer, and was replaced by Peter Lanfranchi.

There was a protracted rail strike during July. National Express suddenly had to cope with a massive increase in demand, and a number of Hants & Dorset vehicles and staff were drafted in to help out. Hants & Dorset managers and clerical staff were also seconded to act as customer care and booking clerks at locations including London's Victoria Coach Station.

In the autumn, proposals were agreed with the National Bus Company for the reorganisation of Hants & Dorset into four operating companies, together with a secretarial services unit and an engineering unit. Details were given in a letter to all staff, dated 14 October 1982 and signed by General Manager Peter Hunt. From 1 April 1983 these would be:

Wilts & Dorset Bus Company
led by Mr A S Rolls with 207 vehicles

Hampshire Bus Company
led by Mr B Hewkin with 186 vehicles

Provincial Bus Company
led by Mr T D McQuade with 75 vehicles

Shamrock & Rambler
led by Mr J Heasman with 70 vehicles

The secretarial unit was led by Hugh Malone and engineering by Peter Lanfranchi.

Lulworth Cove is a popular beauty spot on the Dorset Coast, and below is Bristol LH6L LJT 943P having just arrived from Swanage, Wareham and Wool railway station on 28 August 1981. Note the prominent South Wessex branding.
DAVID PIKE

After the body carried by 1973 Bristol LH6L NLJ 516M was badly damaged in an accident, it was replaced in 1982 by this replica charabanc body built by Hants & Dorset's Central Works at Barton Park. Its new registration number TR 6147 had previously been carried by a Leyland Lion single deck bus that had been in service with Hants & Dorset from 1929 until 1939, followed by a year or so with Wilts & Dorset. This replica was first painted in Hants & Dorset's traditional Tilling green but passed to Shamrock & Rambler when Hants & Dorset was divided into smaller units in 1983.
DAVID PENNELS

A Hants & Dorset bus becomes a Wilts & Dorset bus in the picture above; this was one of the first jobs in April 1983.

Hants & Dorset was divided into smaller units from 1 April. The new managers in the picture above right were (left to right): Allan Rolls (Wilts & Dorset), Bob Hewkin (Hampshire Bus), Tom McQuade (Provincial), Hugh Malone (Secretarial Services), John Bodger (Acting General Manager, Hants & Dorset; Mr Hunt had taken an appointment with the National Bus Company in London), Jim Heasman (Shamrock & Rambler) and Peter Lanfranchi (Engineering Services).

On the right Poole depot driver George Giles looks on as giraffes take a keen interest in his bus and passengers on one of the first Explorer Special trips to Longleat Safari Park in July 1983. The Explorer Specials were soon very popular..

the late C J BURT collection

1983

Early in 1983 20 former London Transport DMS buses joined the Hants & Dorset fleet. The company bought them from vehicle dealer Ensign, by whom they had been modified from separate entrance and exit doors to a single front door although the staircase was still in the middle.

Premises at 20 Gervis Place, Bournemouth, were acquired for a combined bus travel shop and National Travelworld travel agency, the travel shop at 31 The Triangle having been closed.

On 1 April, 11 years after being totally subsumed into Hants & Dorset, the Wilts & Dorset name was re-born. Taking over the erstwhile Hants & Dorset routes in Wiltshire, Dorset and South West Hampshire, the new Wilts & Dorset had depots at Poole, Salisbury, Pewsey, Ringwood, Lymington, Blandford and Swanage. One of the first jobs was to change the fleetname on its 200 vehicles - workshop staff set about the task of replacing HAN with WIL so altering HANTS & DORSET to read WILTS & DORSET.

in 1983

Breakfast television starts.

One pound coin introduced in England & Wales.

Conservative majority of 144 seats (42% of the total vote) in the general election.

Vehicle registrations start to use letter prefixes.

No 1 hits included Karma Chameleon by Boy George and Uptown Girl by Billy Joel.

Inevitably, some buses had to take a turn in service with the process only half complete, and ran for a trip or two as TS & DORSET. General Manager of the new company was Allan Rolls. Andrew Bryce was Traffic Manager and Rodney Luxton Fleet Engineer. Initially the Head Office remained at The House of Travel in Oxford Road, Bournemouth, but moved to Towngate House, Poole, in December.

The summer of 1983 saw the first of the seasonal services that were to prove very popular over the next few years. Marketed as Summertime Explorer Specials, this year they ran from Poole and Salisbury to attractions like Marwell Zoo, Yeovilton Air Museum and Longleat House and Safari Park.

Ordinary double deck buses were used, but the great value offered by Explorer tickets and the superb views from the top decks tempted many people to enjoy a day out on a Summertime Special rather than take a coach tour - relief buses were soon needed on many of the journeys.

The new Travel Centre in Gervis Place, Bournemouth, combined a booking and enquiry office for local buses with a world-wide travel agency. On the right is the interior.

the late C J BURT collection

Photographed at Weymouth on 6 August 1983 below, KUC 223P was then a recent addition to the Wilts & Dorset fleet. The rural run on the 186 route would have been quite a contrast to the teeming streets of London where this vehicle had first entered service.

BRIAN JACKSON

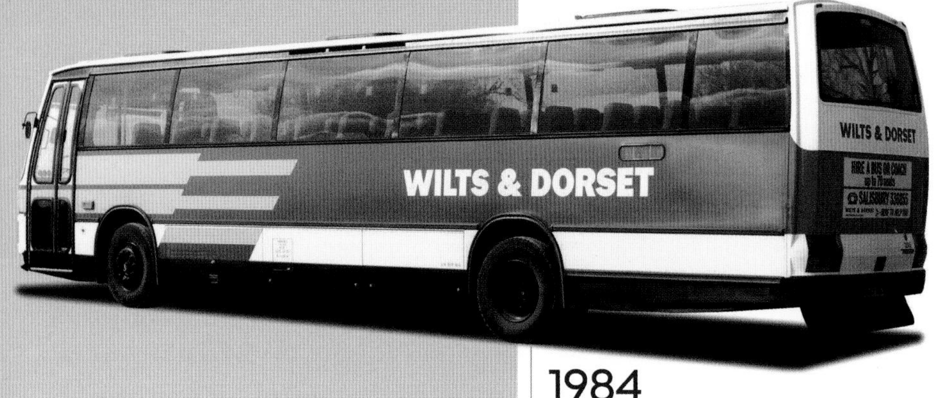

B205 REL on the left shows off the livery adopted for coaches in the mid- 1980s. This was the late National Bus Company so called 'local coach' paint layout.

the late C J BURT collection

New in 1984, Leyland Olympian A902 JPR had 70 comfortable coach seats and was ideal for the X41 route from Salisbury to Bristol. Below it was in Trowbridge heading towards Bristol in September 1985.

DAVID PIKE

1984

Five new Leyland Olympian double deck buses arrived at Salisbury depot. With comfortable coach seats, these were used for private hire and excursions as well as on limited stop bus routes such as the X3 from Salisbury to Bournemouth.

A talking point in the bus industry was the White Paper published by Transport Minister Nicholas Ridley, with proposals to deregulate local bus services and, it was felt, eventually to privatise the National Bus Company. These plans were to have far reaching effects.

The great success of Explorer Summertime Specials in 1983 led to more extensive programmes for 1984 from Poole, Bournemouth and Salisbury. Destinations included Wookey Hole, Bognor Regis, Lyme Regis, Weston-Super-Mare and Blenheim Palace. Some journeys were so popular that three buses were needed. The company got many letters praising the organisation of the trips, the range of destinations and especially the helpfulness and courtesy of the drivers.

1985

To mark 70 years since the foundation of Wilts & Dorset Motor Services Limited, a Bristol RE single deck bus (NLJ 871G, fleet number 1615) was repainted into the old red and cream livery. As well as being used in normal service this bus attended a number of rallies through the year.

The privatisation and deregulation of the nation's bus services – the most significant change to affect the industry for over 50 years – loomed nearer at the beginning of 1985 with the publication of the Transport Bill for putting these Government plans into effect.

in 1984

Miner's strike begins; this would last for a year in some areas and led serious confrontations.

London's Thames Barrier flood defence was opened by the Queen.

In the early hours of 12 October an IRA bomb exploded inside the Grand Hotel, Brighton, where members of the Conservative Party were staying during their conference. 5 people were killed and 31 injured.

British Telecom was privatised.

No 1 hits included Relax by Frankie Goes to Hollywood, I Just Called To Say I Love You by Stevie Wonder, Hello by Lionel Richie and Do They Know it's Christmas by Band Aid.

in 1985

The Sinclair C5 battery assisted personal conveyance was launched, but production ceased after less than seven months.

East Enders started on BBC television.

A fire at Valley Parade Stadium in Bradford claimed the lives of 56 football supporters, and injured more than 200 others.

A British Airways Boeing 737 burst into flames before take off from Manchester Airport resulting in the death of 55 people.

No 1 hits included Nineteen by Paul Hardcastle, The Power of Love by Jenifer Rush and Saving All My Love For You by Whitney Houston.

Wilts & Dorset was 70 years old in 1985, and to celebrate Bristol RE dual purpose NLJ 871G was given this special livery.

BRIAN JACKSON

Crucial to the success of the privatised companies would be identifying networks that could be registered for commercial operation without any form of subsidy. A huge survey, called Bus Driver was carried out during 1985. Similar to the Market Analysis Project survey seven years earlier, twelve teams covered the Poole, Bournemouth, Swanage and Lymington area between mid-February and mid-March, while another eight teams worked in the Salisbury and Pewsey area during April and May. In order to assess the effect of summer holiday traffic, the Poole, Bournemouth, Swanage and Lymington area was surveyed again in July and August. Project Manager was Ivor West, the Survey Controller was Chris Harris, assisted by Alan Thomas in the Poole area and by Alan Pearce in Salisbury. The survey results were processed and coded by a small team headed by Tony Dayman before being analysed by a special computer programme to provide the basis for future service planning.

Salisbury depot got ten new coaches; six for private hire and use on the limited stop X41 between Salisbury and Bristol, four were in National Express livery for the Salisbury to London contract.

A new service was introduced in Poole providing a 20 minute headway between Poole bus station and Poole Quay during the summer months. A Bristol LH single deck bus was given a special livery for the Poole Quay Shuttle which publicised the attractions on offer at the Quay.

In his Christmas message to staff General Manager Allan Rolls said, *"1986 is likely to pose a challenge to our abilities such as we have never before experienced. Let us go forward with optimism and with the will to succeed."*

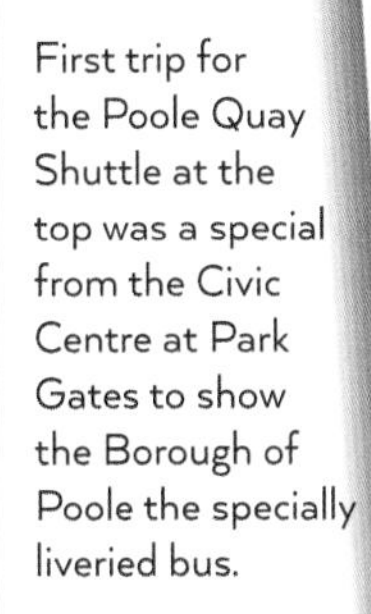

First trip for the Poole Quay Shuttle at the top was a special from the Civic Centre at Park Gates to show the Borough of Poole the specially liveried bus.

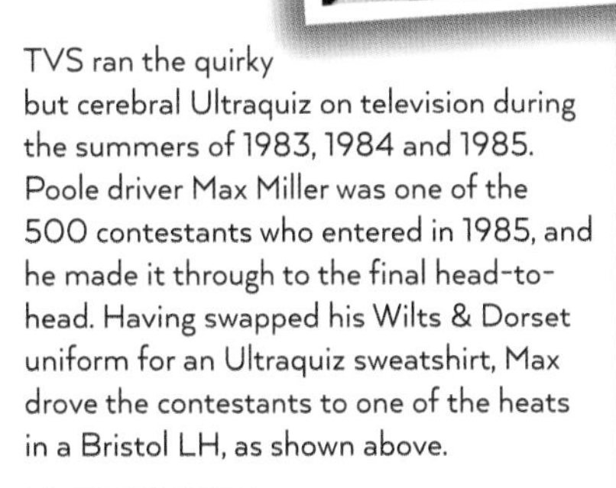

TVS ran the quirky but cerebral Ultraquiz on television during the summers of 1983, 1984 and 1985. Poole driver Max Miller was one of the 500 contestants who entered in 1985, and he made it through to the final head-to-head. Having swapped his Wilts & Dorset uniform for an Ultraquiz sweatshirt, Max drove the contestants to one of the heats in a Bristol LH, as shown above.

MICKEY BRITTON

On the left by Whaddon Post Office is dual-purpose Bristol RE XLJ 729K on the 36 to Romsey via Lockerley ahead of Bristol VR GEL 683V on the 37 to Southampton. This photograph was taken on 26 October 1985, exactly a year before deregulation took effect.

DAVID MANT

Deregulation enabled Badgerline to register bus networks in the summer of 1987 to compete with Wilts & Dorset in Salisbury and Poole.

In the photograph above passengers travelling from Poole to Hamworthy had a choice between Wilts & Dorset Leyland National MLJ 918P or Badgerline Eastern Coach Works bodied Bristol RE AHT 206J.

JOHN CUMMING

In the 50 years between 1930 and 1980 legislation affecting the provision of bus and coach services changed little. And yet the circumstances under which the industry operated had altered considerably during those times, especially with more and more people switching to owning and using private cars from the 1960s onwards.

By the mid-1970s most bus companies faced a shortfall between revenue from fares and the cost of operating services. In most cases this shortfall was made good by subsidy payments from local authorities, provided that agreed levels of service were maintained. The Transport Acts of 1980 and 1985 aimed to halt what was then seen as a gradual decline and to put the industry onto a more commercial footing.

coach deregulation

The 1980 Transport Act deregulated both express coach services and excursions and tours. Previously it was necessary to apply for a licence to run any of these and it was easy for a rival operator to object. The railway companies often objected simply on principal. The coach company applying had to demonstrate a need. It had become cumbersome, costly and not really in the customers' interests or spirit of consumer choice.

It also provided for three trial areas to be set up – in parts of Norfolk, Hereford & Worcester and Devon – in which Road Service Licences would not be required for local bus services, with operators being free to run services as they saw fit.

bus deregulation

Far more significant for local bus services was the 1985 Transport Act. From 26 October 1986 this abolished the requirement for Road Service Licences in Britain (except within London). Now an operator could run any service by giving the Traffic Commissioner 42 days notice of the intention to do so. Similarly, 42 days notice had to be given of the intention to discontinue or modify any such service.

It was intended that as many routes as possible would be provided on a commercial basis by operators registering services in this way. However, if there was a clear social need for a service that no operator was prepared to provide commercially, local authorities were empowered (but not obliged) to seek competitive tenders for the provision of additional routes. The period of notice was later increased to 56 days.

privatisation

By now much of the British bus network was in public ownership, either by the state owned National Bus Company or by municipal owned bus operators. Another section of the 1985 Transport Act allowed for the break up and sale of the National Bus Company. Privatisation was big in Margaret Thatcher's Conservative Government.

Some while before the sell-off began the Government ordered NBC to break up some of its larger companies into smaller units to make them more attractive to buyers (especially their local management teams) and encourage competition. For example, in April 1983 Hants & Dorset was split into smaller units, with one of the operating companies being Wilts & Dorset Bus Company. The NBC Board actually wanted NBC to be sold off as one entity but the then Secretary of State for Transport, Nicholas Ridley, was having nothing of it.

The sell-off started with National Holidays being sold to Shearings in July 1986 and ended with London Country North East going to the AJS Group in 1988. As mentioned elsewhere in this book, Wilts & Dorset was sold to its own management in June 1987. Quite a number of NBC subsidiaries went to their management teams. Some quite quickly sold their companies to the large bus groups that were forming, while others lasted a bit longer as independents. In 2015 East Yorkshire and Trentbarton (originally Trent) were the last two remaining former NBC companies still owned by themselves.

The commercial environment has certainly encouraged the industry to innovate, experiment and be more commercially astute. This has been well received by customers and, in many areas, the number of people choosing to travel by bus has grown significantly. Of course, in some very rural areas buses are simply not commercial and local authorities don't always have the funds to support such operations.

There were few passengers travelling when Badgerline Eastern Coach Works bodied Bristol RE DAO 294K was photographed below at Canford Heath in the Autumn of 1987, while operating its route 7 to Poole via Stanley Green.

Badgerline ended its operations in both Poole and Salisbury during the spring of 1988.

JOHN CUMMING

To provide extra resources to help combat the competition from Badgerline in 1987, 15 former West Midlands PTE 1974/5 Bristol VR double decks with MCW bodywork were acquired. Looking smart in Wilts & Dorset new livery, GOG 682N on the left was in Westover Road, Bournemouth, on the 108 to Sea View and Canford Heath.

PHIL DAVIES

1986

Every route the company would operate on a commercial basis following deregulation on 26 October had to be registered with the Traffic Commissioners by 28 February. Wilts & Dorset registered around 75% of its existing mileage. Some services were enhanced - for example in the Bemerton Heath, Harnham and Bishopdown areas of Salisbury, although there were also reductions and withdrawals, especially in rural areas.

Local authorities were required to examine the registered networks, and where they felt there was a need for a bus service that no company would provide commercially they were empowered, but not obliged, to invite competitive tenders for any extra routes or journeys thought necessary. Wilts & Dorset did well in gaining many tenders in Dorset, reasonably well in Wiltshire, but several routes in the Lymington area of Hampshire were awarded to Maybury Coaches of Cranborne.

From September onwards, season tickets bought by local authorities for school and college students were issued by computer rather than each ticket having details written in by hand and then date stamped.

Colleagues were shocked when popular Swanage Depot Manager Bob Smith collapsed at work and was found to be dead on reaching hospital. He was 54. Bob's role at Swanage was then filled by John Williams, a long serving inspector with the company.

In his Christmas message to staff, General Manager Allan Rolls wrote that 1986 had been, *"one of the most memorable years."* and went on to add that 1987 would, *"in all probability prove to be an even greater challenge to our initiative, our innovative abilities and our resource flexibility,"* words that were soon to be proved very true.

in 1986

Two new national newspapers, Today and The Independent were launched.

Prince Andrew, Duke of York, married Sarah Ferguson at Westminster Abbey.

Estate Agent Suzy Lamplugh disappeared without trace in London.

Courses for GCSE exams replaced those for GCE O Level or CSE.

British Gas privatised (tell Sid!).

No1 hits included Don't leave me this Way by The Communards, Lady in Red by Chris DeBurgh and Chain Reaction by Diana Ross.

1987

Staff returning from a Long Service Award dinner at the Dormy Hotel at Ferndown on 18 March had a more memorable evening than they'd bargained for. The snow that was falling caused no problems until the coach turned onto a minor road between Downton and Alderbury. In deep snow the coach slithered to a standstill on Alderbury Hill. Eventually they got going again but it was 0230 before they reached Salisbury through snow now around a foot deep. Staff making for Hindon and Bulford spent the rest of the night at the garage and went home by bus the next morning.

Wilts & Dorset was privatised on 23 June, with a successful bid from the management team. Allan Rolls had been associated with a rival bid by Southern Vectis, and he left the bus industry when Wilts & Dorset was privatised. The new leadership team was Hugh Malone (Managing & Finance Director), Andrew Bryce (Operations Director) and Rodney Luxton (Engineering Director) with Douglas Smith as non-executive Chairman.

A distinctive new livery and corporate identity was quickly introduced, and not a moment too soon, because Badgerline started serious competition in Salisbury from 28 June on the routes to Bemerton Heath and soon extended to other Salisbury city routes. Then in September Badgerline in association with Southern Vectis registered eight competitive routes in the Poole area. Moreover, Charlie's Cars minibuses had also registered three routes into Poole.

in 1987

The ferry Herald of Free Enterprise capsized at Zeebrugge.

British Rail renamed Second Class as Standard Class.

Conservatives won the General Election.

Hurricane force winds battered Southern England during the night of 15/16 October causing devastation; the cost of the damage was estimated to total £100 million.

There was a serious fire at Kings Cross Underground Station in London.

No1 hits include It's a Sin by The Pet Shop Boys and Never Gonna Give You Up by Rick Astley.

THE TIMES

Demand for Met Office report as 18 die in night of disaster

Wasted warnings of the storm

Insurers expect

On the left, competition! - Badgerline minibuses and a Wilts & Dorset Bristol VR were photographed in Salisbury's Blue Boar Row on 5 September 1987.

DAVID MANT

Wilts & Dorset's response was swift and decisive. Some stored Bristol RE single deck buses were quickly brought back into service, while additional double decks brought into the fleet included five Leyland Olympians from West Yorkshire and 15 Bristol VRTs with MCW bodywork that had started life in 1974-5 with West Midlands PTE. More significant, no less than 45 MCW Metrorider 23-seat buses branded as Skippers were quickly ordered and delivered between October and December and initially entered service at Poole. Following a huge recruitment and training programme, by October 40 extra drivers had been taken on at Poole and 20 at Salisbury. Every move made by the competition was more than matched by Wilts & Dorset, and the loyalty of customers and staff during this period was most heartening.

The summer saw the first two double deck open top buses on the through route from Bournemouth to Swanage via Sandbanks Ferry. The popular Explorer Summertime Specials programme continued to be expanded with more destinations.

Another landmark during this eventful year was the introduction of Wayfarer electronic ticket machines. Lymington was the first depot to be changed over, followed by Swanage. Salisbury had been completed by mid-December, with the rest of the company programmed for conversion early in 1988.

In the top black and white picture Hugh Malone (Managing & Finance Director) seated right, finalises the management buy out in June 1987. Standing, left to right, are Douglas Smith (Chairman), Andrew Bryce (Operations Director), David Mitchell (Minister for Public Transport) and Rodney Luxton (Engineering Director).

Hugh is launching the new livery on a newly converted open-top Leyland Olympian at Shell Bay in July 1987 in the middle picture.

the late C J BURT collection

To drive the new Skipper buses, it was necessary to recruit many extra staff. Driving Instructor Peter Russell (centre) was helped by several drivers to train the influx of new recruits, as seen on the right with two of the new vehicles at Poole garage in October 1987.

MICKEY BRITTON

Ready to leave New Canal, Salisbury, for Wilton and Ditchampton on 21 May 1988 in the picture on the right, Skipper bus E347 REL no longer had to contend with competition from Badgerline.

In the picture at the bottom of this page, stacked high into the air and stored for the 1988 summer season at Salisbury garage, are the roofs from the convertible open-top buses.

DAVID MANT

1988

MCW Metrorider Skippers were introduced in Salisbury in January and proved popular with many customers. During the final weekend in January conversion of the entire Wilts & Dorset fleet to Wayfarer electronic ticket machines was completed by converting 136 buses (111 at Poole, 14 at Ringwood and 11 at Blandford) between 4pm on the Saturday and 8am on the Sunday.

On Friday 25 March Badgerline announced it would be closing down its competitive networks in Salisbury and Poole from 7 May, giving the six weeks notice of deregistration then required by the Traffic Commissioners. In the event, Badgerline services in Poole ceased four days later (this later led to the Traffic Commissioner taking action against that company), while those in the Salisbury area were reduced before final expiry in May.

Operations Director Andrew Bryce said, *"We are absolutely delighted. We decided at the start that the only way to compete was to compete hard, and we demonstrated our determination by investing £1million in minibuses alone and by taking on many extra drivers. That policy has now been completely vindicated."* Managing Director Hugh Malone endorsed this, thanking all staff for their efforts and while warning that Wilts & Dorset still faced competition from Charlie's Cars in Poole he added, *"If any other company thinks they are going to take over Wilts & Dorset's share of the market, they are going to have a real fight on their hands."* In further justification of this policy, all of the Charlie's Cars operations were withdrawn in December 1988.

Five more Leyland Olympians were converted with detachable roofs to run as open tops during the summer months, with their suspension modified to allow operation over the Sandbanks ferry. This meant that most journeys on routes 150 (Bournemouth -Swanage), 151 (Bournemouth-Compton Acres-Poole) and 152 (Poole-Sandbanks)

in 1988

The first BBC Red Nose Day raised £15million for charity.

Piper Alpha oil rig exploded in the North Sea, with the loss of 167 lives.

The first 16 year olds sat the GCSE exam, which had replaced GCE O Level and CSE exams.

A train crash at Clapham claimed the lives of 35 people.

Pan Am flight 103 exploded in mid air over Lockerbie in Scotland, killing all 259 on the flight plus a further 11 people on the ground.

No 1 hits included I Should be so Lucky by Kylie Minogue, Heaven is a Place on Earth by Belinda Carlisle and Orinoco Flow by Enya.

in 1989

British Midland Boeing 737 crashed onto the M1 motorway; 44 people were killed.

The first satellite television service in Britain, Sky Television, started broadcasting.

In a crush at Hillsborough Stadium, Sheffield, 95 football fans lost their lives.

The Berlin Wall fell in November.

No 1 hits included Sealed with a Kiss by Jason Donovan and You'll Never Stop Me Loving You by Sonia.

would normally be open top in the summer, and laid the foundation for the extremely popular Purbeck Breezer operation introduced 21 years later.

The travel interchange by the 'down' side of Bournemouth railway station was officially opened by Lord Digby, the Lord Lieutenant of Dorset, on 23 November, although it had come into use three days earlier. There were bays for express coaches and local bus services. And in December Maybury Coaches withdrew its routes in Lymington.

1989

A small network of minibus routes centered on New Milton, operated under tender to Hampshire County Council, started running in January. Drivers and buses were based at Lymington. Also, Coombe Hill Coaches withdrew from local bus operations in the Salisbury area, giving Wilts & Dorset some additional contracts, although unfortunately not that for the Chalke Valley route between Salisbury and Shaftesbury, which was won by Maybury Coaches. Wilts & Dorset also began operating some journeys previously provided by Verwood Transport, and a Bristol VRT double decker was painted in blue Verwood Transport livery for that purpose.

A further 25 new Skipper minibuses joined the fleet, although the withdrawal of the final Bristol RE single deck buses was deferred, while some recently delicensed vehicles were kept as a small reserve fleet.

Mr Raymond Longman, former Managing Director of Wilts & Dorset until his retirement in 1962, died on 17 February aged 94. Company representatives were among those who attended a memorial service at St Boniface Church, Woodgreen, to pay tribute to one of the most respected figures in the transport industry.

In November staff from Lymington depot undertook a 2,100 mile bus trip around Britain in aid of the BBC Children in Need appeal. Leyland Motors, who the team had approached for sponsorship, lent a single deck Lynx demonstrator bus for the trip, while Gulf oil made a donation of £1,000 as well as picking up the bill for all of the fuel used on the trip. Wilts & Dorset donated £2,500. In total this fantastic trip raised of £15,000, a superb effort!

In the picture below on the left you can see a new Wayfarer ticket machine in use on a Skipper bus at Poole in January 1988.

MICKEY BRITTON

Following damage sustained from a falling tree during the hurricane force winds in October 1987, Bristol VR OEL 232P was converted into a permanent open top bus.

On 4 June 1989, in the picture below, it was used in a fun role, taking part in the Salisbury Carnival procession..

DAVID MANT

1990

Across Southern England Thursday 25 January 1990 will long be remembered for what people called the Burns Day Storm. Winds reached sustained speeds of 75mph - hurricane force - and because it was during the day the effects were rather worse than the nocturnal October 1987 storm. In Wilts & Dorset territory Salisbury was probably the worst hit; debris in Endless Street, Winchester Street and Salt Lane meant the bus station was closed for two hours; country services had to terminate in Blue Boar Row, while inspectors made sure that people did not miss their buses. At one point fallen trees meant that all roads into and out of Salisbury were blocked, while double deckers were prohibited from crossing Salisbury Plain because the gale was so fierce.

Four buses were actually blown off the road. A bus returning from Swindon to Salisbury was caught by a 90mph gust at Figheldean and ended up with two wheels in the ditch; it took the breakdown lorries from both Salisbury and Poole depots to pull the bus out. Two buses were blown off the road on the A338 south of Salisbury – one on a Woodfalls service at Bodenham and one on the X3 route at Charlton. At Stoney Cross in the New Forest a double decker returning from Southampton was blown across a 14 foot verge and a 4 foot ditch. Fortunately no passengers or drivers were injured.

Lymington depot was brought to a standstill for two hours with every road out of town blocked. With no trains running either, Brockenhurst College was badly hit, but despite significant delays, Lymington depot in due course managed to get buses through, even laying on an extra bus to Christchurch for students who normally used the train.

In a number of instances in Poole, Wimborne and Blandford buses were delayed or diverted owing to fallen trees, and several were damaged – windows shattered, roofs hit by fallen branches and so on. Engineering Director Rodney Luxton said 'Everyone involved in this emergency and in the recovery of vehicles did a great job. Through their endeavours all vehicles were safely home by the early hours of Friday morning, refuelled and with repairs carried out, ready for service by the morning run out.'

A postscript occurred on the following Sunday evening, when a Leyland Olympian double deck bus had its roof severely damaged by the heavy branch of a tree on the narrow Nunton-Odstock road. Four passengers on the top deck escaped with minor cuts and bruises. The tree, growing on the edge of a churchyard, had been made unstable by the wind; the branches originally blown over the road had been pruned, but it was unfortunate that the tree had not been more extensively lopped.

Just arrived at Salisbury bus station from Durrington on 14 July 1990, Bristol VR NRU 307M had entered service with Hants & Dorset in 1974..

DAVID MANT

in 1990

A mass demonstration in London protested about the Community Charge (Poll Tax).

Aldi opened its first store in Britain – in Birmingham.

The BBC launched Radio 5.

Margaret Thatcher resigned as Prime Minister and leader of the Conservative Party; she was replaced by John Major.

No 1 hits included Sacrifice by Elton John, Vogue by Madonna and Show Me Heaven by Maria Mckee.

in 1991

The Gulf War began.

The IRA launched a mortar attack against 10 Downing Street – without casualties.

The UK economy was in deep recession.

No 1 hits included I do it for You by Bryan Adams and The One and Only by Chesney Hawkes.

As an experiment, Band 3 two-way radios were fitted to twelve buses – a mixture of double decks, single decks and Skipper minibuses – operating in the Poole/Bournemouth/Ringwood area and linked to a base station in the inspectors' office at Poole..

1991

The Gulf War had direct implications for Wilts & Dorset. Left luggage provision at travel shops was discontinued on police advice, and staff were also warned to be vigilant and suspicious of packages left around depots or on buses. An unofficial service for dog owners also had to cease; on the long 184 route from Salisbury to Weymouth it had been the practice for dogs (and their owners) to be dropped off at the entrance to Blandford Camp and picked up again to continue their journey after the bus had circuited the Camp.

After eight years in Gervis Place, Wilts & Dorset's Bournemouth travel shop moved to the Triangle, a couple of doors down from the premises previously occupied in 1976 following the Bournemouth bus station fire.

In April, the 75th Anniversary of the launch of Hants & Dorset in 1916 was celebrated at an event organised by the Wessex Transport Society in Poole Bus Station. Mrs Lory Hawker, daughter of Hants & Dorset founder William Wells Graham, was invited to cut a special Anniversary cake, slices of which were sold for charity.

The harsh economic climate sadly resulted in some redundancies at head office when the accounts function was reorganised. In his Christmas message to staff Managing Director Hugh Malone said, *"Lowering costs and supplementing revenue became key issues in ensuring Wilts & Dorset survived the recession. When the recovery takes place, we are well placed to take advantage of it."*

TTT 173X had started life in Plymouth in 1982, and had also been in the Stevensons fleet before coming to Wilts & Dorset. Above, on 6 July 1991, it was in Salt Lane, Salisbury, at the start of a journey to Bournemouth and Poole on the X3.

The half-timbered building on the corner is the Pheasant Inn, one of Salisbury's most historic buildings, was once the Shoemakers' Hall, part of a complex of buildings on the corner of Salt Lane and Rollestone Street, which was left to the Guild of Shoemakers by Philip Crewe in 1638, and it was these that later became an inn, known as the Crispin Inn from at least 1743. Saint Crispin was the patron saint of cobblers, curriers, tanners, and leather workers.

By the late 18th century this was being made available as a meeting room. In the early 19th century the complex was leased and then sold, subject to covenants that the Shoemakers' guild could still use the hall for its meetings. A lease of 1821 refers to the inn now being known by the name and sign of the Pheasant.

DAVID MANT

Specially liveried for the Swanage Railway, refurbished Bristol FS6G Lodekka XSL 228A (originally 866 NHT in the Bristol fleet) was here at Swanage station prior to entering service in the summer of 1992

the late C J BURT collection

1992

Wilts & Dorset bought a 30-year old open rear-platform double decker to run a special service on behalf of the Swanage Railway between Harman's Cross and Corfe Castle/Bovington Tank Museum. Named 'Nelly', this Bristol Lodekka FS was refurbished in the workshops at Salisbury and painted in a special Swanage Railway livery. A detachable roof allowed open-top operation during the summer.

The passenger waiting and boarding area at the Rollestone Street end of Salisbury bus station was refurbished and brightened up.

On Saturday 14 November, Lymington Depot Manager Alan Smith, together with fitter in charge Ken Woodford and drivers Dave Kitcher and Derek Budden, set off on a week long tour around Britain in a brand new Optare Spectra double decker that had been loaned by the manufacturer for the trip. During the epic journey, which took in Ipswich, Luton, Leeds, Hull, Lancaster and Morecambe, a total of £7,842.57 was raised for the BBC Children in Need appeal; our intrepid busmen presented the cheque at HMS Victory in Portsmouth on BBC television.

1993

The tenth anniversary of the re-birth of the Wilts & Dorset name was commemorated by the publication of a special 48-page booklet in conjunction with the Wessex Transport Society, which was also 10 years old in 1983. The booklet told the history of the company, with particular emphasis on the 10 years from 1983 to 1993. Printed by Pindar Graphics, the limited edition of 1,000 copies sold like hot cakes at £2 each.

Below are Wilts & Dorset staff at the event at Thruxton celebrating the first 10 Optare Spectra double deckers in April 1993. From left to right they are:

Hugh Malone (Managing Director), Kevin Dolan (Administration Officer), Chris Whelan (Driver, Pewsey), Sarah Holloway (Traffic Clerk, Poole), Barry Quince (Driver, Poole), Andrew Bryce (Operations Director), Bob Wood (Inspector, Salisbury), Pete Russell (Driving Instructor), Kevin Spreadbury (Inspector, Salisbury), Terry Muspratt (Driver, Poole), Bob Newbury (Driver, Salisbury), Steve Chislett (Staff Manager, Salisbury), Brian Hoare (District Manager, Poole), Carole Buckle (PA to OD), Chris Harris (Marketing Officer), Allan Kitson (Driver, Poole), Rodney Luxton (Engineering Director).

CHRIS HARRIS collection

in 1992

The Conservative Party won the general election, but with a much reduced majority.

Neil Kinnock resigned as leader of the Labour Party, and was replaced by John Smith.

On 'Black Wednesday' (16 September) the Government suspended Britain's membership of the European Exchange Rate Mechanism.

Windsor Castle damaged by fire.

Daily Mirror

QUEEN WEEPS FOR WINDSOR

No 1 hits included Stay by Shakespear's Sister and I Will Always Love You by Whitney Houston.

in 1993

IRA bombs went off at Warrington and at Bishopgate, London.

The economy was coming out of recession.

UK Independence Party was formed.

No 1 hits included Young at Heart by the Bluebells, and Pray by Take That.

On the left is one of the Spectras on the Thruxton race circuit at their launch event.

CHRIS HARRIS collection

Ten new Optare Spectra double deck buses entered service in April, the first double deck buses to be bought new for more than 10 years. On 20 April the new buses were launched in style with a special event at Thruxton circuit which included a carefully orchestrated 'race', as well as the opportunity for officers and councillors from Wiltshire, Dorset and Hampshire County Councils to try their hand at driving a new bus around the circuit. More new buses arrived during the summer, including six Optare Delta single decks - the first new full size single deck buses for 13 years. Launches were held at Merley House in August, Beaulieu in September and Embley Park in October.

As well as new buses, Wilts & Dorset was also buying coach companies in 1993. In May Damory Coaches of Blandford was purchased, Ian Gray being appointed manager of this operation. This was followed in November by Oakfield Travel and the Stanbridge & Crichel Bus Company. The bus services provided by these concerns became part of the Damory operation.

The takeover of Oakfield Travel and Stanbridge & Crichel in November brought a collection of bus services into the Damory Coaches operation, and in consequence a number of vehicles were cascaded from Wilts & Dorset into the Damory fleet.

One of the first transfers was dual-purpose Leyland National TEL 492R, new to Hants & Dorset in August 1977, transferred to Damory in November 1993. This winter scene below was taken in the Dorset village of Milton Abbas.

The Damory bus routes were subsequently reorganised, and this photograph was later used on the front cover of the first printed timetable for the network, which was dated 1 May 1994.

TONY DAYMAN

Three new 49 seat Bova coaches entered service in January 1994 liveried for use on the National Express route from Yeovil and Salisbury to London, which was operated by Wilts & Dorset. In this publicity photograph on the right the newly delivered trio was lined up at Wilton House on 31 December 1993 prior to entry into service the following day.

RICHARD WEAVER

In the middle of the opposite page is what may now be a collectors item – the 1995 Wilts & Dorset Fleet Handbook.

Where shall we go this Sunday? next to the Fleet Handbook is one of the leaflets produced to encourage families to take days out on both the Explorer Specials and the regular service buses running from the Salisbury area on Sundays.

1994

Three new Bova Futura Club coaches entered service at the start of January on National Express route 005 (Yeovil- Salisbury -London) for which Wilts & Dorset had the contract. Later in the year Wilts & Dorset came top of the performance league of the 36 operators who provided National Express coach services at that time.

There were more new buses, with launches for Optare Spectra double decks at Poole Grammar School and Breamore House, and for 31-seat single-deck buses at Northaw School, West Tytherley. A cartoon of an Optare Spectra with the motto ***Be Cool - Go By Bus*** was put on T-shirts sold in the company's travel shops for the summer season.

Services previously operated by Oakfield Travel and Stanbridge & Crichel were fully integrated into a revised network of Damory bus routes from 1 May.

The 23-mile Stour Valley Way footpath from Christchurch to Sturminster Marshall was opened in September,designed so that people could enjoy walking it in sections using public transport; Wilts & Dorset sponsored the Stour Valley Way leaflet pack and also provided a bus for the opening ceremony. And in November a double decker was needed to transport everyone who attended when naturalist and television presenter Chris Packham opened the Mude Valley Easy Access Path.

1995

On 1 February Tourist Coaches of Figheldean was acquired. Its main business was coach hire and contract work and, responsible for a fleet of 20 vehicles, Chris Mills was appointed to run Tourist as an autonomous unit within the Wilts & Dorset family.

New vehicles at the beginning of 1995 included four Optare Spectra double decks with comfortable semi-coach seats. These were painted into coach livery and used for private hire as well as operating on some of the longer routes from Salisbury.

The company brought out an illustrated 24-page Fleet Handbook costing £2, containing full details of all of the vehicles operated by Wilts & Dorset, Damory and Tourist as at April.

A new route, X5, from Bournemouth to Southampton, only stopping at nine stops along the way and making use of the M27 and M271 motorways, began on Monday 5 June. It was operated jointly with Solent Blue line with a scheduled end to end running time of only 50 minutes.

in 1994

The Channel Tunnel between England and France opened.

Labour Party Leader John Smith died suddenly from a heart attack; Tony Blair took over.

Sunday trading restrictions were eased.

UK National Lottery began.

No 1 hits included Love is All Around by Wet Wet Wet and Always by Bon Jovi.

in 1995

Former Labour Party Leader Neil Kinnock resigned from Parliament to take up a new role as a European Commissioner.

The national daily newspaper Today ceased publication.

Former Prime Minister Harold Wilson died.

No 1 hits included Some Might Say by Oasis and Country House by Blur.

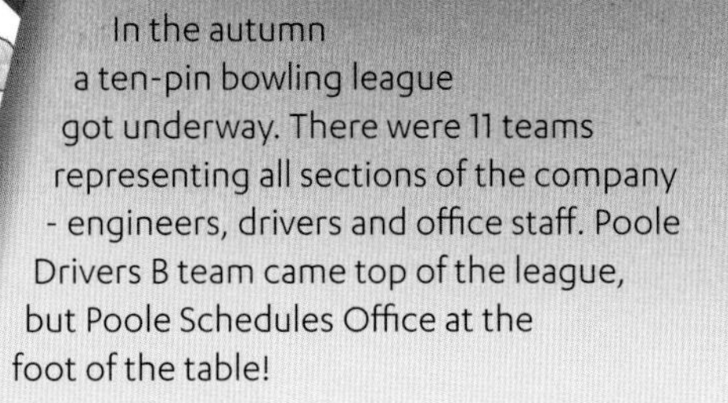

In the autumn a ten-pin bowling league got underway. There were 11 teams representing all sections of the company - engineers, drivers and office staff. Poole Drivers B team came top of the league, but Poole Schedules Office at the foot of the table!

Above is Tourist Duple Dominant bodied Leyland Tiger coach YPD 124Y photographed at Stratford Bridge on a wintry day in February 1995 carrying pupils from Leadenhall School in Salisbury.

RICHARD WEAVER

By now fitted with 77 bus seats, 1984 Leyland Olympian A901 JPR in the picture below carried a special livery for the Stonehenge Tour. It was leaving Salisbury bus station on 6 May 1995. There's more about the Stonehemge Tour on pages 144-5.

DAVID MANT

1996

Increased pedestrianisation of Bournemouth town centre brought changes in the road layout and the locations of many of the main bus stops, so revised stopping arrangements came into use during April.

A rebuild of the Tourist Coaches premises at Figheldean was completed during the autumn. The Tourist fleet then consisted of ten full-size coaches, four minicoaches and eight 8-seat minibuses.

By 1996 all of the Bristol VR double deckers in the fleet were at least 16 years old, but it was evident that these reliable buses would need to remain in service for some years longer. So a refurbishment programme got underway in December, with Wilts & Dorset working together with Hants & Dorset Trim to effect this transformation. At the time it was estimated that the refurbished VRs would last at least another five years, but as events turned out some remained in the fleet rather longer than that.

1997

Allan Rolls, General Manager of Wilts & Dorset from 1983 to 1987, died on 20 February 1997. Allan had left the industry in 1987 when Wilts & Dorset was privatised. A memorial service at Victoria Park Methodist Church on Monday 3 March was attended by many staff.

No longer required by the Swanage Railway, 1961 Bristol FS Lodekka Nelly was repainted into the old Tilling style open top livery (cream with red wings) and ran between Poole Quay and Sandbanks during the summer months. The open rear platform body meant that she had to run with a conductor – the first time that a crew operated bus had been used on an ordinary scheduled service since November 1980.

In the picture in the middle passengers on the 150 from Bournemouth to Swanage have just crossed the mouth of Poole Harbour on the chain ferry on one of the most exciting open top bus rides in the country. The picture was taken taken in the summer of 1996 at Shell Bay from the top deck of a similar bus going the opposite way.

Below is Optare Delta L503 AJT setting down passengers in Newbridge Road, Salisbury, while on an afternoon journey on route 40 from Salisbury to Fordingbridge in September 1996.

BOB MILES

in 1996

IRA bombs exploded in the London Docklands, on a London bus and in Manchester city centre.

A gunman gained access to a primary school in Dunblane, Scotland, and killed 16 children, their teacher and himself. A further 13 children and another teacher were injured.

A serious fire occurred on a train in the Channel Tunnel.

No 1 hits included Wannabe by the Spice Girls and Return of the Mack by Mark Morrison.

in 1997

Television Channel 5 was launched.

Labour won a landslide victory in the general election on 1 May; Tony Blair became prime minister.

Princess Diana and Harrods heir Dodi Fayed died in a motor accident in Paris.

No 1 hits included Who Do You Think You Are by the Spice Girls and Barbie Girl by Aqua, but the tune that was heard everywhere during the late summer and into the autumn only got to No 2 in the charts – Tubthumping by Chumbawamba.

The Mail ON SUNDAY
4am: Tragedy for Princess as Dodi is killed
DIANA VERY GRAVE AFTER CAR CRASH

The bus station at Amesbury was completely remodelled, with redundant buildings demolished and five boarding bays provided. It considerably changed the look of that corner of the town.

At the Bus & Coach Show, held at the National Exhibition Centre in October, the Optare Solo single deck bus was unveiled. Andrew Bryce and Rodney Luxton from Wilts & Dorset had worked closely with Optare in the development of the Solo, and it was announced that Wilts & Dorset would start receiving some of these buses in the spring of 1998.

Wiltshire Council's Paint-a-Bus competition was won by 13-year-old Rachel Hamlin, a pupil at South Wilts Grammar School. A 23-seat Skipper bus, used on Salisbury city routes, was painted in Rachel's eye-catching livery, as shown at the top of this page.

Optare Spectra double deck M143 KRU was photographed during the autumn of 1996 in the picture below, having paused outside the Drax Arms in Spetisbury on a route 139 journey from Blandford to Bournemouth.

By 2015 Spetisbury had the regular hourly X8 bus to Poole and to Blandford, while the Drax Arms has been renamed The Woodpecker.

The one item remaining the same is the bus stop, which is in the traditional Hants & Dorset green and cream design. This stop was somehow missed when all bus stops were given National Bus Company corporate identity in the 1970s, and it has since then been kept as a heritage feature.

M JAY BROWNE

1998

Late in 1997 Wilts & Dorset had acquired Levers Coaches of Fovant; then from 1 February 1998 it also bought Kingston Coaches of Lopcombe Corner. The Kingston vehicles were transferred to Salisbury but the name was kept as a subsidiary of Tourist Coaches. Levers continued to run from Fovant.

Saturday 31 January was the last day of operation for the Leyland National in the Wilts & Dorset fleet. The last example in the fleet, FPR 61V, was used on a number of routes across the Wilts & Dorset network on that day, the final journey for the 18-year old bus being the 8pm X3 from Bournemouth to Salisbury.

In June the Travelwise Paint-a-Bus competition came to Dorset and attracted more than 2,000 entries from local children. The winner was 11 year old Jacob Chapman from Lytchett Minster Upper School; a 23 seat Skipper bus from Poole depot was painted in his Clean Green Travel Machine design.

The first Optare Solo low-floor single-deck buses entered service on the routes between Poole and Canford Heath in May, but the big event of the year was the conversion of all Salisbury city services to low-floor operation, making Salisbury the first place in Britain to achieve a city-wide network of easy-access bus services. There was a special launch in Salisbury Market Square on Wednesday 26 August, followed by lunch at the Red Lion Hotel. Invited guests heard Mrs Veronica Palmer, Director General of the Confederation of Passenger Transport, praise this initiative by Wilts & Dorset. The Mayor of Salisbury, Cllr Mrs Olwen Tanner, proposed the toast - Salisbury's future is riding on it.

1999

Saturday 27 February was the last day of operation for the Bristol LH single-deck bus in the Wilts & Dorset fleet. These basic lightweight buses had been built with a seven year life in mind, but the last Wilts & Dorset example had seen a very creditable 19 years in service. On the last day it operated on a number of routes around the patch.

Strategically positioned in a gap in the Purbeck Hills, Corfe Castle dates from the time of William the Conqueror in the 11th century.

A Royalist stronghold at the time of the English Civil War, the castle was heroically defended by its widowed owner Lady Mary Bankes and her men, but captured by the Parliamentarians in 1646 after Lady Bankes was betrayed by one of her own officers. Much of the castle was then demolished, some of the stone being used to build cottages in the village.

Standing sentinel over the village, the castle's craggy outline rises majestically above Optare Spectra M146 KRU as it passes through Corfe on its way from from Poole to Swanage in August 1998 in the picture on this page.

DAVID PIKE

in 1998

The £2 coin went into general circulation.

Car manufacturer Rolls Royce was acquired by BMW.

DVDs went on sale in the UK.

No 1 hits included Never Ever by All Saints and Because We Want To by Billie (Piper).

in 1999

A national minimum wage was introduced for the UK.

Television presenter Jill Dando was shot dead on the doorstep of her home in Fulham, London.

A rail crash at Ladbroke Grove, near Paddington, claimed the lives of 31 people.

No 1 hits included Baby One More Time by Britney Spears, Perfect Moment by Martine McCutcheon and Livin' La Vida Locha by Ricky Martin.

The Daf with a Plaxton Prisma coach body on the left, R214 NFX, had been new in 1998 but did not wear this rather attractive, experimental livery for very long.

PETER COOK

Further expansions to the coach side of the business came when Wilts & Dorset acquired Bell's Coaches of Winterslow, near Salisbury. Bell's became a subsidiary of Tourist Coaches, whose head office moved from Figheldean to Castle Street, Salisbury, although the office and garage at Figheldean remained in use.

In May a new bus route was introduced, running from Poole via Ferndown, West Moors, Verwood and Ringwood to Bournemouth, providing a regular link to the conurbation for the extensive new housing areas around Verwood. Meanwhile, Damory Coaches introduced the Blackmore Vale Rider, giving the towns and villages in that part of the world rail connections at Gillingham station.

Wilts & Dorset supported the Salisbury Walking Forum to sponsor a set of bus walks leaflets. These proved very popular and certainly provided more passengers on a number of rural routes as people travelled to the starting point of the walks.

Launch of the city-wide network of easy-access bus routes using Optare Solo and low-floor Spectra buses took place in Salisbury Market Square on Wednesday 26 August 1988, as can be seen in the photograph below taken from the roof of the Guildhall.

RICHARD WEAVER

Having travelled in from Amesbury via the Woodford Valley, Optare Solo R617 NFX on the right was about to turn from Castle Street into Blue Boar Row when caught by the camera in Salisbury in March 2002.

MALCOLM AUDSLEY

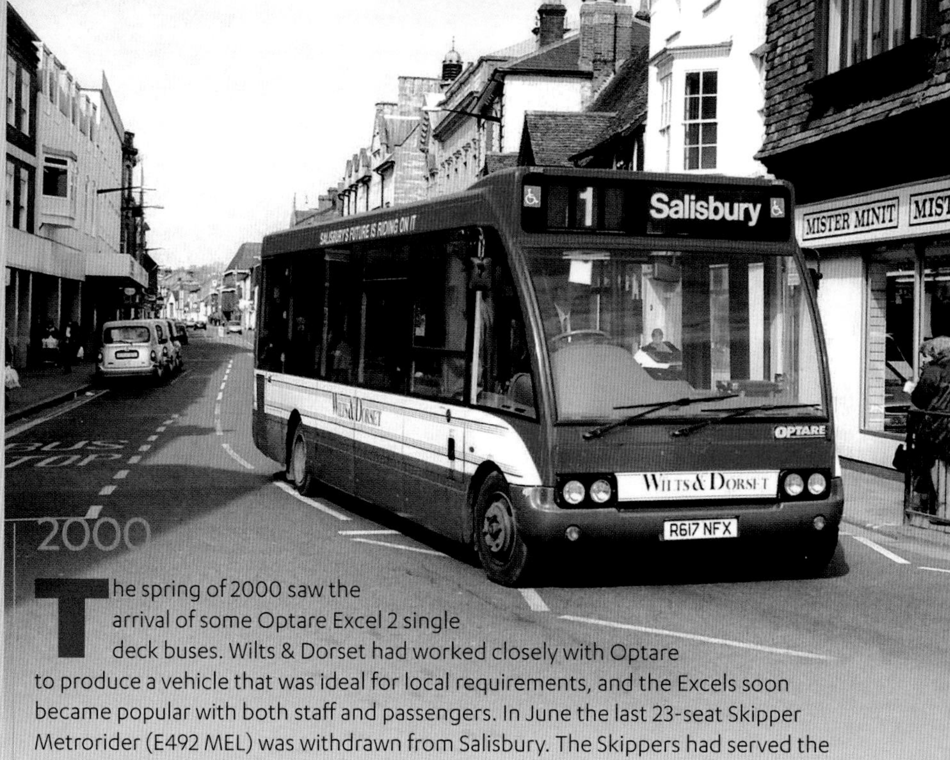

in 2000

The Queen officially opened the Millennium Dome at North Greenwich.

The Tate Modern opened in London.

High fuel costs led to protesters blocking access to refineries - combined with panic buying there were severe fuel shortages during the early autumn.

No 1 hits included Pure Shores by All Saints and It Feels So Good by Sonique.

in 2001

Walking and other leisure pursuits in the countryside was restricted owing to outbreaks of foot and mouth disease.

The Eden Project opened in Cornwall.

William Hague resigned as leader of the Conservative Party, replaced by Ian Duncan Smith.

Terrorist attack on World Trade Centre in New York, on 11 September.

No 1 hits included Whole Again by Atomic Kitten and Pure and Simple by Hear Say.

in 2002

It was the Queen's Golden Jubilee. Princess Margaret and the Queen Mother both died.

BBC 6 Music was launched, available only on digital media.

Baltic Centre for Community Arts opened in Gateshead.

No 1 hits included Round Round by Sugababes, The Tide is High by Atomic Kitten and Sound of the Underground by Girls Aloud.

2000

The spring of 2000 saw the arrival of some Optare Excel 2 single deck buses. Wilts & Dorset had worked closely with Optare to produce a vehicle that was ideal for local requirements, and the Excels soon became popular with both staff and passengers. In June the last 23-seat Skipper Metrorider (E492 MEL) was withdrawn from Salisbury. The Skippers had served the company well from their introduction in 1987-8, and in some ways were a victim of their own success - bigger vehicles were now needed on many journeys.

During the early hours of Sunday 8 October buses outstationed in the High Street car park at Lyndhurst were targeted by arsonists; a Spectra double deck was a complete write-off, while another and an Optare single decker were badly damaged. There was a further attack early on Monday 13 November at Poole, where another Spectra double deck, a Solo, an Ikarus single decker and two Leyland Tiger coaches were burnt out, and a Bristol VR double deck damaged. The total cost of these attacks was over £1million.

Staff shortages were an ongoing problem, but a special recruitment day at Salisbury cattle market, in which people were encouraged to try driving a bus, produced a number of applications.

2001

Wilts & Dorset's own building maintenance department built a new workshop at the Castle Street garage in Salisbury. This was completed on time and on budget, and the new workshp was used to prepare vehicles for MOT testing.

Four Ikarus bodied DAF SB220 49-seat single-deck buses had been acquired secondhand from Walls of Manchester at the beginning of 1998.

On the left, at the start of a journey to Verwood on route X36, N16 WAL approaches bus stop P in Bournemouth's Gervis Place in August 2000.

MALCOLM AUDSLEY

Wearing the distinctive Salisbury Park & Ride livery, Optare Excel X606 XFX was passing Salisbury's main Post Office in Castle Street on the left, while operating Park & Ride route 501 between the Beehive and the city centre in March 2002.

MALCOLM AUDSLEY

The first of Salisbury's park & ride sites was officially opened on Thursday 1 March at the Beehive, near Old Sarum. Wilts & Dorset provided the bus link to and from the city, using new specially liveried Optare Excel single deck buses.

Engineering Director Rodney Luxton became Chairman of Wilts & Dorset on 1 August, Douglas Smith having retired. Geoff Parsons, formerly Fleet Engineer, became Engineering Director.

2002

Changeover to the new Wayfarer TGX 150 ticket machines was a huge task during the summer. 320 new ticket machines had to be installed on vehicles and new computer systems brought into use, while behind the scenes traffic assistant Mike Robins input more than 300,000 fares for the new fare charts.

A three way Quality Partnership was signed between Wilts & Dorset, Salisbury District Council and Wiltshire County Council when three new Optare Excel single deck buses were launched at Wilton House for the X4 route between Salisbury and Bath, thus introducing low floor easy access buses to this corridor.

To mark 50 years the Queen's reign, an Optare Spectra double deck bus was painted in a special Golden Jubilee livery and kept its gold livery until the end of the year.

A great advantage of travelling by double-deck bus is the view of the passing scenery from the top deck.

Optare Spectra K106 VLJ, new in April 1993, was below on a route 6 journey from Salisbury to Pewsey via Amesbury, Netheravon and Upavon in July 2001.

This route followed the valley of the River Avon north of Amesbury.

DAVID PIKE

For a few years Wilts & Dorset experimented with magazine style A4 timetable books for the Dorset and South West Hampshire area. The issue on the right is dated 6 April 2003 and featured buses in various locations on the cover.

For several years, two journeys on the X8 Blandford to Poole route were extended to Bournemouth via Lower Parkstone and Branksome. Eastern Coach Works bodied Bristol VR ELJ 216V, new in January 1980, was photographed below arriving at Bournemouth Square on 12 June 2004.
MARK LYONS

in 2003

The London congestion charge came into operation.

Ian Duncan Smith resigned as leader of the Conservatives, replaced by Michael Howard.

Final commercial flights by Concorde.

The temperature reached a record high of 101.3 Fahrenheit (38.5 Celsius) on Sunday 10 August (recorded at Brogdale, Kent).

No1 hits included Hole in the Head by the Sugababes and Where is the Love by the Black Eyed Peas.

in 2004

A prominent addition to the London skyline was 30 St Mary Axe (the Gherkin).

On 16 August flash floods destroyed buildings and swept cars out to sea at Boscastle, Cornwall, but thanks to a huge rescue operation, no lives were lost.

The Wales Millennium Centre opened in Cardiff.

On Boxing Day a tsunami in the Indian Ocean resulted in many deaths, including those of a number of British holidaymakers in Thailand and Indonesia.

No 1 hits included Thunderbirds by Busted and Call on Me by Eric Prydz.

2003

Lymington's refurbished bus station was completed early in the year and formally opened on Monday 9 June by Hampshire County Councillor Tim Knight and the Mayor of Lymington and Pennington, Cllr Mrs Jean Clarke.

One of the most significant events in the recent history of the company was announced in a notice to staff issued on a hot summer morning. It read: *"We wish to inform all staff that at 0900 this morning, Monday 11 August 2003, it was announced in the City that the Go-Ahead Group has acquired the Wilts & Dorset Group, including Wilts & Dorset Bus Company Limited, Damory Coaches, Tourist Coaches and Levers Coaches."*

"Hugh Malone, Managing & Finance Director and Andrew Bryce, Operations Director, will be retiring with immediate effect, to be replaced by Managing Director Alex Carter and Operations Director Andrew Wickham. We wish to express our personal gratitude for the support we have received from all staff since acquiring the Company in 1987. We welcome the new owners and Directors, and wish them every success in taking the Company forward within the Go-Ahead Group."

Go-Ahead had acquired the Wilts & Dorset family of companies for £31,600,000 and the new directors acted quickly to reassure staff that the takeover was good news. A leaflet a few days later pointed out: *"Go-Ahead was keen to buy Wilts & Dorset because it is a very sound, well run business, and as the saying goes, 'if it ain't broke, don't fix it'. But there are also real opportunities to further improve public transport in our area; we want to share in those opportunities and lead new initiatives. We look forward very much to working together with you and building on Wilts & Dorset's success to make our Company the best."*

2004

From 1 March the X33 Bournemouth-Ringwood-Southampton limited stop route was increased to hourly and operated with specially branded coaches cascaded from the Oxford Bus Company.

Wilts & Dorset also won a 4-year contract from Hampshire County Council to run an improved service between Salisbury and Winchester via Stockbridge. Provided by specially liveried buses, the route was marketed as The Cathedral Connection and was launched at Winchester on Monday 19 April by Cannon Edward Probert, Cannon Chancellor of Salisbury Cathedral and the Venerable John Guille, Archdeacon of Winchester Cathedral.

Staff shortages were a problem and recruiting events were held at Salisbury on 17 April and 9 October, and at Poole on 5 June. Publicity for these used the strap line ***Good Pay... Good Times...Good Jobs - on the Buses***, and a number of new drivers were taken on.

Monday 26 July saw the introduction of a new town centre bus service in Poole, RouteONE, initially run with two specially branded Optare Solos, while from September Wilts & Dorset began a major new contract with Bournemouth University to provide a network of services. And popular with bus users was the increase in frequency of the X3 between Salisbury and Bournemouth from hourly to every 30 minutes from July.

Working in conjunction with local authorities, real-time information displays started to come into use at bus stops, while the distinctive glass and aluminium Cityspace 'Cibeles' bus shelters began to appear in Salisbury.

A new logo and corporate image for Wilts & Dorset was launched during the summer of 2004, and a very significant development was the launch of the More brand on routes m1 and m2 between Poole and Bournemouth in December, using new Volvo single deck buses in a distinctive blue livery. There's more about More on the next page.

Three coaches were given a purposeful livery by Best Impressions for the X33 route between Bournemouth and Southampton when this was enhanced to an hourly frequency. Unfortunately, this upgrade did not prove commercially viable and the route was subsequently withdrawn.

Above, R812 NUD, a Plaxton Premier bodied Volvo B10M-62, was nearing journey's end at Southampton on 16 March 2004. The fine building behind the coach is Southampton Civic Centre, built to the design of Ernest Berry Webber, and for which the foundation stone was laid by the Duke of York in July 1930.

Three new routes for Bournemouth University, branded as Unilinx, started operation on 27 September 2004. Route A took Wilts & Dorset buses into new territory at Alum Chine, where Optare Spectra L112 ALJ, which had entered service in August 1993, was showing off the new dedicated Unilinx livery on 1 October 2004.
MARK LYONS

On Sunday 12 December 2004 a new era for public transport began in Poole and Bournemouth. A fleet of 30 new Volvo single deck buses - an investment of £4million by the Go-Ahead Group - launched More.

One innovation was the forward area inside the buses had two plus one seating across the gangway rather than the usual two plus two, giving passengers a bit more personal space and room to put a child in a buggy alongside.

A vital element in the development of More was getting the service plan right. Previously there had been a bus every five minutes between between Poole and Bournemouth, but running over five different routes (101-105) and whose evolution could be traced back to the days of Hants & Dorset. This variety of routes meant that while it was possible to travel more or less from anywhere to anywhere between the two towns, none of the individual routes were very frequent. To a casual user it was quite complicated and less than customer-friendly; a radical new approach was needed to spark passenger growth.

So the five direct routes between Poole and Bournemouth became two (m1 and m2), which gave in effect a turn-up-and-go level of service on weekdays.

On the right is HF54 HGC loading up in Gervis Place on its way to Westbourne and Poole in the first summer of More operation, 2005. Better vehicles, strong branding and good publicity, promotion and information, as shown on this page, helped make More the success it was soon to become.
THE IMAGE TEAM

At the top of the opposite page is HF55 JZR, one of the Mercedes Benz Citaros passing the Kings Arms restaurant in Castle Street, Christchurch, on 28 July 2006 while operating on route m2 between Poole and Burton.
MARK LYONS

Travelling via Lower Parkstone the m1 went to Bournemouth Travel Interchange, while the m2 omitted Lower Parkstone and continued from Bournemouth centre to Boscombe, Christchurch and on to Burton. Routes 155, 156 and 157 to Canford Heath were also given new More-branded buses as routes m5, m6 and m7.

The vehicles used on the 101-105 had varied from Optare Solos (with peak-period capacity problems) to the occasional Bristol VR. The new Volvos were a major improvement on anything that had been provided before, so they were given a new livery, making them stand out from the rest of the fleet.

Marketing and promotion was expertly handled by Best Impressions, and this included leaflets for door-to-door distribution, press advertisements, 48-sheet billboards and a new website. The 'Looks like a bus, Works like a dream' campaign caught the imagination and won the prestigeous marketing award at the 2005 UK Bus Awards in London. And to kick-start the new service, all travel was free on the first day of operation.

Passenger numbers picked up immediately; by the spring of 2005 there had already been an increase of 20% in the usage of the improved services.

More continued to go from strength to strength. In August 2005 the m1 extended from Bournemouth Travel Interchange via Charminster to serve the new Castlepoint Shopping Centre, while on the m2 beyond Christchurch a number of journeys now terminated at Somerford rather than Burton.

To cover the increase in buses needed on the m1 and m2, the more branded Volvo single deckers were taken off the Poole to Canford Heath routes at this time. Some of the Mercedes Citaro single-deck buses delivered in 2006 were used on the m1 and m2 and also on the routes between Poole and Canford Heath in replacement for the transferred Volvos. All of Go South Coast's Citaros eventually got repainted and reallocated to the Bluestar fleet over in Southampton.

Timetable changes in May 2008 saw the eastern terminus of the m2 route cut back to Boscombe bus station, but a plus was the introduction of m1 and m2 night buses on Fridays and Saturdays. Then, on 19 September 2011 it was extended to Southbourne Fisherman's Walk.

Then in 2012 a new fleet of 36 buses were delivered for More. These had free wi-fi onboard and, later on, USB charging points beside the seats to enable passengers to top up their phones or tablets while on the bus. By December 2014, ten years after introduction, passenger numbers on the m1 and m2 had soared by 110%.

The More brand name has now replaced Wilts & Dorset as the fleetname for buses in the Poole, Bournemouth, Lymington and Ringwood areas. It won the Medium Size Bus Operator of the Year category in the 2014 Route One Excellence Awards, and officials from the Department of Transport have visited to look at the success of the operation.

With new buses for More a little way off, and the original ones in need of a repaint, it was decided in 2010 to simplify the livery and change the blue to the same brighter blue that Bluestar used. HF54 HHB shows this in Longfleet Road on its way to Poole on 26 June 2010 in the small picture at the top of the opposite page.

The new order for More routes m1 and m2 was the Wright bodied Volvos that arrived in 2012. HF12 GXG shows off the new livery and logo on the left, while negotiating Lansdowne roundabout in Bournemouth on 8 July 2013.
MARK LYONS

Right from the very start of More, rears have been used to advertise and promote features of the service and reasons to travel on these routes. Above is HF12 GVZ extolling the usefulness of night buses. Going the other way in Gervis Place is one of the original More buses repainted into the new livery and heading off for Southbourne.
GARETH JOHN

There was plenty of room on the top deck for the queue of passengers on the right boarding this Northern Counties Palatine bodied DAF open topper in Gervis Place in Bournemouth on 29 June 2006.

It was heading off for the scenic trip over the Sandbanks chain ferry to Swanage. The vinyl covering between the decks promoted this route - what a contrast to the duties on which this bus had been used when new in the Manchester area for Walls.
PETER COOK

in 2005

The television series Dr Who was revived by the BBC, having previously been discontinued in 1989.

The general election on 5 May was won by Labour, with a majority of 66.

Terrorists exploded bombs on three London Underground trains and a London bus during the morning peak period on 7 July, causing a number of deaths.

Michael Howard resigned as leader of the Conservatives, replaced by David Cameron.

No 1 hits included Is this the way to Amarillo? by Tony Christie and You're Beautiful by James Blunt.

in 2006

Charles Kennedy resigned as leader of the Liberal Democrat Party, and was replaced by Sir Menzies Campbell.

Natascha Kampusch, an Austrian girl who'd been kidnapped and held captive in a cellar for eight years, escaped and told her story.

No 1 hits included Crazy by Gnarls Barkley and Smile by Lilly Allen.

The Daily Telegraph
BRITAIN'S BEST-SELLING QUALITY DAILY
Al-Qa'eda brings terror to the heart of London

2005

Salisbury's park & ride was extended to include the car parks at Wilton and Britford as well as the Beehive, and the new services quickly proved to be very popular.

The Tsunami that had devastated large areas of Sri Lanka and Indonesia on Boxing Day 2004 had left those countries with the daunting task of rebuilding virtually every aspect of life for the communities involved. Buses were needed, so the Asia Bus Response originated by Mitch de Faria appealed for surplus older but robust vehicles. Wilts & Dorset and Levers contributed towards the total of 100 vehicles from various parts of Britain and these were handed over at Marwell Zoo, Hampshire in June.

In July the work of the former district traffic offices at Poole and Salisbury was centralised into a single commercial team based at Towngate House, Poole.

In Bournemouth and Poole More route m1 was extended from Bournemouth rail station to Castlepoint in August, soon well-used by both shoppers and workers at Castlepoint. Recognition of the success of the More brand came in November, when it won the award for Bus Marketing Campaign of the Year at the 2005 UK Bus Awards in London.

On 25 & 26 November the Broadstone Memorial Hall resounded to laughter and applause as Wilts & Dorset staff presented the pantomime Serviced with a Smile, which was written by Poole depot drivers Graham Leyland and Neil Mitchener. Staff of all grades were in the cast – including Managing Director Alex Carter.

The Go-Ahead Group bought Isle of Wight bus operator Southern Vectis during 2005, which also owned Eastleigh-based Solent Blue Line and, and from 1 December Wilts & Dorset Managing Director Alex Carter, Operations Director Andrew Wickham and Engineering Director Geoff Parsons' responsibilities included Solent Blue Line and Southern Vectis.

The Wilton Park & Ride bus link to Salisbury started on 7 March 2005, normally operated by special liveried Opatre Excel single-deck buses, but when this photograph on the left was taken at Blue Boar Row exactly two months later on 7 May standard liveried Excel X608 XFX had been allocated to the route. Of course, once on board the bus, the accommodation was just as comfortable.

2006

In February the Bemerton Heath-Salisbury city centre-District Hospital route was branded as Pulseline with the introduction of new specially-liveried Mercedes Citaros. There was a door to door distribution of timetables, and existing bus stops replaced with branded ones. Citaros were introduced on a number of other routes, including the X4 between Salisbury and Bath, and on a new fast route between Poole and Wimborne.

While driving home from a meeting he'd attended at Towngate House, Poole, on the afternoon of Monday 19 June, Salisbury Depot Manager Chris Gordon had a fatal heart attack; he was only 53. Less than three months later, on 12 September, Chris Moyes OBE, Chief Executive of the Go-Ahead Group, died at the age of 57 as the result of a brain tumour that had only been detected a few months previously. One of the group of managers who had bought Northern General in 1987 when the National Bus Company was being privatised, Chris had become Chief Executive of the Go-Ahead Group in 2005.

A major revision of services in the Poole and Bournemouth area came into effect from June. This was the biggest change since February 1978 and was designed to match the services more closely to the changing demands of bus users.

Expansion came in October, when Marchwood Motorways, based at Totton, was acquired. This company had operated some local bus services under the Solent Blue Line name as a franchise arrangement, but also had a coach hire operation in its own name, which was retained for this section of the business.

On 4 March 2006 Mercedes Citaro HF55 JZG below was heading south along Newbridge Road on its way from Bemerton Heath out of Salisbury city centre off towards Salisbury District Hospital. It shows the newly introduced Pulseline branding for this route.

Salisbury Cathedral, seen in the background, was built over a period of 38 years between 1220 and 1258 and, unique among gothic cathedrals was built entirely in one style that became known as Early English Gothic architecture.

The spire, added around 1320, is the tallest church spire in the United Kingdom at 404 feet. Inside the Cathedral, the organ is a magnificent Father Willis dating from 1877 and well worth hearing in recital.

MARK LYONS

Volvo B10B with Alexander Strider bodywork L527 YDL, shown on the right, had started life with Southern Vectis on the Isle of Wight but had been transferred to Wilts & Dorset by the time it was photographed on 13 September 2007 in Salisbury's Brown Street at the start of its journey on the 184 to Blandford and Weymouth.

It is a contractural requirement that vehicles on National Express duties carry correct livery and branding. This is exemplified by YN307 EWS below, a Scania K340EB4 with 49-seat Caetano Levante body, that had entered service with Wilts & Dorset in March 2007 and photographed when new on National Express route 032 in Southampton

MARK LYONS

in 2007

Three year old British girl Madeline McCann was reported missing in Portugal.

Tony Blair stepped down as Prime Minister and was succeeded by Gordon Brown.

The High Speed 1 railway line was completed between London and the Channel Tunnel.

Sir Menzies Campbell resigned as leader of the Liberal Democrat Party. He was replaced by Nick Clegg.

No 1 hits included Umbrella by Rihanna and Bleeding Love by Leona Lewis.

2007

The Salisbury-Tidworth-Andover service, run jointly with Stagecoach, was relaunched as Activ8 in an event at Tidworth in February. Buses used on the route were given their own livery, and a marketing campaign rolled out to attract new customers. Colonel Richard Aubrey Fletcher, Tidworth's Deputy Garrison Commander, praised the Route 8 Quality Bus Partnership which involved both bus companies, the local authorities and the Ministry of Defence.

Hants & Dorset Trim, a very successful coachwork company, had been acquired early in 2006, and in March 2007 it was moved from Southampton to Barton Park, Eastleigh, where (like Solent Blue Line) it occupied part of the former railway carriage works.

During the year the name Go South Coast first came into use as a collective title for Wilts & Dorset, Solent Blue Line, Southern Vectis, the associated coach companies and Hants & Dorset Trim. Within Solent Blue Line a number of key routes had been branded as Bluestar from 2004 onwards; this branding was reinforced by the issue of a network timetable book under the Bluestar title in the autumn of 2007, and the Solent Blue Line name passed out of use early in 2008.

Staff at Salisbury depot formed a new branch of the Royal British Legion, formally recognised at the regional launch of the annual Poppy Appeal on Saturday 27 October. Driver Len Blake, Chairman of the Wilts & Dorset Royal British Legion Branch, said that recruiting members had not been difficult with a considerable percentage of staff at Salisbury being former service personnel.

Steve Hamilton replaced Geoff Parsons as Engineering Director,

2007

Operated jointly by Wilts & Dorset and Stagecoach, route 8 from Salisbury to Andover via Amesbury, Bulford, Tidworth, Ludgershall and Weyhill was branded Activ8 in February 2007.

The design was originated by LMA Marketing & Advertising, and was applied to the Stagecoach and Wilts & Dorset buses normally allocated to that route. Easy access Optare Spectra T160 ALJ, caught by the camera when entering Salisbury bus station from Rollestone Street on 17 March 2007 shows the branding as initially applied.
MARK LYONS

To show the company's support for the Bournemouth Air Festival, Volvo saloon HF54 HFY used on More services was given a special livery to publicise the event.

Pride of the Damory fleet in 2008 was the twin-deck coach shown below. Tourist Coaches also received an identical vehicle, and they were particularly useful for school outings.
MARK LYONS

2008

Wilts & Dorset was named as the title sponsor for the new 4-day Bournemouth Air Festival taking place between 28-31 August. A Volvo single deck bus used mainly on the m1 & m2 routes in Bournemouth and Poole was given a special livery designed by Best Impressions to promote the event. The Morebus Bournemouth Air Festival was a resounding success, attracting more than 750,000 visitors to the town over the 4-day period. Resources from every company in the Go South Coast family were needed to help provide transport for visitors. Everything went smoothly and many letters of commendation were received praising the friendly and helpful staff.

Another successful innovation in Bournemouth and Poole was the introduction of nightbus services on the m1 and m2 on Fridays and Saturdays from Friday 30 May. A very effective campaign by Wilts & Dorset in conjunction with Best Impressions saw the night routes quickly carrying encouraging numbers of passengers, and the new service won the award for Tourism Marketing Initiative of the Year at the Bournemouth Tourism awards on Thursday 27 November 2008.

Wilts & Dorset named Salisbury Hospital's Stars Appeal as its chosen charity in the Salisbury area; an Optare Solo single deck bus with a special livery to help raise the profile of the Stars Caring 4 Kids campaign was launched at the Hospital. Transport was also provided for the Walk for Wards event.

in 2008

Heathrow Airport Terminal 5 opened.

Great Britain won 19 gold, 13 silver and 15 bronze medals at the Beijing Olympics.

A financial crisis developed and the economy went into recession.

No 1 hits included Don't Stop the Music by Rihanna and Use Somebody by Kings of Leon.

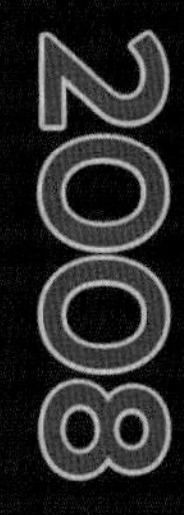

The Southampton based Uni-link operation became part of the Go South Coast family from 28 September, after Bluestar was successful in its bid to the University to run these services.

Five new Scania Irizar PB coaches joined the Marchwood fleet ready for the Low Emision Zone regulations introduced in London from July 2008, while the Tourist and Damory fleets each received a new East Lancs bodied twin-deck coach-seated bus. These all carried a new coach livery by Best Impressions in tones of blue. This livery would be common to all Go South Coast mainland coach units, with slightly different styled fleetnames for each one.

Go South Coast invested over £5 million in 34 new Scania double-deck buses which came into service during the autumn of 2008. Seven of these new vehicles were allocated to the Wilts & Dorset fleet and were allocated to Ringwood depot and given distinctive branding with chrome highlights to work the X3 route between Bournemouth and Salisbury.

Marchwood on the motorway – one of the new Scania Irizar PB coaches is above at speed, showing off the stylish livery designed by Best Impressions for the company's coach operations.

New Scania double deck buses that came into service in the autumn of 2008 were put to work on the X3 between Bournemouth and Salisbury, shown by HF58 GYZ when new.

GARETH JOHN

2009

In the 2009 New Year Honours list, Damory Coaches driver Jim Newton was given an MBE for his services to public transport in Dorset - his story is on page 154.

Poole bus station got a facelift at the beginning of the year, with Wilts & Dorset, the Borough of Poole and Grosvenor Estates investing a total of £300,000 on improvements that included better lighting and raised kerbs at the departure stands.

Ten new Scania Omnicity double deck buses took to the road at Salisbury in March; one of these new buses was named Chris Gordon in honour of Salisbury's past Depot Manager, who died from a heart attack in June 2006.

The year saw the final withdrawal of Bristol VRT double deckers from active scheduled service in the Wilts & Dorset and Damory fleets; some of the last examples had been in daily use for 30 years.

A highlight for the summer was the arrival of 13 new double deck buses for routes on the Isle of Purbeck. Six were open-toppers with removable roofs, three semi open tops with a small enclosed saloon at the front and one permanent open top. The other three had fixed roofs for use on the 40 route between Swanage and Poole. And in August two new Optare Solo SR buses arrived for RouteONE, the Poole town service operated by the company under contract to the Borough of Poole.

Operations Director Andrew Wickham was appointed Managing Director of Plymouth Citybus from 1 December following the sale of the former municipally-owned company to the Go-Ahead Group. Andrew had been Operations Director for Wilts & Dorset since August 2003.

To mark the withdrawal of the last Bristol VR buses from scheduled service, a number of relief journeys were operated by this type in the Salisbury area on Saturday 28 March 2009. BFX 666T, which had been new in March 1979, is on a route 5 journey at Sharcott near Pewsey in the picture above. Following withdrawal the company decided to keep this bus as a heritage vehicle.

New Optare Olympus bodied Scania double deck HF09 FVR was photographed at the departure point at Swanage station forecourt on 4 June 2009 in the picture to the right. It was shortly to leave for Corfe Castle, Wareham and Poole. This bus was one of the closed-top Purbeck Breezers branded specifically for the 40 route with Corfe Castle imagery included in the livery.
MARK LYONS

in 2009

Woolworth's stores ceased trading in the UK.

Many television areas were switching from analogue to digital transmissions.

Publication of MPs expenses ignited controversy.

ITV's Teletext service ended.

No 1 hits included Just Dance by Lady Gaga, The Fear by Lilly Allen and Meet Me Halfway by Black Eyed Peas.

HF09 BJZ was one of ten Scania Omnicity double deck buses new to Wilts & Dorset in March 2009; when photographed on 19 March, seen above in Salisbury on a route 5 journey from Marlborough. Best Impressions designed a number of generic themes for the buses in this batch that did not carry specific route branding.

Having started life in the Southern Vectis fleet on the Isle of Wight, Volvo Olympian M748 HDL had been cascaded to the Damory bus fleet when this photograph was taken in Blandford Road, Upton, on 19 December 2009. The coach-seated Northern Counties body provided ample accommodation for passengers travelling into Poole from the Lytchett Matravers area.

MARK LYONS

With the well-known ruins of Corfe Castle and the village spread out beneath, a Purbeck Breezer bus on route 40 to Poole was caught gliding through this beautiful area in the picture on this page.

MICHAEL H C BAKER

Opposite is the epitome of a English summer holiday with a Purbeck Breezer 50 bus, having just crossed the mouth of Poole Harbour on the chain ferry, heading off from Shell Bay on its way from Bournemouth to Swanage. To the left of the bus in the distance within Poole Harbour can be seen Brownsea Island, famous for its red squirrel population.

MATTHEW WOOLL

The Isle of Purbeck is not actually an island at all but it feels like one when you approach it from the Bournemouth direction, for the most obvious way to reach it is on the chain ferry across the entrance to Poole Harbour. And there is no better way to do this than on an open-top bus ride over to Shell Bay, Studland and Swanage.

The Isle of Purbeck is a beautiful corner of England. It has dazzling white high chalk cliffs, heathlands that stretch to the horizon, picturesque villages with quaint pubs, a charming seaside resort that still has steam trains and, to cap it all, a romantic castle ruin perched high on a hill.

For many years Purbeck was served by the buses of Hants & Dorset from Bournemouth and Southern National from Wareham. Southern National's Swanage operations (although by then renamed Western National) were transferred to Hants & Dorset in 1974 when they were both part of the National Bus Company.

Until the mid-1980s only single deck buses could be used on the route from Bournemouth to Swanage via Sandbanks ferry. In the 1950s and 1960s extra

high on a hill
an ancient castle stands sentinel
while a rolling English road
winds through gentle folds
of green Dorset hills

capacity was provided during the summer by running open-top double deckers from Bournemouth to Sandbanks, so passengers could go on foot on the ferry to catch two waiting single deckers at Shell Bay for the onward journey to Swanage. Thanks to more sophisticated suspension, open-top double decks could begin running all the way through from Bournemouth to Swanage in 1987, and this proved a popular move.

Bus services in Purbeck were relaunched as Purbeck Breezers in 2009, with the open-top Bournemouth -Sandbanks-Swanage and closed top Poole-Wareham-Corfe Castle-Swanage routes both being operated by vehicles carrying very stylish branding maximising the tourist potential of these routes. This was designed by Best Impressions, who also gave the bus stops a makeover. The revitalisation of these routes has made them much more aligned to the character and spirit of this special place and proved very successful.

The Optare Visionaire bodied Scania double decker on the right, HF09 FVY, is a convertible and can run with the roof fitted during the winter months. Here it's in summer open top form heading towards the chain ferry in Sandbanks on 26 June 2010 on Purbeck Breezer route 50 from Bournemouth to Swanage.

Sandbanks is colloquially known as Millionaire's Row, for houses here - some of which are clearly built to impress - attract some of the highest prices outside London. In July 2009 a 1,393 sq m empty plot of land on the peninsula was put up for sale for £13.5 million - that's nearly £10,000 per square metre!

MARK LYONS

in 2010

A cloud of volcanic ash following an eruption in Iceland cased great disruption to air travel.

The general election resulted in a hung parliament. David Cameron became Prime Minister, leading a coalition government.

Gordon Brown stepped down as leader of the Labour Party, replaced by Ed Miliband.

University students mounted protests against increased tuition fees and cuts in expenditure on higher education.

No 1 hits included Good Times by Roll Deep and Forget You by Cee Lo Green.

2010

Wilts & Dorset gained the contract to run the Bournemouth University bus services for a further five years. Six new Alexander-Dennis Enviro 400 bodied double-deck buses were taken into stock, plus one new Wright bodied single decker and a single-deck bendy-bus that had previously been in service with Go-Ahead London. Bournemouth University wanted a new look for this fleet and, working closely with the University, Ray Stenning from Best Impressions came up with a rather striking pink and white livery.

The Salisbury city bus network was re-launched on 21 March as Salisbury Reds, to make the local bus network more associated with the city. The new Reds image was also designed by Best Impressions. Vehicles, timetable books, publicity and bus stops all received a makeover, and a ticket promotion encouraged people to sample the new product. There's more about Salisbury Reds on pages 138-9.

Two splendid dinners at the Village Hotel, Bournemouth during April and May were attended by employees and retired employees who between them were celebrating a total of 1,665 years of service with the company.

In August Ed Wills, who had previously worked for Yellow Buses in Bournemouth and who had been Young Manager of Year runner-up at the 2009 UK Bus Awards, joined Go South Coast as Divisional Director. Also, on Monday 2 August Wilts & Dorset's new depot at Salisbury Road Business Park, Pewsey, was officially opened.

A new bus lane at Poole College was opened by Olympic medallist Liz Yelling on 29 September, with new pedestrian footways and easily accessible bus stops. On the same occasion, a single deck bus was named Liz Yelling in honour of the athlete, who said that using public transport encouraged a higher level of fitness than hopping in a car; *"Just the walk to the bus stop each day is great for health and wellbeing,"* she added.

The new Bournemouth University livery is shown above by HF59 FAM, one of the Alexander E400 double decks taken into stock at the beginning of 2010. On 11 February it was photographed in Wallisdown Road, near the Talbot Campus of the University, having just set out on route U1 to Bournemouth Lansdowne.
MARK LYONS

Unique in the Go South Coast fleet was BX02 YYZ, a bendy bus that had previously been used by Go-Ahead London. On the left it's at Bournemouth University Talbot Campus on a wintry day in January 2010.

At the bottom of the opposite page the Salisbury Fire Brigade Red Watch help Managing Director Alex Carter launch Salisbury Reds in March 2010.

And all smiles as Managing Director Alex Carter declares the new Pewsey depot open on 2 August 2010
GARETH JOHN

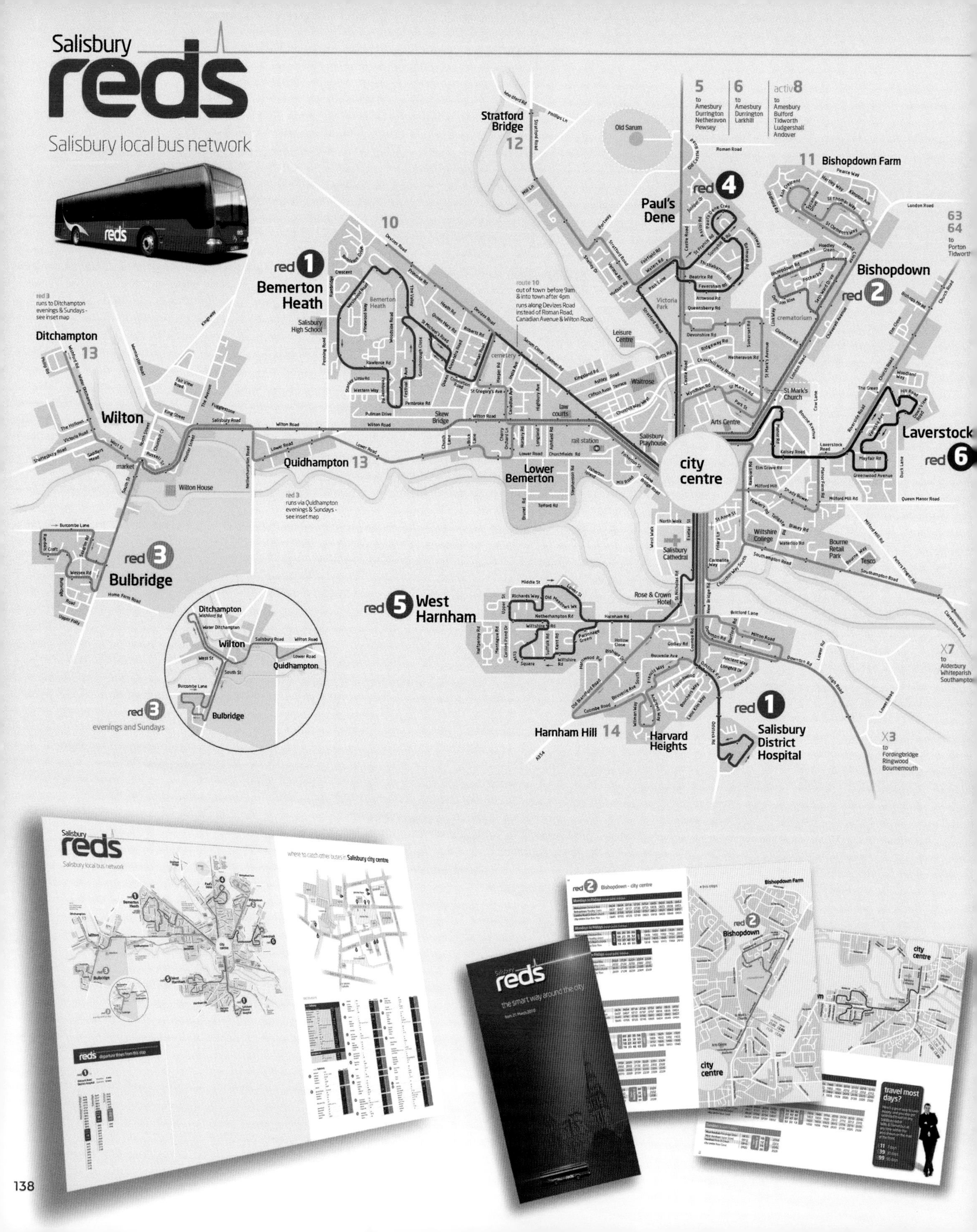

Salisbury
reds
Salisbury local bus network
red 1
Bemerton Heath
red 2
Bishopdown
red 3
Bulbridge
red 4
Paul's Dene
red 5
West Harnham
red 6
Laverstock
red 1
Salisbury District Hospital
city centre
Stratford Bridge
12
10
11 Bishopdown Farm
Ditchampton
13
Wilton
Quidhampton 13
Lower Bemerton
Harnham Hill 14
Harvard Heights
Old Sarum
Wilton House
Salisbury Cathedral
5
to Amesbury Durrington Netheravon Pewsey
6
to Amesbury Durrington Larkhill
activ8
to Amesbury Bulford Tidworth Ludgershall Andover
63
64
to Porton Tidworth
X7
to Alderbury Whiteparish Southampton
X3
to Fordingbridge Ringwood Bournemouth
red 3
runs to Ditchampton evenings & Sundays - see inset map
red 3
runs via Quidhampton evenings & Sundays - see inset map
route 10
out of town before 9am & into town after 4pm
runs along Devizes Road instead of Roman Road, Canadian Avenue & Wilton Road
red 3
evenings and Sundays
Ditchampton
Wilton
Quidhampton
Bulbridge
Salisbury High School
Leisure Centre
Victoria Park
crematorium
Waitrose
law courts
rail station
Salisbury Playhouse
Arts Centre
St Mark's Church
Wiltshire College
Bourne Retail Park
Tesco
Rose & Crown Hotel
Skew Bridge
market
cemetery
reds
the smart way around the city
travel most days?

During 2009 it was obvious that the local bus network in Salisbury was in need of a bit of invigoration to stimulate the market to make bus travel more appealing for both local trips into the city and out of Salisbury, too. Management turned to Best Impressions to come up with a new identity, better information and promote the network more actively. Thus Salisbury Reds was born.

At city centre stops there was clear, stylish, comprehensive information about which buses went where, when they ran and where to catch them. Centrepiece of this was the easy-to-understand network map with routes colour coded and all bus stops shown. A Salisbury Reds timetable booklet was distributed and this gave information about places to go from Salisbury, too.

Salisbury Reds came into operation on Sunday 21 March 2010. Initially this branding applied only to the Salisbury city route network, but a couple of years later the brand was extended to include all Go South Coast bus routes in the Salisbury region with the exception of the X3 to Ringwood and Bournemouth, which runs under the More name.

In 2014 and 2015 a significant number of new buses joined the Salisbury Reds fleet, and the brand image was refreshed to be a simpler, allover deeper red with revised fleetname.

On 21 March 2010, the first day of Salisbury Reds, HW54 BTX was photographed running into Salisbury city centre on a red 3 journey from Wilton.

This Plaxton Pointer bodied Dennis Dart MPD (short for Mini Pointer Dart) had been new to Southern Vectis and was later transferred to Salisbury.

The spire partly visible in the background is part of Salisbury United Reformed Church, and dates from 1879

MARK LYONS

2011

New ticket machines were rolled out across the Go South Coast companies in the Salisbury area from Sunday 20 February and at the other Wilts & Dorset depots a week later, enabling a wider range of tickets to be sold and speeding up boarding times. Also introduced from 27 February was new X5 route from Salisbury to Durrington then to Larkhill or to Pewsey, Marlborough and Swindon with a regular headway and a more easily understood timetable. It replaced the former routes 5, 6, 16, 95 & 96 and gave a bus every 30 minutes during the day on weekdays as far as Durrington, then hourly on each onward leg.

A new Operations Manager at Salisbury from 9 May was Andrew Sherrington, who came from Stagecoach at Northampton.

A new Bus Walks map was produced by Wiltshire Council, detailing 17 walks that could be enjoyed using Wilts & Dorset buses from the city. Updating the map was done by Pam Rouquette, volunteer co-ordinator of Walking for Health in Salisbury. To launch this, Wilts & Dorset provided a special bus to take walkers to Pitton for the enjoyable 5-mile walk back along the Clarendon Way footpath.

A team from Salisbury depot (Scott Bailey, Alex Makwana, Tony Topham, Martin Harkins and Jo Trigwell) raised £656 for Wiltshire Air Ambulance in an It's a Knockout tournament. They handed over their cheque to Clinical Team Leader Richard Millar at the Wiltshire Air Ambulance base in Devizes on 7 November.

At the end of the year Andrew Wickham returned to Go South Coast as Managing Director, Alex Carter having left the business.

2012

A big innovation in paying for bus travel, the key contactless smart card, was introduced in the Salisbury area from 13 February and across the rest of Wilts & Dorset from 5 March. At Bournemouth on Monday 5 March Government Transport Minister Norman Baker was one of the first people to use a key in the conurbation. He said, *"Smart ticketing is about making it easy, quick and simple for bus users, giving them more choice and better offers."* This was part of a very successful roll out of the key across the Go-Ahead Group.

in 2011

Prince William married Catherine Middleton at Westminster Abbey.

The News of the World ceased publication.

During the summer there were serious outbreaks of rioting in London and several other cities.

Sudden fog on a November evening led to a pile up of 34 vehicles on the M5 near Taunton which resulted in seven deaths and many injuries.

No 1 hits included Someone Like You by Adele and All About Tonight by Pixie Lott.

in 2012

Queen Elizabeth II celebrated her Diamond Jubilee.

Britain hosted the 2012 Summer Olympic Games.

It was agreed that a referendum would be held in Scotland during the Autumn of 2014 on Scottish independence from the UK.

Retail chain Comet went into administration.

No 1 hits included Call Me Maybe by Carly Rae Jepson and Gangnam Style by Psy.

On the left are David Brown, Go-Ahead's Chief Executive, Andrew Wickham, Go South Coast's Managing Director and Norman Baker, Minister, launching the Key smartcard in Bournemouth.

GARETH JOHN

Below is one of the then brand new Wright bodied Volvo buses with its new Best Impressions' livery, photogreaphed in April 2012.

MARK LYONS

36 new Wright bodied Volvo single-deck buses - an investment of £5.5 million - began being delivered during the spring for More routes m1 and m2. Some entered service immediately, but the rest were initially used as part of the fleet providing transport for the 2012 Olympic Games events at Weymouth - Go South Coast had won the contract. At its peak this operation, based at Osprey Quay beside the Portland Beach Road, used 77 drivers and 14 support staff per day, with separate services provided for athletes, site workers, technical officials and the media. Coach links to Heathrow Airport and Stratford were run on a round-the-clock basis.

On Wednesday 25 July Wilts & Dorset was one of the signatories to Salisbury Quality Bus Partnership along with other operators, local authorities and the Vision for Salisbury Board. This was to make sure Salisbury had good public transport facilities and there were measures to help buses run reliably and punctually.

Ed Wills, shown at the bottom of this page on the right, was promoted to Operations Director and Nick Woods appointed as Finance Director.

In the picture on the left Engineering Director Steve Hamilton (right) and Managing Director Andrew Wickham (left) make a retirement presentation to Swanage fitter-in-charge Brian Davies in December 2012. Brian had joined Southern National as a trainee fitter at Swanage in October 1965, and for the whole of his service had worked in the same garage in King's Road West.

GARETH JOHN

Before the new More buses arrived, HF54 HGC, was painted in an adaptation of the interim More livery (see page 124) to celebrate the Queen's Diamond Jubilee. It's in Holdenhurst Road, Bournemouth, on 21 July 2012 in the picture at the bottom left.

MARK LYONS

On the opposite page on the left is Andrew Sherrington newly arrived as Operations Manager at Salisbury.

GARETH JOHN

To the right of Andrew the Salisbury depot It's a Knockout team are handing a cheque for £656 to Wiltshire Air Ambulance Clinical Team Leader Richard Millar at Devizes on 7 November 2011.

CHRIS HARRIS

On Sunday 18 May 2008 open-top East Lancs bodied Volvo B7TL HF05 GGO was photographed on the left at Beaulieu in the green - the first - New Forest livery. Rather appropriately the name literally means 'beautiful place'. The bus is passing beside the Beaulieu River on the way from Exbury Gardens to Lyndhurst.

GARETH JOHN

Additional Volvo/East Lancs open-top buses were given colour-specific liveries when the red and blue routes were introduced on the New Forest Tour. A vehicle for the blue route is shown at the top of the opposite page, as is one of the posters also designed by Best Impressions.

CHRIS HARRIS

The countryside we today call the New Forest has a history that dates back to the 11th century AD when it was used as a royal hunting ground by King William I and his noblemen. Around 150 square miles in size, much of this area of open heaths and ancient woodlands has changed very little over the centuries, making the New Forest a very special place. To help retain the uniqueness of the area, the New Forest Tour was designed to encourage visitors to explore by open top bus rather than by car.

The tour was started in 2004 by Solent Blue Line and City Sightseeing, using one bus on a circular route. In 2006 a payment from Hampshire County Council and funding from the National Park Authority enabled the tour to run hourly using two open-toppers.

With the association with City Sightseeing ending in 2007, the tour was now run by Go South Coast in conjunction with the New Forest National Park and Hampshire County Council using two Volvo open-toppers in a distinctive green livery and based at Totton.

The original Tour route ran from Lyndhurst via Brockenhurst, Lymington, Beaulieu and Exbury. From the summer of 2011 another route was added to take in the north west corner of the Forest designated the red route and operated by Wilts & Dorset out of Ringwood depot, the original route becoming the green route. It is shown on the map on the opposite page.

Then for the 2013 season the blue route was added, taking in some of the coastal attractions of the New Forest. All three of these popular open top bus tours have run between June and September, and proved to be a popular way of seeing this beautiful area without the need to use a car.

To encourage connections from trains, Brockenhurst and New Milton stations had the New Forest Tour added to their platform signage.

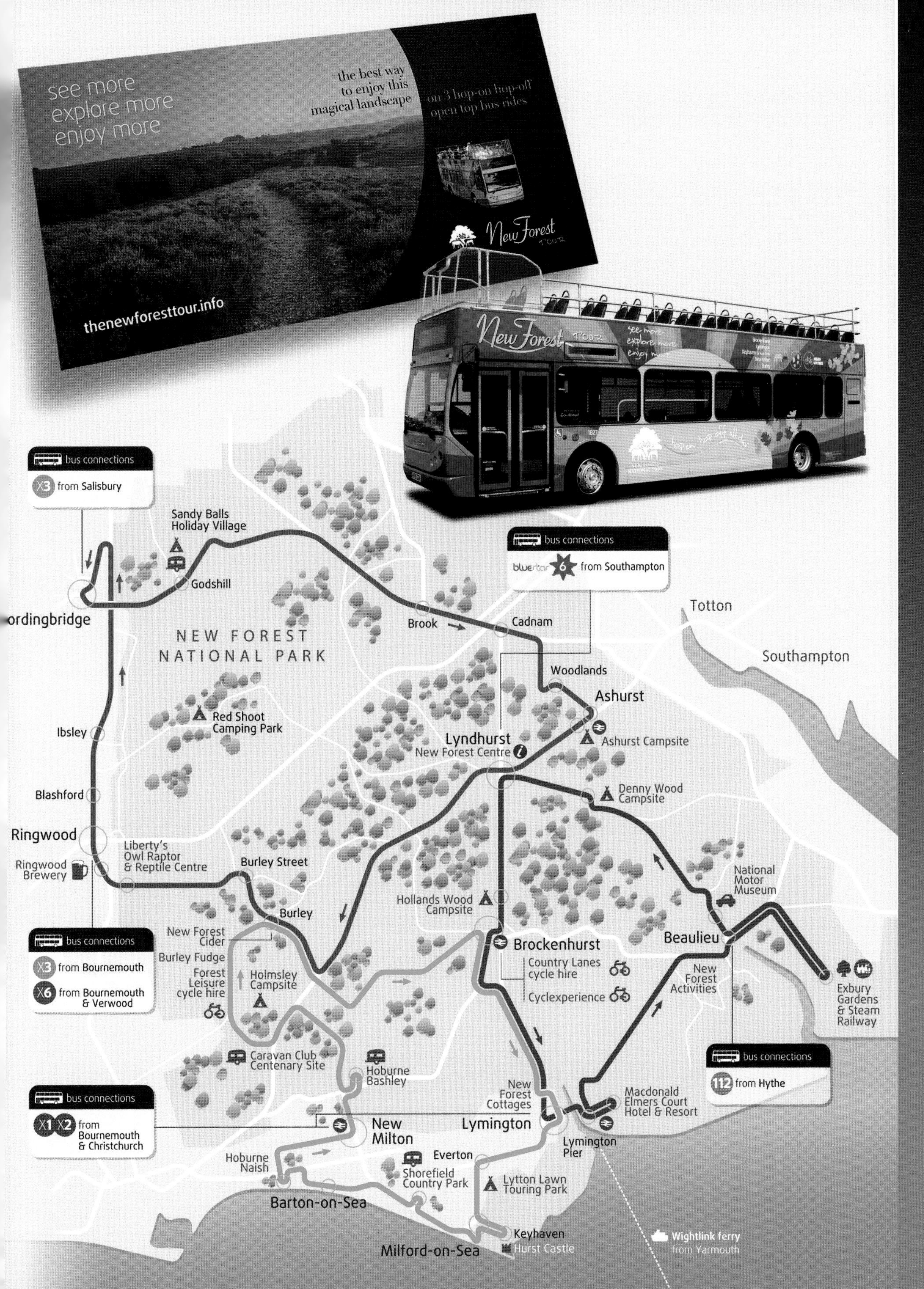
see more
explore more
enjoy more
the best way
to enjoy this
magical landscape
on 3 hop-on hop-off
open top bus rides
New Forest
TOUR
thenewforesttour.info
New Forest
TOUR
see more
explore more
enjoy more
hop on hop off all day
bus connections
X3 from Salisbury
Sandy Balls
Holiday Village
Godshill
ordingbridge
NEW FOREST
NATIONAL PARK
Brook
Cadnam
bus connections
bluestar 6 from Southampton
Totton
Southampton
Woodlands
Ashurst
Ashurst Campsite
Lyndhurst
New Forest Centre
Red Shoot
Camping Park
Ibsley
Blashford
Ringwood
Ringwood
Brewery
Liberty's
Owl Raptor
& Reptile Centre
Burley Street
Denny Wood
Campsite
National
Motor
Museum
Hollands Wood
Campsite
Burley
New Forest
Cider
Burley Fudge
Forest
Leisure
cycle hire
Holmsley
Campsite
Brockenhurst
Country Lanes
cycle hire
Cyclexperience
Beaulieu
New
Forest
Activities
Exbury
Gardens
& Steam
Railway
bus connections
X3 from Bournemouth
X6 from Bournemouth
& Verwood
Caravan Club
Centenary Site
Hoburne
Bashley
New
Forest
Cottages
bus connections
112 from Hythe
Macdonald
Elmers Court
Hotel & Resort
bus connections
X1 X2 from
Bournemouth
& Christchurch
New
Milton
Lymington
Lymington
Pier
Hoburne
Naish
Everton
Shorefield
Country Park
Lytton Lawn
Touring Park
Barton-on-Sea
Keyhaven
Hurst Castle
Milford-on-Sea
Wightlink ferry
from Yarmouth

STONEHENGE

EXCURSIONS FROM SALISBURY BUS STATION
Depart daily at 1100 and 1500*
EXCURSIONS FROM SALISBURY RAIL STATION
Depart daily at 1045 and 1445*
EXCURSIONS FROM AMESBURY BUS STATION
Depart daily at 1115 and 1515*
Additional excursions to Wilton House and Stonehenge, Longleat House and Safari Park, and New
are operated on certain days during the summer from Salisbury Bus and Rail Stations.
CODE: *—Summer only.

mysterious stones thousands of years old stand silent . . . were they put there to trace an ancient sun across ancient skies or to talk with long-forgotten gods?

The stone circle on Salisbury Plain known as Stonehenge is possibly one of the best known prehistoric monuments in the world, and has fascinated and intrigued man for centuries. The original purpose of this ancient site, despite numerous theories and archeological investigations, is still a mystery.

Stonehenge is about two miles west of Amesbury in the heart of the Wilts & Dorset area, and during the 1920s the company was advertising daily coach excursions from Salisbury, departing at 11am and 2.30pm for a fare of 2/6 (12.5p). Apart from during the Second World War, twice daily excursions to Stonehenge, using standard vehicles, continued for a further 60 years.

During the 1990s and into the early years of the 21st century Wilts & Dorset operated the Stonehenge Tour from Salisbury bus and railway stations in conjunction with Guide Friday, a company well-known for running open-top sightseeing tours in historic cities all over Britain. The double-deck buses used on the now far more frequent departures to Stonehenge were give a special Guide Friday livery. Guide Friday was taken over by City Sightseeing in 2002, and in due course Wilts & Dorset's Stonehenge Tour buses were painted in the City Sightseeing red livery for the start of the 2005 season.

However, for 2008 the operation was back fully under Wilts & Dorset control, and the Stonehenge Tour was re-launched with a stylish new livery and branding by Ray Stenning of Best Impressions. With new leaflets, posters and advertising, plus a dedicated Stonehenge Tour website, the revitalised service was a great success with passenger number soon showing a significant increase.

The livery was given a further update by Best Impressions in time for the 2013 season, with a revised, brighter colour scheme. Also, the long-overdue visitor approach to Stonehenge was changed in 2013, with the entrance, decent catering and proper state-of-the-art interpretation centre now over a mile from the stones to give visitors a better sense of occasion when visiting the monument. The previous facilities were, frankly, a disgrace for a designated World Heritage Site, and English Heritage had been lobbying the Government about this for years.

At the top is a Stonehenge excursions ad from the 1979 Salisbury bus timetable.

Optare Spectra L131 ELJ above right is in the City Sightseeing livery.
MARK LYONS

Above is Optare Spectra M132 HPR in Guide Friday Stonehenge Tour livery heading away from Stonehenge in July 2003.
RICHARD WEAVER

On the right is an Optare Solo in the English Heritage livery for the Stonehenge Shuttle service
PETER COOK

Although many visitors would enjoy the sense of drama the walk to and from stones would fulfill, English Heritage wanted to provide suitable transport for those who didn't want to or couldn't walk. So shuttle buses

between the visitor centre and the monument were needed, and some Optare Solos that had been cascaded into the Tourist Coaches fleet were re-liveried in pale gold for this purpose.

In 2015 the Stonehenge Tour was running every half hour during the main summer season, and was routed to give visitors the opportunity to explore Old Sarum and Salisbury Cathedral as well as Stonehenge.

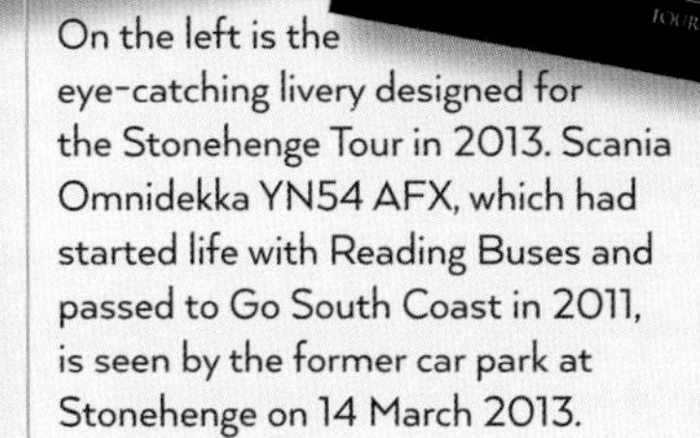

On the left is the eye-catching livery designed for the Stonehenge Tour in 2013. Scania Omnidekka YN54 AFX, which had started life with Reading Buses and passed to Go South Coast in 2011, is seen by the former car park at Stonehenge on 14 March 2013.

MARK LYONS

It would not be possible in 2015 to photograph a bus in the location of that seen below, as this section of the A344 road passing Stonehenge thankfully was closed and grassed over after the new visitor centre opened in 2013. It ran perilously close to the monument and was a visual and aural distraction from the solemnity of the site. The Optare Spectra shows the Stonehenge Tour livery introduced in 2008.

The standard of cleanliness and presentation of buses in the Salisbury area came in for praise early in 2013. The credit for this achievement was due to Salisbury depot's Fleet Hygiene Team, a group of perfectionists whose job is to ensure that every nook and cranny of a bus is thoroughly cleaned. Above, members of the team are seen at work at Salisbury Garage.
DAVE HOSKINS

A team of staff and buses was mustered to provide transport for the Bournemouth University Ball on 8 June 2013. A total of 10,500 passengers were carried by the buses laid on for the event, and the whole process went without a glitch. There was even time for a team photograph, as you can see in the picture above right.
ADAM KEEN

2013

Early in 2013, a letter from a gentleman who said he was an occasional user of bus services praised the presentation of the Wilts & Dorset bus he had recently caught which he said was *"immaculate inside and out, and smelled fresh and clean."* He also commended the *"smartly dressed, friendly and helpful driver."* The gentleman added that since that journey he'd noticed that Wilts & Dorset's buses were generally cleaner than those of other operators serving the area and applauded the high standards maintained. This was a great credit to Salisbury's fleet hygiene team, a group of perfectionists who had done a great job in driving up standards of vehicle cleaning and presentation.

A number of staff from Poole and Bournemouth depots had formed a dramatics group, which presented a stage adaptation of the film Alien in Wimborne on four dates in February, and then, on Saturday 1 June, at the Leicester Square Theatre in the West End of London.

For the 2013 summer season a third route was added to the New Forest Tour. This was a summer season only hop-on-hop-off open-top bus tour through this attractive National Park, the Blue Route, which included coastal views as well as the traditional New Forest scenery. A further innovation was the 112 Beach Bus, operated by Optare Solos in a special livery, this provided links to a number of attractions in the south east of the New Forest, including Buckler's Hard, Exbury Gardens and Lepe Beach.

in 2013

A helicopter crashed in central London, resulting in 13 injuries and 2 deaths.

Prince George, third in line to the throne, was born.

Same sex marriage became legal in England.

Firefighters in England and Wales began a serious of strikes in protest over changes to their pensions.

No 1 hits included Mirrors by Justin Timberlake and Wake Me Up by Avicii.

DAILY Mirror
SOUVENIR EDITION
OUR LITTLE PRINCE
8lb 6oz son born at 4.24pm after 11-hour labour

At the bottom of the opposite page passengers are getting off the route 112 Beach Bus at Hythe Ferry on Saturday 27 July 2013, the first day of operation. When the bus left again for Lepe, Exbury, Bucklers Hard and Lymington it was carrying almost a full load.
CHRIS HARRIS

In September 2013 route-branded Alexander Enviro 400 double deckers were introduced to the fleet.

On the left, photographed the following year, HJ 63 JKN shows off the new darker red colour of Salisbury-based vehicles. It's liveried for the Activ8 service and because these buses were required to carry external third-party adverts, a calmer version of the Activ8 branding was designed.

In September, new Alexander Dennis Enviro 400 double deck buses entered service on the X3 Salisbury- Bournemouth, X5 Salisbury-Marlborough-Swindon and Activ8 Salisbury-Tidworth- Andover routes as part of an investment of £8.74million in new buses by the Go South Coast companies.

More won the Transport category in the 2013 Bournemouth Tourism Awards; it was thanks to the first class team who worked hard to deliver what was recognised as a great product and helped the company to win this prestigious award.

Below is one of the More liveried double deckers on the X3 route in Ringwood on the way to Bournemouth on 24 September 2013. For the occasions when third-party adverts might be absent, promotional messages were permanently carried within the advert frames
MARK LYONS

Above the Bishop of Salisbury is cutting the ribbon held by Managing Director Andrew Wickham and Finance Director Nick Woods to formally open the new Salisbury Reds travel shop in New Canal on 9 May 2014.
DONNA VINCENT

Enviro 400 HW63 FGN in the lower picture was photographed in Bemerton Heath on 19 January 2015. Free onboard WiFi by now was beginning to be expected on new buses and this was clearly being promoted on the bus.
MARK LYONS

2014

Saturday 4 January 2014 was the last day that timetabled service buses used Salisbury bus station, the last scheduled departure of all being the X3 journey to Ringwood at 10 minutes past midnight. At the Vintage Day on the Sunday marking the end of an era more than 20 preserved buses ran free services on seven different routes. The final departure carrying passengers from Salisbury bus station was a convoy of four former Wilts & Dorset buses dating from 1956 to 1970 which left for a circular trip via Alderbury at 1545.

The ageing bus station no longer provided satisfactory accommodation for customers or staff and it was logical to move longer distance services to terminate at city centre stops in the same way as local routes had done for many years. This involved a general reorganisation of the Salisbury city centre bus stops, which was achieved very smoothly. Staff accommodation was moved to a building that had been built for the Wilts & Dorset Bank in 1901, and the area used by Salisbury Reds on the ground floor was refurbished to provide offices and a drivers' room much more fit for purpose than the old bus station.

A new Salisbury Travel shop in New Canal was formally opened by Nicholas Holtram, Bishop of Salisbury, on Friday 9 May 2014. The war memorial plaque, honouring 12 staff from Wilts & Dorset Motor Services Ltd who gave their lives in the Second World War, has been positioned in the new shop.

When Hatts went into administration, Salisbury Reds acted quickly and from 25 July until 30 August operated a number of scheduled services that had previously been provided by Hatts. A few years previously Hatts had won the Salisbury Park & Ride contract, but from Saturday 2 August 2014 Salisbury Reds and Stagecoach took this over, and following re-tendering the entire operation passed to Salisbury Reds on 1 June 2015.

New buses entering service in 2014 included eight ADL Enviro 200 single decks in early September, while in November eight new Enviro 400 double deckers took over the busy r1 linking Salisbury District Hospital, the city centre and Bemerton Heath.

in 2014

Severe storms early in the year caused much damage and destruction, including the complete washout of the rail line at Dawlish.

Russia annexed Crimea.

The Church of England voted to allow women bishops.

In the referendum on 18 September, the people of Scotland rejected independence by 55% to 45%.

No 1 hits included Ghost by Ella Henderson and Am I Wrong by Nico and Vinz.

Optare Solo SRs came into the fleet in 2015. HF64 BRZ, shown on the left, was put to work in the Ringwood area.
MARK LYONS

2015

It was on Monday 4 January 1915 that Wilts & Dorset Motor Services was registered at Companies House, therefore centenary celebrations started in January 2015 when two Scania double deck buses from the current fleet were repainted in heritage liveries. One was in the red and grey colour scheme carried by the company's buses in the 1930s, the other in the red and cream used from the late 1940s until the early 1970s. Inside the buses the seats were reupholstered in the Tilling style moquette once found in many buses throughout the country, while the cove panels highlighted Wilts & Dorset's 100 year history. They're shown on page 160.

By the end of February six more Enviro 200s plus five OptareSolo SR short single deckers had entered service with Salisbury Reds. Five more Solo SRs went into the Damory fleet, and another went to More at Ringwood.

Below is the new order for Salisbury Reds in 2015. On the left is an Optare Solo SR and on the right an Enviro 200 at Hindon on 13 February.
PAULA WOOD

The end of an era; Ringwood driver Will Degan waits to depart with the last scheduled service journey to run from Salisbury bus station; the X3 at 0010 on Sunday 5 January 2014.
BRIAN JACKSON

During the Vintage Day to mark the closure of Salisbury bus station, preserved former Wilts & Dorset Bristol LD6G OHR 919 above was turning right into Endless Street. This bus had entered service with Wilts & Dorset in 1956
MARK LYONS

POINTS OF INTEREST—

Southampton Route. Service No. 4.

LEAVING Salisbury and proceeding *via* Petersfinger we reach Alderbury, standing on the east bank of the Avon—3 miles S.E. of Salisbury. At Ivychurch near the village, formerly stood the Augustinian priory of St. Mary—founded by King Stephen. Passing on we reach Newton Corner, near White-parish. In the latter village is the 13th century edifice of All Saints—containing several monuments to the Eyre and St. Barbe families. From Dean Hill, extensive views of the New Forest and surrounding Country, and Isle of Wight can be obtained. We next pass the village of Landford, on the Hampshire border, on a branch of the River Test. Continuing the road we pass West Wellow and on to Ower, a junction for Romsey, Ringwood and Christchurch, &c., &c. Pretty views along this section of the road are had of the Forest and surrounding country. Then on through Testwood and Totton, we enter Southampton—23 miles S.E. of Salisbury. To the N.E of the present town where Bitterne now stands, the Romans had a military station called "*Clausentum*." *King Canute* made this town his occasional residence. Southampton in Norman days derived its importance from being the Port of Winchester. Henry V., previous to the battle of Agincourt, marshalled his army here. Of the ancient parts of the town, the most notable remains are West Gate, South Gate, and Bar Gate, and portions of the old walls and round towers. The town can be reached comfortably and quickly by the Company's fast and reliable Bus Service every day in the week.

Char-a-banc Excursions

SEE THE BEAUTY SPOTS

Wilts and Dorset Motor Services Ltd.

27

In the pioneering days of bus operation, Wilts & Dorset did promote its bus services in the timetable booklets produced, as in the description of points of interest on the route between Salisbury and Southampton shown in the 1925 timetable booklet on the left.

Note, at the bottom of the page, the correct spelling of the plural of char-a-banc in a company advert from the same booklet.

Of course, third-party advertising in timetable books helped to offset the cost of producing them, although Wilts & Dorset, like many bus companies in days gone by, charged for its books. The one issued in November 1939 cost 1d and on the back cover was the charming advert below.

The blue printed advert dates from 1949 when, of course, petrol was still rationed and there was a big demand for bus travel.

WHILE YOU'RE WAITING

FOR A 'BUS—

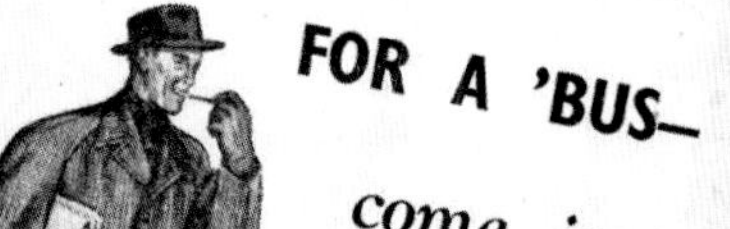

come in and see our new range of Winter overcoats!

W. RANDALL

The Shop for Men's Wear

ENDLESS STREET, (Opposite New Bus Station) - SALISBURY

PHONE 3894

Published by White & Carter Ltd., Carlton House, Regent St., S.W.1 and Printed by The Salisbury Press Ltd., Salisbury

HELP US—

—AND HELP YOURSELF

BY ADJUSTING YOUR BUS TRAVEL TIME

IF POSSIBLE

TO AVOID THE PEAK HOURS OF THE DAY

7-30 a.m. to 9 a.m. 4 p.m. to 6-30 p.m.

You will enjoy a less crowded and more pleasant journey if you

DON'T TRAVEL at these times

WILTS AND DORSET MOTOR SERVICES, LTD.

Chars-a-banc Excursions.

For all Chars-a-banc Excursions to the BEAUTY SPOTS and Places of Interest in the South and Western Counties, book your seat in one of our up-to-date "De Luxe" Motor Coaches.

We give the Largest and Best Selection of Drives out of Salisbury.

Chars-a-banc may be hired by Private Parties and Clubs for Picnics, Race Meetings, Employees and School Outings, etc. All enquiries for Private Hire should be addressed to the **Traffic Manager, 4, St. Thomas Square, Salisbury; 'Phone Salisbury 313.**

EARLY BOOKINGS ADVISED.

selling the service

It's all very well putting on bus services for people to get to where they want to go, but they do need to be promoted, which means producing easy-to-understand information and eye-catching, imaginative advertising that sells what's on offer.

Advertising and marketing in bus operating companies has not always been accorded the importance it deserves, and when decline in bus usage was getting worse year-by-year as the 1950s turned into the 1960s and beyond, cost-cutting seemed to be the prime business mantra and advertising and promotion almost a dirty word.

So here we present a selection of advertising and marketing material produced by Wilts & Dorset and Go South Coast over the years from the what seems to modern eyes to be a simple, almost naïve approach of the early days to the professionally-produced examples of recent times.

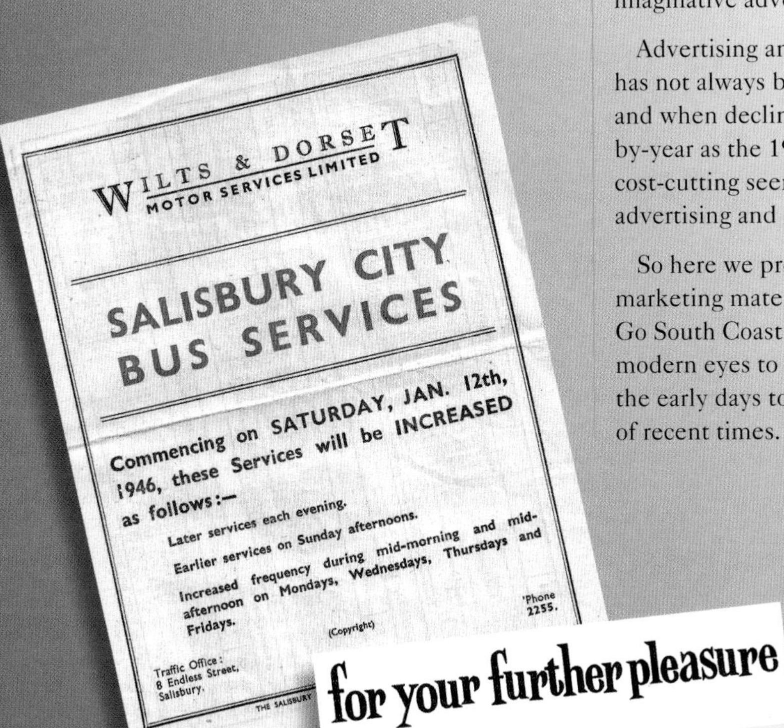

WILTS & DORSET MOTOR SERVICES LIMITED

SALISBURY CITY BUS SERVICES

Commencing on SATURDAY, JAN. 12th, 1946, these Services will be INCREASED as follows:—

Later services each evening.

Earlier services on Sunday afternoons.

Increased frequency during mid-morning and mid-afternoon on Mondays, Wednesdays, Thursdays and Fridays.

(Copyright) 'Phone 2255.

Traffic Office: 8 Endless Street, Salisbury.

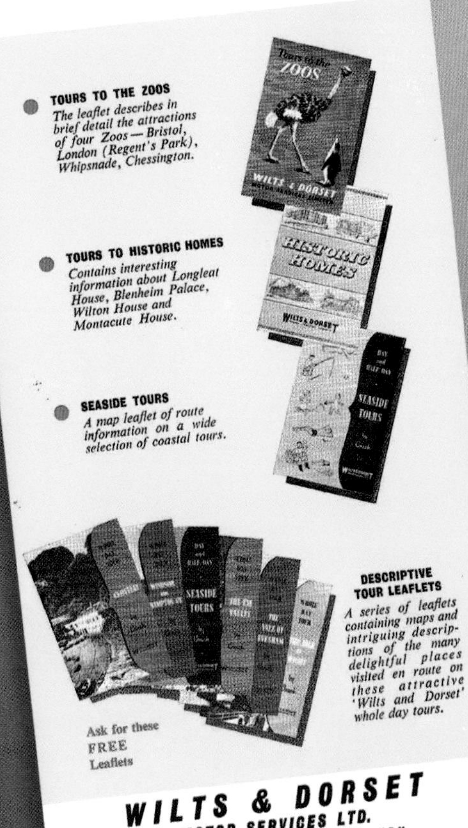

Above is a pamphlet mentioneing improved bus services for Salisbury in 1946.

By the early 1960s design was being used to promote bus services in a contemporary style. Language was less stilted and formal than the earlier examples.

The X3, X5 and X7 routes radiating out of Salisbury have huge potential for leisure travel opportunities, and instead of just producing a simple timetable, these examples show how attractive publicity with useful information about destinations and ideas of things to do can have pick-up appeal and increase awareness of these routes. Helpful, but pretty basic, stuff like showing where bus stops are located along the route and in towns and cities has given potential customers greater confidence in using bus services.

As well as ordinary leaflets and flyers available to be picked up on bus or in travel shops and tourist information centres, Go South Coast used a comprehensive marketing mix to reach customers, involving online activity and doordrops with redeemable vouchers that has helped the company understand its customers better. The doordrops on the opposite page were distributed widely in the appropriate catchment areas.

The Keep Cool was a summer promotion (the More buses had air-conditioning), while the Whooosh one was after the company had made some changes to routes from Wimborne into Poole.

we need motivated experienced engineers

Help keep our buses in perfect shape . . .

Wilts & Dorset is looking for experienced PCV/HGV engineers to join its Poole garage.

We have both day and evening shifts available.

Contact Kenny for more information.

01202 339216

kmcdonald@wdbus.co.uk

closing date 31 May 2011

Wilts Dorset

Technological advances in both design and print processes, coupled with a more enlightened attitude as to how good design and advertising can actually help to grow patronage and revenue has meant Wilts & Dorset and Go South Coast has been marketing itself far more actively since Go-Ahead bought the company.

These clever bus rear promotions for More, developed by Best Impressions working closely with the Go South Coast marketing team, helped to create a good buzz around the product and highlighted how bus travel is actually in tune with how people like to run their lives.

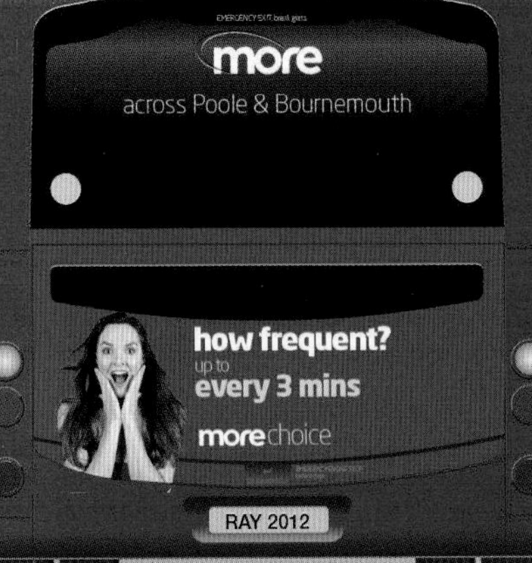

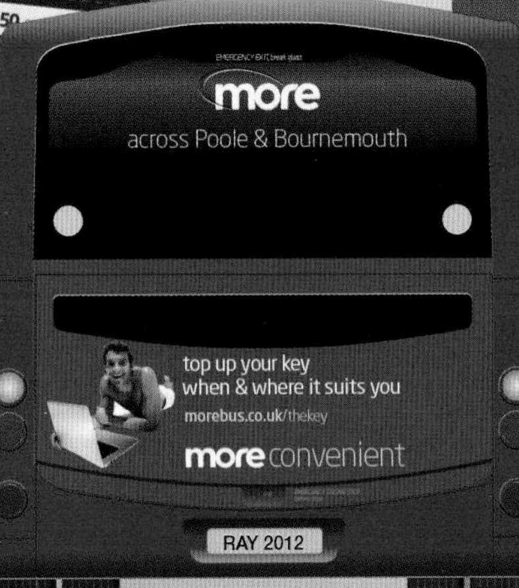

Without doubt the people vital to the success of Wilts & Dorset throughout the company's hundred years are the staff. The company has always had loyal staff, many of whom have stayed with the company for many years. The input made by each and every person who works or has worked for the company is of great value. Here are a few of them.

Jim Newton MBE

Jim started as a conductor with Wilts & Dorset at Blandford depot in September 1951 aged 21. He became a driver in October 1959 and quickly progressed to driver only operation, spending many years mainly on the long 34 route between Salisbury and Weymouth via Blandford and Dorchester. A reorganisation after the amalgamation with Hants & Dorset saw Jim also working on the routes from Blandford to Shaftesbury, Bournemouth and Poole. He retired at 65 in the autumn of 1994, taking a break of just one week before joining the associated Damory Coaches operation. He continued to work for Damory for a further 15 years, latterly part time mainly driving school buses.

Jim was awarded the MBE in the 2009 New Year Honours List for his services to public transport in Dorset. At the time he said, *"I have never thought that I'd be honoured in this way, and I am delighted to accept the award. I still very much enjoy the job, and it is nice to have been recognised as a driver."*

On Friday 17 July 2009 Jim completed his final run in service, having decided to retire after 58 years in the bus industry. He was given presents by children at Puddletown first and middle schools before returning to the Damory depot, where he was met by then Operations Director Andrew Wickham, who paid warm tribute to Jim's 58 years of dedicated service and wished him a happy retirement. At that time he was believed to be Britain's longest serving bus worker.

Above, in classic pose on the rear platform of a Bristol K, Jim Newton is conducting during the early 1950s.

TOM BOLT

On the right, Jim is at the wheel of an ex-Maidstone & District Leyland Panther leaving Weymouth for Salisbury in 1973.

BRIAN JACKSON

WILTS & DORSET MOTOR SERVICES, LTD.

WORKS NO. NAME
548 KING, A.E.

HOURS RATE (INCLU. WAR WAGE)
1 1/10-1/4

INSURS. 2/10	NAT. SAV.	DEPOSIT
SOC. CLB.	HOSP. 6	RED X	PENSION 10
	TAX 35/-	

	£	S	D
88½ hrs. GROSS WAGES	8	4	1
TOTAL DEDUCTIONS	1	19	0
NET WAGES £	6	5	1
SUBSISTENCE			
INCOME TAX REFUND			

W.E. 10-1-47
PAID 16-1-47

Retain this Pay Envelope for reference.

Arthur King

For the whole of his distinguished 50 years service, Arthur King was a conductor at Hindon outstation. He joined as a 15-year old in 1929, and apart from service in the Military Police during the Second World War, enjoyed working for the company until his retirement in 1979. He wore the Wilts & Dorset badge, his PSV conductor's badge and long service medals with great pride.

He had an exemplary record throughout his time with Wilts & Dorset. With little day-to-day supervision, outstation staff have to be highly motivated. Arthur certainly met this requirement, and on several occasions received personal letters from the Managing Director praising the way he had handled various situations.

For a number of years Arthur was the staff representative at Hindon, and when Wilts & Dorset won important bus transport contracts for RAF Chilmark - the majority of which it was found expedient to run from Hindon - Arthur willingly took on the extra responsibility of ensuring that these vital journeys were properly and efficiently operated each day. He was so effective in this role that the Area Manager at the time (Mr Peter Fairweather) commented that he could not recall ever receiving any complaints about the RAF Chilmark journeys provided by Hindon outstation.

Arthur was held in very high regard by his colleagues, and also by passengers. On his last morning at work he was puzzled as the bus ran into Salisbury because he noticed that people were not getting off at their usual bus stops but remained on board until the bus station. On arrival, Arthur's regular passengers made a presentation to show their appreciation of his excellent service and to wish him a happy retirement. Arthur was the last conductor employed at Hindon outstation when he retired in 1979 at the age of 65.

The top picture shows Arthur King on the day of his retirement and the one above when he first joined Wilts & Dorset.

courtesy of ALICE KING

Maury Coombes

Not to be confused with Wilts & Dorset founder Edwin Maurice Coombes, Maury Coombes joined Wilts & Dorset at 16 in 1929 as a conductor at Salisbury. He became a driver 10 years later in 1939.

During the Second World War women joined Wilts & Dorset as conductresses. Maury and one of the conductresses struck up a friendship that led to marriage, and he and his wife Annie worked together as a crew after the wedding. Here they are on the left. Maury continued as a driver until April 1963, when he transferred to Salisbury garage in Castle Street. He retired in March 1978.

Bert Cooper

In the section of the book dealing with 1919, we note that Bert Cooper brought Wilts & Dorset's very first double deck bus from Worthing to Salisbury (he can be seen in the 1919 photograph of the bus, leaning on the mudguard of the vehicle), and on arrival remained in that fair city to work for the company.

Bert was still a driver with Wilts & Dorset in the 1950s when this photograph above on the right was taken in Salisbury bus station canteen.

Fred Mitchell & George Jocelyn

Driver Fred Mitchell and conductor George Jocelyn were photographed with their bus while operating a Salisbury city service to Milton Road around 1930 in the picture below.

George Jocelyn later became an Inspector, while Fred Mitchell was later one of the senior coach drivers based at Salisbury. Here is Fred on the left with immaculate Bristol L6B coach GAM 216 at Chichester on 12 July 1958.

Although we have picked out these worthy characters, sincere thanks go to each and every member of staff, past and present, all of whom have played their own part in helping to make the Company what it is today.

If there is one person who can be said to synonymous with Wilts & Dorset Motor Services, that person is surely Mr Raymond Ilfred Henry Longman. Raymond was born at Winfrith in Dorset, and served during the First World War with the Royal Flying Corps at Upavon on Salisbury Plain. After demobilisation in 1919 he worked for the Salisbury estate agent George Davis, who was also joint Secretary and Managing Director of Wilts & Dorset Motor Services Limited.

George Davis died in 1924 and Raymond Longman then took up the position of Secretary of Wilts & Dorset. With the exception of vehicle specification and purchase, he effectively ran the company as Secretary. Perhaps his most notable achievement was sourcing secondhand vehicles to more than double the size of the fleet in the run-up to the Second World War in order to transport construction workers to Blandford Camp and other military sites.

Raymond Longman was made General Manager in 1942, Mr R E Herridge (who came from Western National) being appointed Secretary the following year. In 1946 Mr Longman was redesignated as Managing Director, the position he would hold until his retirement from Wilts & Dorset in 1962.

Wilts & Dorset had become part of the Tilling Group in 1942, and in October of that year Raymond Longman joined the executive staff of Thomas Tilling Limited. When the Tilling bus operations passed to the British Transport Commission in 1948 he became a member of the Tilling Group Management Board of the BTC. He held directorships of a number of bus and coach undertakings, including Hants & Dorset, Southern Vectis, Brighton Hove & District, Eastern National, United Automobile Services, United Counties, London Coastal Coaches, Samuelson New Transport, A Timpson & Sons and Bourne & Balmer.

Raymond was a member of the Road Operators' Safety Council, and also served as Vice-Chairman of the Public Transport Association, Chairman of the Conference of Omnibus Companies and Chairman of the National Council for the Omnibus Industry.

Raymond Longman died at the age of 94 on 17 February 1989. He had been one of the best known and most widely respected figures in the transport industry. Representatives from Wilts & Dorset were among the many who attended his memorial service at St Boniface Church at Woodgreen.

WILTS & DORSET

Photo of Maury and Annie Coombes courtesy of
WENDY HARRIS

Photo of Fred Mitchell standing by coach in 1958.
DAVID PENNELS

Photo of Bert Cooper in canteen, photo of Fred Mitchell and George Jocelyn standing by bus around 1930, and photo of Raymond Longman from the
DAVID PENNELS COLLECTION

1910	
1915	Wilts & Dorset formed by Alfred Cannon,Douglas Mackenzie & Percy Lephard
1920	formed into a public limited company
1930	
1931	equal shares acquired by TBAT & the Southern Railway giving them a joint majority shareholding
1940	
1942	TBAT shares passed to Tilling
1948	railways nationalised & Tilling sold to the state - Wilts & Dorset now part of the British Transport Commission
1950	
1960	
1963	British Transport Commission became Transport Holding Company
1969	National Bus Company formed - Wilts & Dorset one of 54 operating companies
1970	
1980	
1987	Wilts & Dorset sold to its management
1990	
2000	
2003	Wilts & Dorset sold by management buy-out team to the Go-Ahead Group
2010	

The name Wilts & Dorset was first seen on the sides of a bus in August 1914, when Edwin Maurice Coombes started a route between Amesbury and Salisbury using that title. Discussions started between Coombes and two directors of Worthing Motor Services, Alfred Cannon and Douglas Mackenzie. These talks culminated in Alfred Cannon, Douglas Makenzie and Percy Lephard registering Wilts & Dorset Motor Services Limited at Companies House in London on 4 January 1915. Coombes received 100 shares in the new company and was employed as manager at Amesbury. He was subsequently called up to join the Armed Forces, but when he returned from war service he found that his position with the company had been filled in the meantime, and that there was no job for him.

In 1920 Wilts & Dorset changed from being a private limited company to a public limited company, to be able to access the funding needed for expansion and development, and also to fight off competition - not least from the (understandably) disgruntled Edwin Coombes during 1920 and 1921. The 1920s was a period of financial stringency for Wilts & Dorset, but developments at the end of the decade and into the 1930s did much to secure the future of the company, although at the cost of its independence.

Meanwhile, Thomas Tilling Limited and the British Electric Traction Company had acquired considerable stakes in the bus industry in various parts of the UK, though not in Wilts & Dorset, and in 1928 the bus interests of both organisations, totalling 25, were brought together as the Tilling and British Automobile Traction Company (TBAT). TBAT effectively became the principal force in the British bus operating industry at that time. Also in 1928 the Railways (Road Transport) Acts allowed the four main line railway companies to buy into bus operations within their respective territories. In general the railway companies exercised this right by buying equivalent numbers of shares to those held by TBAT in the bus operations in question.

Partly because of slight complications that arose because the Great Western Railway, as well as the Southern Railway, had expressed some interest in becoming involved with Wilts & Dorset, it was not until 1931 that the Southern Railway and TBAT each acquired 9,800 ordinary shares in Wilts & Dorset, which gave them a joint controlling interest in the company. An immediate sign of this change was the appearance of the strapline 'In association with the Southern Railway' on Wilts & Dorset's publicity material.

The TBAT 'marriage', although operationally successful, was not altogether a happy one, and managerial disagreements led to TBAT being wound up in 1942, with the bus companies involved being allocated to either Tilling or the British Electric Traction Company. The railways were nationalised from 1 January 1948, bringing their bus company shareholding into public ownership. Believing nationalisation of bus services might not be far behind, Tilling sold out to the British Transport Commission, also in 1948, and so Wilts & Dorset, which had passed to Tilling in 1942, became wholly state owned.

The National Bus Company (NBC) came into being on 1 January 1969. It consisted of the existing state owned former Tilling undertakings, plus the UK bus operations of the British Electric Traction Company, which by now had sold out to the state. At formation, NBC totalled 54 bus operating companies.

The management of Wilts & Dorset had already been merged with that of neighbouring Hants & Dorset in 1964, and while part of NBC Wilts & Dorset was completely subsumed into Hants & Dorset from 1972, but the name was reborn in 1983 when NBC decided to break up its larger operating companies into smaller units.

The 1985 Transport Act provided for the privatisation of the NBC, and Wilts & Dorset was sold to its local management team in 1987. For 16 years the company remained locally owned and managed until August 2003, when the management team decided to sell to the Go-Ahead Group. The origin of Go-Ahead was a management buy out of Northern General from NBC in 1987, but it began expanding when it bought Brighton & Hove in 1993 and Oxford Bus Company in 1994, both previously management buy-outs from NBC.

Almost 30 years later, the Go-Ahead Group has grown from a regional bus operator in North East England to become one of the UK's leading providers of passenger transport, bus and rail. Since acquisition in 2003, Go-Ahead has invested significantly in Wilts & Dorset, bringing modernisation and innovation. In turn this has led to an encouraging growth in the numbers of passengers carried in many areas.

An important feature of the Go-Ahead Group is that individual operating companies are given a high degree of autonomy. Local identities and branding are encouraged and valued – the recent development of Wilts & Dorset into more and Salisbury Reds is a good example. Most importantly, the networks continue to be managed by locally based people who have a good knowledge of the area and who are passionate about providing a first class service.

In the picture on the opposite page there's no mistaking who ultimately owned this Eastern Coach Works bodied Ford R1014, RRU 594N, one of 25 which had been new to the company in 1974.

By that time the Wilts & Dorset name was no longer in use, as the former Wilts & Dorset operations had all been completely absorbed into Hants & Dorset two years earlier (management had been combined in 1964).

There was a concerted effort at that time to promote the 'brave new world' that the National Bus Company was intended to be, but many will argue that the loss of local identities made the companies seem more remote from their customers, and adhering to corporate diktats became more important than responding to local market conditions and concerns.

JOHN CUMMING COLLECTION

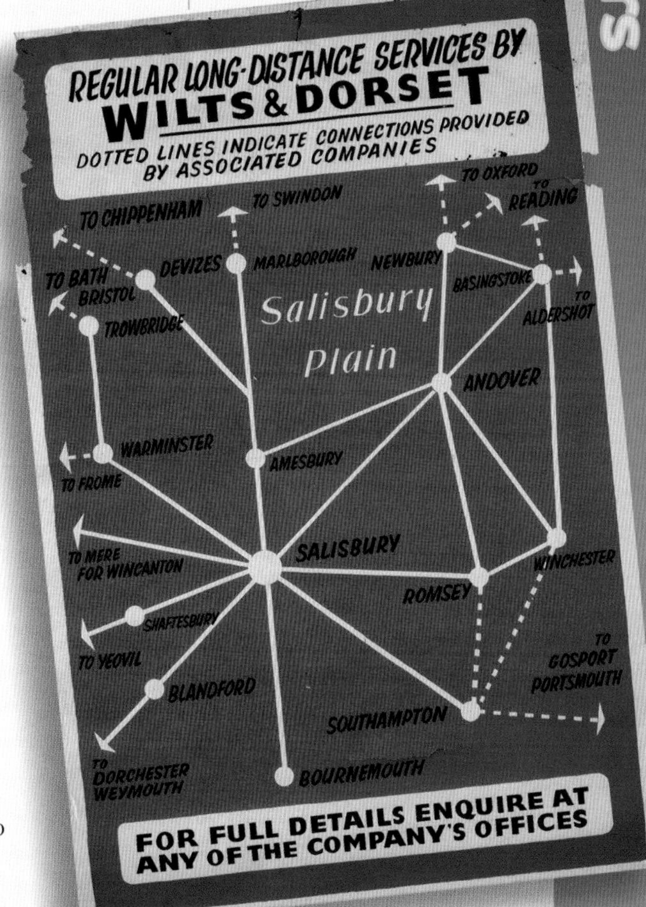

into the future

It's impossible to know beyond a shadow of a doubt what the future might hold for any business. Writing this in 2015, there is no doubt that the company will continue to face challenges as lifestyles change and, therefore, demands from customers continue to change.

New technology has enabled the company to introduce such features as smartcard ticketing and real time bus information direct to a customer's mobile phone, even buying tickets directly onto your phone, ideas that would have seemed incredible even 25 years ago. In a wider context who can predict the future of local authority spending or government transport policy?

Nonetheless, there are grounds for optimism. People travelling by bus - indeed, choosing to travel by bus - are now growing in number in many areas. Poole has shown the highest level of growth in the country at 72%, and the company has responded where appropriate with more frequent and better quality services.

A hundred years after the name Wilts & Dorset was first seen on the sides of buses, the company remains on the forefront of developments, investing in the latest technology and planning for the future. The vehicles in the photographs on the early pages of this book appear quaint and old fashioned in 2015, but if a copy of this book should survive for 100 years, what would a reader in 2115 think of the new vehicles llustrated just a few pages back?

. . . so, here's to the next hundred years!

It would not have been possible to have produced this book without the wonderful assistance of the many people who have loaned precious photographs and other material or helped in various ways following appeals in the company's staff magazine Coaster and the Salisbury Journal newspaper. These include

Ian Gray	Jacky Fall	Andrew Waller	Dave Andrew
Ivor West	Mike Daly	Ken Wigmore	Mike Caldicott
Peter Cook	Bill Smith	Barry Rolf	Debbie Potter
Wendy Harris	Lindsay Proctor	Roger Kerley	Mike Robins
Sally Goddard	David Mant	Mark Lyons	Donna Vincent
Malcolm Scott	Phil Davies	Tony Gallagher	

I would like to extend special thanks to Brian Jackson and to David Pennels for the wonderful help and guidance they have provided in addition to making available many evocative photographs. Also the Wilts & Dorset Fleet History, compiled by David Pennels in 1963, has been an invaluable work of reference, while for more recent events back issues of the company's staff magazine have also been very useful.

Ian Scott and the staff at Salisbury Photo Centre in Catherine Street have been most obliging, and Ray Stenning at Best Impressions has done a great job with the design and layout.

Thank you to Andrew Sherrington Operations Manager at Salisbury Reds, Ed Wills Operations Director and Andrew Wickham Managing Director, for inviting me to write this book, and a particular thank you to Andrew Wickham for providing the foreword.

Of necessity a book of this nature has to be somewhat selective in content to keep within a reasonable number of pages and to retain appeal for the general reader. I have thus tended to concentrate more on the human and commercial side of the history than the engineering and technical.

Buses and coaches have been identified by their registration numbers rather than by their company fleetnumbers; this is mainly to keep the story simple as in many cases vehicles have carried different fleet numbers during their lifetime when the fleet has been renumbered, and in the same way a given fleetnumber may have been carried by more than one vehicle. The various types of buses and coaches operated over the years have been described and illustrated in some detail, but to keep the narrative appealing for all readers I have not set out to tabulate every vehicle operated by the company during its 100 year history.

Corfe Mullen
Highfield Estate
Broadstone
Hillbourne
Creekmoor
Waterloo
Fleetsbridge
Canford Heath
Bearwood
West Howe
Alderney
Tower Park
St Aldhelm's Academy
Newtown
Foxholes
Oakdale
Stanley Green
Upper Parkstone
Sea View
Park Gates
Lower Parkstone
Penn Hill
Poole
Holes Bay
Upton House
Upton Country Park
Twin Sails Bridge
Poole Bridge
Poole Park
Hamworthy Park
Poole Harbour
Lilliput
Compton Acres
Parkstone
Waitrose
Co-op
Asda
Tesco
The Pilot
cemetery
The Fleetsbridge
Sweet Home Inn
The Red Lion
New Harbour Road West
New Quay Rd
The Quay
school summer holidays only